Reappraisals
Essays in the history of youth and community work

Edited by
**Ruth Gilchrist, Tony Jeffs, Jean Spence,
Naomi Stanton, Aylssa Cowell, Joyce Walker
and Tom Wylie**

Russell House Publishing

First published in 2013 by:
Russell House Publishing Ltd.
58 Broad Street
Lyme Regis
Dorset DT7 3QF

Tel: 01297-443948
Fax: 01297-442722
e-mail: help@russellhouse.co.uk
www.russellhouse.co.uk

British Library Cataloguing-in-publication Data:
A catalogue record for this book is available from the British Library.
ISBN: 978-1-905541-88-1

Typeset by TW Typesetting, Plymouth, Devon
Printed by IQ Laserpress, Aldershot

About Russell House Publishing

Russell House Publishing aims to publish innovative and valuable materials to help managers, practitioners, trainers, educators and students.

Our full catalogue covers: families, children and young people; engagement and inclusion; drink, drugs and mental health; textbooks in youth work and social work; workforce development.

Full details can be found at www.russellhouse.co.uk and we are pleased to send out information to you by post. Our contact details are on this page.

We are always keen to receive feedback on publications and new ideas for future projects.

Contents

Acknowledgements

Like the previous volumes this collection predominately comprises papers presented at the most recent bi-annual *History of Youth and Community Work Conference*. Held at Northern College, near Barnsley, this was the seventh such conference to take place in the United Kingdom. The essays contained in this book reflect not only the enthusiasms and interests of the authors but also that of the many delegates who helped shape the content via their contribution to the debates and workshops that took place during that weekend at Northern College.

The editors would like to record their thanks to Geoffrey Mann at Russell House. His encouragement and patience have made our task much easier than it would otherwise have been. Also we wish to express our appreciation to Tracey Hodgson who organised and managed the Northern College gathering with her usual efficiency. Without her hard work and energy this text would never have materialised.

Aylssa Cowell, Ruth Gilchrist, Tony Jeffs, Jean Spence, Naomi Stanton, Joyce Walker and Tom Wylie

About the Authors

Bernard Davies has been involved in youth work as a practitioner, manager, trainer, policy maker, researcher, writer and trade unionist.

Dod Forrest is now retired after working in the voluntary and local government sectors, and contributing to the youth research and evaluation work of the Rowan Group, School of Education University of Aberdeen.

Tony Jeffs teaches at Durham University. He is a member of the Institute for Social Research, University of Bedfordshire and the *Youth and Policy* Editorial Board.

Helen M. F. Jones is a lecturer at the University of Huddersfield and a Trustee of the The Youth Association.

Robert McCloy was director of education and chief executive of the Royal Borough of Kingston upon Thames, and adviser to the Association of Metropolitan Authorities. Earlier roles included that of community centre warden in Birmingham and assistant education officer in Cambridgeshire. A life-long transport enthusiast, he is currently chairman of the Roads and Road Transport History Association.

Judith Metz is professor of urban youth work, Amsterdam University of Applied Sciences.

Juha Nieminen is Development and Training Manager at the National Youth Center Marttinen in Virrat in Finland. He is a part-time teacher at the University of Tampere and his teaching and research areas relate to the history, theory and system of youth work.

Keith Popple teaches at the London South Bank University, Department of Social Work. He was a founding editor of the journal *Youth and Policy*.

Naomi Stanton teaches at the George Williams YMCA College, London. She is a member of the Editorial Board of the journal *Youth and Policy.*

Tony Taylor is Co-ordinator of the In *Defence of Youth Work Campaign.*

Aniela Wenham teaches at the University of York, Department of Social Policy.

Tom Wylie was Chief Executive of the National Youth Agency (1996–2007). Previously he was Assistant Director of Inspection for the Office for Standards in Education having become one of Her Majesty's Inspectors of Education in 1979. Currently he is a trustee of various charities including the Paul Hamlyn Foundation and Rathbone.

CHAPTER 1

'Not For One, But For All': The First Decades of Leeds Association of Girls' Clubs (1904–1935)

Helen Jones

Leeds Association of Girls' Clubs (LAGC) was founded in 1904. It still exists after a series of name changes and is now The Youth Association (TYA) with offices in Wakefield and Leeds. TYA holds the organisation's archives which date back to the creation of LAGC. The earliest handwritten minutes book records that 'The first General Meeting of the Leeds Girls Clubs Union was held on Friday December 9th 1904'. During the months that preceded that meeting, a small self-appointed committee representing 'some half a dozen Girls Clubs' had contacted sixty Leeds clergymen and ministers asking whether they knew of any other local girls' clubs which they could contact. Twenty-seven years later, Hilda Hargrove reminisced about the birth of the organisation:

> *It was whilst on a holiday in North Wales in 1902 that the idea of such an Association first entered my mind . . . I had the good fortune of getting to know an enthusiastic worker from the Bristol Union of Girls' Clubs. Until then I had never heard of such an organisation and I determined to do all that was in my power to found a similar organisation in Leeds.*

(LDAGC, 1931)

The fact that other cities already had associations whose work was reported in their newspapers demonstrates the fact that the media of the day were essentially local. Leeds residents had a choice of newspapers which published exhaustive accounts of Leeds's civic, cultural and religious life together with items of national and international interest. However, coverage of news from other provincial cities and towns was limited. Hence even a well-informed young woman in Leeds conceivably might have little knowledge of developments in other regions.

Hilda explained two functions which an association of girls' clubs would play. These comprised holding competitions and joining together for lectures and classes. LAGC brought together girls' clubs which were associated mostly with chapels and churches and, later, a synagogue. Each autumn the Association issued a programme of classes for the annual competition which became its primary raison d'être. This provided members with several months' notice to work on their entries. The prize-giving event grew to include an exhibition and performance. In summer the girls were invited to a garden party hosted by a local benefactor. Some lectures and other events were provided for clubs which came together. Holidays in the Yorkshire countryside were attempted but with limited success. At the inaugural meeting, Hilda Hargrove had described how Bristol's Union organised a week's holiday in summer. She explained, 'Some of the helpers go with the girls and by this means get to know, understand and sympathise with them as would otherwise be impossible' (LAGC, 1931).

Twenty-seven years later she expressed regret at the holidays' demise: 'they provided an excellent means of workers and members getting together to enjoy the delights of the country' (LAGC, 1931). However saving up and sharing a house in the inauspiciously named village of Blubberhouses did not appeal to the girls of Leeds.

Unlike similar organisations in other cities, the Association had no overt aims concerning girls' working or living conditions. In its early days, Bristol's Association of Working Girls' Clubs had set out not only 'to brighten, cheer, and elevate the lives of the working girls of their city' (*The Bristol Mercury and Daily Post*, 1896) but also to ensure members 'became better acquainted with the Factory Acts and all that affects the conditions of women's labour' (Sherbrooke and Townsend, 1896). Whether Hilda was not aware of this, or whether she chose to keep the information to herself, is difficult to say. Similarly, whether the women in Leeds decided against having any political purpose cannot be ascertained although the decision was taken to be an 'Association' rather than a 'Union'. The first President Dr Lucy Buckley, showed an inclination towards political engagement and certainly will have known about issues concerning young women's health from her medical practice. There may have been tensions between those founders who would have been keen to have a more political and welfare-focussed dimension and those who wanted to focus only on leisure activities. Hilda Hargrove, Dr Lucy Buckley, Mary Harvey and Margaret Harvey: the small group of women who launched the Association, epitomised the different concerns of the time. They were soon joined by other women including representatives of leading local families, the Luptons and the Middletons.

Hilda Hargrove

Hilda Elizabeth Hargrove was born in 1876. The 1901 census gives her occupation as 'Girls' Club Secretary': she was the honorary secretary of Mill Hill Unitarian Church Girls' Club. Her father Charles was the minister and was deeply involved in a range of local cultural and philanthropic activities. He spent half his life in Leeds but his earlier years had not suggested that he would become a long-standing pillar of a local Unitarian community. Born into the Plymouth Brethren he had converted to Roman Catholicism as a young man. Having failed as a schoolteacher, he became a Dominican monk then Catholic priest. The church sent him to a parish in Trinidad but he had not been happy there and struggled, particularly when working through a smallpox epidemic. Effectively burned out, he relinquished his habit on a boat home. Back in England in his early thirties he moved around without a clear purpose for many months. During this time he was introduced to a 16 year old girl. Having met her three times, he married her. Charles secured work in University extension and became involved in Unitarianism. He spoke at Mill Hill Chapel, Leeds and became a candidate for the vacant minister's post. The Chapel elders feared he would 'bolt' again but they took the risk of appointing him (Jacks, 1920: 285).

Charles and his wife settled in Leeds and had four children of whom Hilda was the oldest. She worked closely with her father and took on many of his pastoral duties while he attended meetings of the committees on which he served from the Children's Holiday Fund to the University Council (Jacks, 1920: 309). He also attended public meetings and on 16 April 1890 *The Leeds Mercury* reported that Charles 'made a few remarks' in favour of women's suffrage at a well-attended meeting addressed by the suffragette Isabella Ford. In 1897 he supported women's admittance to degrees at the University of Cambridge (Jacks, 1920: 331). When members of the congregation complained of Charles's indulgence in outside activities, and thus the neglect of the pastoral side of his office, he replied, 'I cannot give up all other work for visiting' (Schroeder, 1924). This was the radical social, political and religious environment in which Hilda was raised.

Hilda reduced her involvement in LAGC in 1906 due to 'the uncertainty of her plans'. Sadly the extant archives contain no clues as to what these plans were but she continued some involvement in the LAGC and returned in 1931 to address the Association. In 1907 Hilda was described as having done 'more than anybody to start the Association' (LAGC, 1907) yet she did not become President. Instead, together with Olive Middleton she became Honorary General Secretary. She also remained as her father's assistant rather than seeking ordination as a Unitarian minister herself. Perhaps Hilda was happiest out of the limelight or maybe she was eclipsed by her larger-than-life father.

Lucy Buckley

LAGC's first President was Dr Lucy Buckley. For her, work with the Association was one aspect of an interesting and busy life. She was born in Oldham in 1868. Her father Samuel was a hat manufacturer in nearby Denton, a centre for the trade. Lucy attended Manchester High School for Girls a few years before the Pankhurst sisters. She went on to achieve a BSc at the University of Manchester in 1891 then went on to study in Glasgow gaining her M.B., Ch.B. in 1900. It is important to emphasise how remarkable this success was: women had only been allowed to study at Scottish universities since 1892 and the first women graduates in medicine had achieved their qualifications in 1894. The University of Glasgow's website shows the exponential growth in the numbers of women studying, from 6 per cent in 1892 to 26 per cent in 1908. Lucy was part of this expansion. When she had completed her studies, Lucy was a Licentiate of the Royal College of Physicians, London (LRCP), a Licentiate of the Royal College of Surgeons, Edinburgh (LRCS) and a Licentiate of the Faculty of Physicians and Surgeons, Glasgow (LFPS). She became a Clinical Assistant at Northumberland County Asylum for a very short period but by 1901 was living in Leeds where she entered private practice, sharing both a home and nearby surgery with Dr Ursula Chaplin. At the time there were only a couple of hundred women medical practitioners in the country.

In Leeds in 1901 Lucy lectured on 'Some Nervous Manifestations of Childhood' to a gathering of people involved in the correspondence-based home-schools set up by Charlotte Mason. Lucy 'emphasised the fact that nervous diseases are becoming more frequent, especially among the educated classes' and added that this applied to children as well as adults. 'We are too apt', she suggested, 'to give [children] a great variety of occupations, and not enough real honest leisure' (Mason, 1901: 68). This sentiment might explain why she did not insist on LAGC having a clearer political dimension: she might have seen greater value in evenings spent in pleasure and relaxation.

Dr Buckley remained as President for only a couple of years. In January 1906 aged 38, she married 35-year old James Wilkinson Pinniger. He had been a curate in Leeds, near Lucy's surgical premises, but subsequently had become the vicar of Crompton, near Oldham. Lucy moved to join him and her involvement in LAGC reduced; she transferred to the post of Vice-President. Sadly she was widowed sixteen months later. The LAGC minutes for the meeting held on 3 July 1907 record unanimous agreement that she should be sent a letter of sympathy. Possibly with a view to supporting her, the meeting also decided to ask her whether she would be willing to formally represent the LAGC at the Girls' Clubs Committee of the National Union of Women Workers (NUWW). Hitherto her attendance seems to have been due to her own personal interest although she probably saw herself as representing the LAGC. Soon she was chairing meetings having returned to Leeds and thrown herself back into her work, both paid and voluntary.

In December 1907 the minutes report that Lucy:

> brought forward a proposal that some attempt should be made to get Club Workers interested in the industrial questions connected with factory and other employment.

She suggested that a conference should be held some time in February and stated that she had received a promise from 'Miss Montagu of London' to address such a conference 'if at all possible'. It was unanimously agreed that such a conference should be organised and also that the Honorary Secretary of the Leeds Industrial Law Committee should be communicated with, in order to secure their co-operation'. The next meeting discussed arrangements but the minutes of the meeting which followed the date agreed for the conference (5 or 6 March 1908) makes no mention of the event. It is notable that the conference was aimed at 'club workers' rather than members: Lucy saw potential in the workers' education so they could provide a resource for clubs, possibly inculcating in members a more questioning approach to working conditions.

In July 1909 Lucy Pinniger resigned from LAGC as she was returning to Oldham. This time her move appears to have been professional: the 1911 census describes Dr Pinniger, who was now 42, as 'medical inspector of school children'. Again Lucy was at the vanguard, this time in terms of the development of a new professional area. Medical inspectors had been introduced by the Education (Choice of Employment) Act 1910. Local Education Authorities were empowered 'to assist boys and girls under seventeen years of age in the choice of suitable employment' (Greenwood, 1911: 62). Hitherto young people had been reliant on families and friends who might only know of a narrow range of possibilities. Young people were also attracted by 'blind alley jobs' which were comparatively well paid but associated with a high turnover as young people were replaced when they reached adulthood (ibid: 5). Greenwood observed, ' "blind alley" occupations lead to a "blind alley" view of life – lack of purpose and hopelessness' (ibid: 73). On the other hand, there was a shortage of entrants to new and progressive industries of which families and friends were unaware. Over a hundred years ago, Greenwood identified the 'cost to the community' of failing to supervise young people between leaving school and achieving adulthood and suggested a model which we might see as a form of mentoring (ibid: 66). This required 'tact' in winning the young people's confidence and 'avoiding exciting the antipathy of parents, and the opposition of employers' (ibid: 71).

The Act also gave Education Authorities the power to set up Juvenile Advisory Committees with two areas of responsibility: industrial and educational. Membership of industrial committees comprised the medical inspector of school children, trades unions, employment associations and social workers and it assisted in identifying appropriate employment for each child. The involvement of the state in guiding young people into occupations and careers marks the birth of the careers service. After-care committees supported young people once they were in employment and involved representatives of voluntary agencies with an educational dimension, including literary and debating societies, uniformed organisations, boys' clubs and girls' clubs.

Lucy remained in the post until the 1920s when she retired with her mother to the village of Woodham Walter, Essex. There she bought a house close to Dr Ursula Chaplin who had also retired to the area with her parents. The Chaplins had already helped to set up various women's community and health organisations and it is likely that Lucy found life there both sympathetic and stimulating. She lived there until her death in 1937.

Mary and Margaret Harvey

Mary and Margaret Harvey attended LAGC's original meeting. Unlike Hilda Hargrove whose family only moved to Leeds in the late nineteenth century and Lucy Buckley who moved there in the twentieth, they were from a well-established Quaker family although their social prominence was recently achieved. Their father had inherited considerable wealth and retired from business in his 30s, thereafter dedicating himself to philanthropic concerns and attending many of the same committees as Charles Hargrove. Their mother Anna was an active temperance campaigner, even visiting police cells on Sundays (Burdett-Coutts, 1893: 396). They had six children of whom Mary and Margaret were the oldest. Their house in Leeds was far larger than those of Lucy or Hilda and numerous servants were employed. Mary, Margaret and their younger sister Helen each took a turn as honorary secretary of Pontefract Lane Girls' Club. They were priv-ileged young women engaging in philanthropic activity but they had been away to the Quaker school in York and nursed during the First World War. Whilst the family was prosperous, their faith was important to them and they were noted for their generosity and hospitality. Mr Harvey proved to be a reliable, long-term donor to LAGC funds.

Margaret, Elinor and Olive Lupton and Olive Middleton

The Middletons and Luptons were long-established Leeds families whose donations were important in the Association's early days. Although she was not at the preliminary meeting Olive Middleton was at the inaugural meet-ing of the Executive Committee of Leeds Association of Girls' Clubs in 1904. She was selected together with Hilda Hargrove as Honorary General Secretary and held this role for two years before transferring to the role of Competitions Secretary for at least two further years. During 1914–15 she was one of three Vice-Presidents.

The Luptons were an established and wealthy Leeds family. Unitarians, they had been involved in Charles Hargrove's appointment as minister. Three cous-ins, Elinor, May and Olive were all involved in the LAGC. Elinor Lupton was involved in the Association for at least thirty years: in 1913 she was a donor and in 1914 she became the Honorary General Secretary, and President in 1919. The archives show she remained as President or Vice-President until at least 1933. As youth work developed, her name re-appeared: in 1943 she was a member of the Advisory Council.

During the First World War Elinor's cousin Margaret Lupton (known as May) was Assistant Competitions Secretary. In 1908 Elinor and May's cousin Olive Lupton were members of the Executive Committee, serving on the Holiday Home Sub-Committee as Honorary Secretary and Treasurer. In 1914–15 Olive Lupton was on the Executive Committee, confusingly now as Olive Middleton: she had married Olive Middleton's brother Richard Noel. Elinor, Olive and Olive were subscribers throughout the 1920s. The Lupton family was gravely affected by the loss of all three of Olive's brothers in the First World War. In conse-quence, she and her sister Ann inherited considerable wealth on the death of their father. Recently Olive and Richard Noel Middleton achieved posthumous fame as the Duchess of Cambridge (née Catherine Middleton)'s great grand-parents and May, Elinor and the other Olive became footnotes as three of her great great aunts.

The first decade

For its first decade LAGC focused on its annual programme and exhibition (Jones, 2011). Increasingly complex sets of rules were published and each competition was followed by judges' reports providing detailed guidance for entries in subsequent years. Classes included numerous forms of needlework and handicraft, Morris Dancing, drill, recitation and singing. Summer sometimes saw swimming classes at one of the recently constructed pools.

In 1908 the Association decided it needed a motto and the Council weighed up the rival suggestions of 'By love serve one another' (a quote from the New Testament's Letter to the Galatians) and 'Not for self but for all' (an English translation of the Latin motto 'non sibi, sed omnibus'), before agreeing to adopt the former. However, by the following meeting it had been discovered that it was already being used by the Young Women's Christian Association. The rejected motto was modified to 'Not for one but for all' and was adopted. In the light of the different faith backgrounds of subsequent affiliated groups this was fortuitous.

By 1913 LDAGC had become a small pebble in Leeds's lively local cultural, artistic, political, educational and religious pond. It had already made its first name change, becoming Leeds and District Association of Girls' Clubs (LDAGC) so that girls' clubs within easy reach of Leeds could affiliate. Since the mid-nineteenth century Leeds had been transformed rapidly into a well appointed dynamic city, proud of its facilities and its commerce, however there were substantial slums and areas of great poverty, but nothing to rival those of Manchester or Bradford. The women associated with girls' clubs came from the families who endowed civic buildings, attended public meetings and founded cultural and educational organisations including the University. Several family names including Lupton, Kitson and Middleton crop up frequently. Many were non-conformists: Quakers and Unitarians in particular. Leeds was an increasingly affluent town, noted for its non-conformism in terms of religion and, particularly in the nineteenth century, its liberalism in terms of politics.

The Association expanded but the pattern of collaborative management continued. The minute book is remarkable for the sheer number of women listed, some just for a year or two and others for more than a decade. There is no sign of a single figurehead: this could explain the Association's stability with its strength resting in its organisational demands being shared. By the outbreak of the First World War LDAGC boasted 36 affiliated clubs. The membership of each was listed in the annual reports and, based on this, around 2,000 girls and helpers were involved: most clubs had between twenty and fifty members.

Nonetheless, the Association's financial status was consistently precarious: it relied on regular subscriptions and ad hoc donations since the clubs' affiliation fees did not cover its running costs.

The Association had no aims related to employment issues or girls' general welfare. The apolitical stance extended to their response in 1910 when the Executive Committee received a request from Mary Fielden, the Yorkshire organiser of the National Union of Women's Suffrage Societies, to 'address the older girls on the suffrage question'. The Committee concluded that the Association 'could take no part whatsoever in political or controversial movements'. However, they agreed to send her the Annual Report which contained the contact details for each club's secretary. Whether this was 'shrewd and strategic thinking' (Jones, 2011: 381) or avoiding the issue can only be surmised. Lucy Pinniger was no longer involved in the organisation and Hilda Hargrove (whose father had spoken in favour of women's franchise many years earlier) was not active. The political position of the committee of the time is not evident from the minutes so whether members were sympathetic to the extension of the suffrage is unclear.

In 1913 the first Jewish club joined the Association. "Evelina Behrens" Girls' Club (the inverted commas appeared in its name) had been founded recently. It offered a range of classes including Jewish history. With over three hundred members, it had a far larger membership and attendance than any other club. It was the only Jewish girls' club affiliated to the LDAGC. Leeds had experienced the arrival of many Jewish refugees around ten years earlier. Another influx of refugees occurred immediately before the First World War: when six thousand Belgian refugees arrived in Leeds (Kushner and Knox, 1999) and were welcomed in a way not afforded to many new arrivals. Some girls' clubs raised money to buy coal and others knitted for them.

Pre-war unrest in Leeds

The LDAGC's 10th Annual Report, published in November 1914, opened with the Executive Committee's report. Hardly surprisingly it focused on the impact of the war but it also hinted at the turmoil which Leeds had seen during the previous twelve months as it opened with:

> *The war, which casts its shadow over every life in Britain, has already caused us to forget the happenings of a few months ago, real and important as they seemed at the time.*

> (LDAGC, 1914)

Before turning to the war and its impact on LDAGC it is interesting to identify the position the Executive Committee and clubs took concerning the widespread unrest in Leeds during the year covered by the report.

Across Britain, the period immediately preceding the First World War was one of militancy, not only concerning women's suffrage but also around workers' conditions and rights, with trades unions playing a central role. This has not entered popular consciousness in the same way as the campaigns for women's suffrage. The majority of strikes occurred at commercial mills and factories but, in Leeds, the corporation employees' strike achieved national significance. It is worth noting that the corporation's range of activities was unusually broad: on 18 December 1913 *The Times* observed that Leeds Corporation:

> *has already undertaken almost every practicable form of municipal enterprise. Besides being responsible for education, baths, cemeteries, markets, parks, allotments, free libraries, highways, sewerage and ordinary municipal services, this one body runs for profit-bearing undertakings – tramways, waterworks, gasworks and electricity works – and employs directly more than 10 000 persons.*

Local ratepayers regarded themselves as employing the corporation's workforce so the strike was not against an identifiable capitalist, but rather divided neighbours against one another. The municipal strike started in December 1913 and lasted five weeks. It originated in demands for a pay rise which several groups believed they had been promised when other municipal workers had received wage increase in July 1913. Bradley (1997) notes that there was a blackout as the gas workers stopped work and 'there were bomb attacks on the gas works and the army barracks'. 'Foreign' police were brought in from Huddersfield, Bradford and Hull (*The Times*, 15 December 1913). At the time, Greenwood (1914) described how the University 'intervened' as students and staff stepped in, alongside local citizens, to help to run essential services. He cited *The Yorkshire Observer* (19 December 1913) which quoted Dr Sadler, the University's Vice-Chancellor, as differentiating between a dispute involving a private employer and the working-classes and one between:

> *municipal employees [who] engage in services vital not only to the convenience, but to the health, safety and well-being of the whole community, not least the working people and women and children.*
>
> (Greenwood, 1914)

Sadler (1914) himself wrote of the 'urgent requests' received by the University 'for aid in both the electricity and gas departments'. In order to avert the 'peril' which would have resulted from the city being 'plunged into darkness', volunteers took on the tasks. Sadler insisted that 'junior members of the University' should have parental permission for their involvement and that all volunteers from the University must undertake their involvement 'in a very serious spirit', without 'irritation', 'anger' or 'any feeling of class antagonism'. He wanted them to gain understanding of 'the ordinary worker's lot'. On 15 December 1913 *The Times* own 'Special Correspondent' observed:

> *All these services are necessary to the corporate life of the city, and if the men employed for that purpose will not do the work the community is bound to take it in hand. University studies, clerical duties and professional work must stand on one side in a domestic crisis of this kind.*

Everybody living in Leeds was affected by the strike and the women who were club leaders and helpers, and the members, were doubtless touched closely. In 1911 the Federation of University Women had established a girls' club which was affiliated to LAGC. It was 'the best way of keeping in touch with the girls whom they had undertaken to visit for the Advisory Committee for Juvenile Employment' under the Education (Choice of Employment) Act. Although LAGC's Executive Committee had links with University circles mainly through male relatives, being apolitical was no longer possible. It is also likely that the club members included some girls whose fathers were involved in the strike alongside others who were volunteering to maintain services. As *The Times* correspondent observed on 16 December 1913, 'every citizen is a potential "blackleg"'. The corporation strike was broken but was followed almost immediately by a rent increase which nearly three hundred tenants refused to pay. The areas affected lay in the neighbourhoods around many of the affiliated girls' clubs suggesting that both members and local helpers again came from families who were involved on both sides.

The 1914 Annual Report hints at these tensions in a throwaway comment- 'in consequence of the general disapproval felt by the Clubs of the action of the Workers' Educational Association at the time of the municipal strike, the LDAGC has discontinued its affiliation to that Society' (LDAGC, 1914). While the WEA presumably supported the Leeds Trades Council and unions in the strike (Chase, 2009) the nature of the 'action' is not known. Although in 1910 LDAGC had declared it could 'take no part whatever in political or controversial movements' (LAGC, 1910), it proved impossible to adhere to these protestations of being apolitical when faced with a situation affecting all local residents. By early 1914 Woodhouse Carr GC's programme included 'an address on Woman

Suffrage' [*sic*] by 'a working girl from Bradford'. On the other hand, Sheep-scar Guild had a programme of 'six lecturettes' concerning 'points of etiquette and general behaviour' which were 'listened to with great interest, and were often followed by a lively discussion'; the content of these discussions was not explored in the archives.

LDAGC in wartime

The widespread discontent across Britain was curtailed abruptly by the outbreak of war in August 1914. Many young women workers' hours increased and fac-tories recruited large numbers. Leeds, which lay at the centre of the woollen industry, produced fabric for military uniforms. Now, as the Executive Commit-tee observed in its report, clubs played an important role in providing 'hours of distraction and cheerful companionship' whilst homes were 'filled with anxiety or sorrow'. The stoical attitude was summed up in the following paragraph:

> *We cannot always be on a stretch of self-sacrifice and self-neglect, and games and music and dancing still have their necessary place at the end of a day's work. But neither girls nor helpers will be content with relaxa-tion and amusement only, and many parcels of clothing and comforts for their poorer neighbours, and for the soldiers and sailors, will be sent from the Clubs this year. We hope that the experience gained by com-petitors in former years in the knitting of socks, coats, and caps, and in the making of clothing of all kinds, will prove its value now.*

(LDAGC, 1914)

The Annual Report in 1915 noted how clubs 'have risen to meet the occa-sion, and have taken their place in war service'. Some clubs had suspended their normal programmes and 'devoted their weekly meeting almost exclusively to the preparation of large parcels of every sort of comfort which have been sent to our troops' (LDAGC, 1915). Burley Church GC members, for example, were 'chiefly occupied in making shirts and knitting for the troops' whilst Hol-beck Unitarians were 'sewing for the soldiers and the Belgians' and Sheepscar Guild members devoted themselves to knitting 'scarves, mittens, belts, etc., for the soldiers'. Leeds Parish Church GC members had even turned their skills to making sandbags. However attendance was affected. For example, Wood-house Carr Girls' Club noted that attendance 'was seriously affected by late hours of work' although members managed to organise a Christmas supper for 40 'poor children' who had 'a good romp' and were each given 'an orange and a toy'. LDAGC's 1915 annual competition was scaled down and concentrated on areas of practical relevance (such as cookery, nursing and laundry work) or ones which required 'little preparation or expense'.

In 1915 LDAGC published a plea for more helpers. The phrasing was clearly intended to suggest that assisting at a girls' club contributed to the war effort:

> We . . . hope that many ladies will give up one night a week, which they would in other years have devoted without compunction to some form of amusement, to helping in a girls' club, and so bringing healthy recreation and interest into lives whose need is greater now than ever before.

It was evident in the following year's Annual Report that this plea had not been answered sufficiently as the Executive Committee reported that:

> Many of the ladies who formerly taught [singing, drilling and dancing] are now fully occupied with some form of war-work, and it is a very difficult problem to find volunteers to take their place.

During the war the nature of young women's employment changed considerably. Numbers in domestic service decreased as munitions work required greater participation and, particularly following the introduction of conscription in March 1916, women took men's places in a range of occupations including the postal service and public transport. Domestic service was associated with lower wages, poorer conditions (including the isolation of being the only young person in a household and the most junior in the pecking order together with personal restrictions which affected choices in clothing, hair styles and social lives): increasingly young women opted for higher wages and greater freedom together with the sense of contributing to the war effort.

Even before the war mistresses were keen to retain their young servants. Founded in 1913 Roundhay Undenominational Girls' Club had an attendance of around 27, all of whom were local domestic servants. Membership was open to 'any girl of good character who will pay the subscription and attend regularly'. It appears members were advised to attend: 'mistresses find that it makes new maids settle better to have somewhere to go to, and make friends' (LDAGC, 1913). For the mistresses, this became more significant when the war started and girls might be attracted to factory work. A greater sense of identification with the young men at the front could be gained from supplying them with uniforms or shells than from working as a servant. In addition, Roundhay Undenominational members were contributing one penny each per week to pay for the coal at the nearby Belgian Refugees' Home. The extent to which the agenda was set by the mistresses can only be supposed.

During the winter of 1914–15 the Lady Mayoress's Committee opened a Recreation Room for girls working in central Leeds and two LDAGC members were appointed to the Committee. During the winter the room was open each evening and Clubs sent both helpers and elder girls to assist. This was a new sort of endeavour for the Association as it showed them taking action to support the welfare of girls working long shifts. Restrictions on street lighting affected clubs' attendance and some reported trying to meet during Saturday afternoons. However the Girls' Friendly Societies' home nursing lectures, which had been poorly attended in earlier years, attracted larger audiences. Middle class young women, including club helpers and leaders like the Harvey sisters, went into nursing but others found themselves nursing family members in their homes.

Wartime also saw the growth of the Girl Guides (founded 1910) who were to prove an increasingly popular alternative to traditional girls' clubs during the post-war period. Even during the war Pontefract Girls' Evening Home, most of whose members were employed in the liquorice works with the rest working on munitions, saw their attendance affected by the recently created Girl Guides.

1918–1934: LDAGC's decline

Unfortunately the LDAGC reports from 1917 and 1918 are not in the archives. The 1919 15th Annual Report outlines the post-war context:

> For the last four years there has been little to report except that the Association was 'carrying on' in a quiet way, marking time till new conditions would allow fresh developments. This was still the case with the session just ended, for though the signing of the armistice in November, 1918, marked the end of the times of greatest stringency, the difficulties under which the Clubs had laboured could not be removed immediately. Time was needed before rooms, which had been commandeered for other purposes, could be secured again for meetings, before fresh helpers could be found, and girls freed from the necessity for 'overtime' work which made their attendance so irregular.

The Association paints a picture of hard-working young women patiently playing their role in wartime. The description conveys a sense of the exhaustion which the war and subsequent influenza epidemic engendered throughout the population. Previous wars had not had the same impact on the civilian population which had faced for the first time food rationing and aerial bombing as well as hitherto unimaginable numbers of dead and injured. However, writing in 1923, Scott expressed a different view of local young women's response to the war. He commented that:

> *If you gain the confidence of returned soldiers they will tell you quietly of the great change which they feel has come over many of our women and girls; of their over-dress or under-dress, their giddiness and flippancy, the frequent veneer of affected masculinity. Exceptions there are, they admit. But, on the whole, they are not favourably impressed with either the tone or the manners of the majority of girls "they left behind". The development of womanhood, in the hands of those who have professed to be its leaders, does not strike them as being on the right lines. They preferred the pre-war feminine atmosphere.*

(Scott, 1923: 70)

Girls' club leaders and helpers may be included among the 'professed leaders' to whom Scott refers with such negativity. The possible tensions between the ex-servicemen and the young women who had worked long hours in hitherto unfamiliar and physically demanding occupations can be imagined from Scott's comment. The comparative independence and income they had enjoyed was replaced by an attempt to return them to pre-war models of domesticity. Women frequently lost their jobs, making way for the returning men.

During the 1920s membership of traditional girls' clubs decreased and the number of clubs affiliated to LAGC declined as some clubs folded or temporarily suspended their meetings. In 1924 twenty-eight clubs were affiliated but ten years later the number had declined to twelve. The LDAGC was alert to this and in 1926 the Annual Meeting heard Miss Atkinson Williams whose 'helpful address' suggested ways to increase club membership. Potential members, she said, 'would be attracted to our Clubs by posters in house and shop windows, and by carefully worded notices from the pulpit' although it appears likely that clubs had tried such measures already. She stressed that clubs should open and close punctually and that helpers needed to be 'ready to start work at the time advertised', suggesting that there were clubs where these things did not happen. A clubs' ethos should demonstrate that their activities were 'a means to an end', nurturing the girls' development into 'better daughters in the home', reflecting the post-war ethos and emphasising the change in girls' lives: a decade ago many had been working overtime in mills and factories. By this time, unemployment in Leeds was increasing. Some workers lost their jobs entirely but more were on reduced hours due to lack of orders. Young women doing piece work found their incomes were not only reduced but also more unpredictable.

In 1928 the Annual Meeting heard an apparently more secular speech from Mrs Schroeder on 'A Girl's Liberty'. She commented that:

> *Much of the freedom the young girls of today are enabled to enjoy had been gained for them by the 'blue stockings' of the former generations who were able to take a long view of life, and by their acts, had gained much for the young people of today.*

However she subsequently turned to the theme of service which generally formed an aspect of annual addresses during the period. 'Liberty' could only be earned through service:

> *If a girl only strives for pleasure she will soon find her life is empty, so club leaders are endeavouring to teach girls the things that will make her life better and more useful.*

It is interesting that Mrs Schroeder gave this speech to LDAGC: presumably the audience comprised club leaders and helpers rather than members as the content appears rather more designed for a middle-class audience.

Each year the Association continued to hold its competition, with classes mirroring contemporary changes: creative writing, dyeing and skipping joined embroidery, knitting and cookery but the number of entries declined reflecting the reduced membership. In 1928 the Annual Report drew readers' attention to the fact that LDAGC had a balance of 'only a few shillings' and 'would be grateful for additional subscribers'. With the exception of references to the financial situation, the annual reports fail to convey any impression of panic, but it seems reasonable to suppose that some consideration must have been given to the Association's future and whether it should carry on.

The organisation had lost its pre-war dynamism although this was scarcely evident when Hilda Hargrove returned to give the address at the 27th Annual Meeting in 1931, bearing greetings from Dr Lucy Pinniger. She spoke of a club as the 'outlet for [girls'] bound up energies and talent' and celebrated the Association's history (LDAGC, 1931). The account of her speech shows her celebrating the growth and development of the organisation, without which 'Leeds would be the poorer'.

1935–6: the turning point

1935 proved to be a time of change: in its thirty-first year LDAGC decided to affiliate to the National Council of Girls' Clubs (NCGC). NCGC invited LDAGC to affiliate and was in turn invited to send a representative to address the Executive Committee and Council. The NCGC's Clubs Expansion Organiser, Mrs Cole, outlined the advantages of affiliation which included training schemes for club leaders, access to campsites and insurance. She also stressed that:

> Clubs were not only to be regarded as play centres or a place for cheap amusement but to make the club a real training for life and to the maintaining of relationships with the World, the Home, other Clubs and with the National Movement.

LDAGC's President Mrs Rich asked members to consider not only what they would gain by affiliating but also 'what we could give'. A motion proposing that LDAGC should affiliate to the NCGC was carried and the next months were a time of change. Mrs Cole urged LDAGC 'to take a wider view of club work by being interested in the clubs all over the county': no clubs from the district beyond central Leeds were affiliated by this time. There is little to suggest that LDAGC had been proactive in promoting the idea of clubs either locally or around the district for many years, despite its aims (which had never been changed). NCGC received £450 from the King George V Jubilee Trust to create new girls' clubs and strengthen existing ones across the county and created a new tier of organisation: Yorkshire Association of Girls' Clubs (YAGC) with a paid worker. Based in Leeds, the worker was expected to work across the whole county.

In public YAGC was presented as linking existing bodies rather than being in competition with them. However there were probably people who saw the large, funded new organisation as presenting a threat to LDAGC's very existence. Pronouncements that YAGC was intended to link rather than swamp existing bodies may not have convinced everyone. Nevertheless, the period saw the revitalisation of LDAGC and during the next year the number of affiliated clubs increased to 20. Mrs Cole encouraged the formation of a members' council which, within a year, was in existence. Hitherto, girls had been involved in the running of some clubs, but LDAGC had not promoted participation in its own governance.

In 1936 LDAGC decided that 'if a mixed club asked to be affiliated we accept it, provided it is not merely a social club'. In the light of the creation of the National Association of Social Clubs for Young People (see Butterfield and Spence, 2009), this was a significant decision. On a national basis, there was greater acceptance of mixed work and, characteristically, Leeds reflected the zeitgeist. Gender relations had been altered by the First World War and segregation began to feel old-fashioned. Nevertheless it is pertinent that LDAGC did not wish to be associated with organisations which were simply established for social purposes but sought to retain an educational dimension.

Conclusion

From its creation in 1904, LAGC was an organisation whose strength lay in the fact that it did not rely on a single figurehead: it depended on regularly changing groups of women, many from established Leeds families. The 1920s saw the Association reach a low point in terms of affiliated groups but the changes wrought by the advent of YAGC in 1935 were to strengthen it for many years ahead. At the time, across Europe young people's participation in organised activities was increasing, as was state involvement in youth matters. Debates were taking place concerning the desirability of making membership of a youth organisation outside school or employment compulsory (Todd, 2005: 216): the role of girls' clubs was changing, as were the structures around them. The advent of training schemes for leaders saw the start of a move towards the professionalisation of youth work.

Over its first three decades LDAGC evolved from being a voluntary organisation relying entirely on volunteers' efforts, into an organisation in a position to secure state funding. It had not been an innovative organisation in itself but during its first decade it was frequently at the forefront of adapting activities for local use. Although the Association had stagnated during the period following the First World War, the changes which followed LDAGC's affiliation to the NCGC and the impact of the creation of YAGC saw a revival. LDAGC and YAGC existed in parallel for several years. With the return of wartime, NCGC discovered that Yorkshire was far too large a county for a single organiser, however capable, and in 1941 the organisation divided to reflect the county's three Ridings.

References

Bradley, Q. (1997) *The Leeds Rent Strike of 1914*. Housing Studies HNC Research Project. Available: http://freespace.virgin.net/labwise.history6/rentrick.htm. Accessed 1 April 2012.

Burdett-Coutts, A. (1893) *Woman's Mission*. London: Sampson Low, Marston and Company.

Butterfield, M. and Spence, J. (2009) The Transition from Girls' Clubs to Girls' Clubs and Mixed Clubs. In Gilchrist, R. Jeffs, T. Spence, J. and Walker, J. (Eds.) *Essays in the History of Youth and Community Work*. Lyme Regis: Russell House Publishing.

Chase, M. (2009) *The WEA and Leeds Municipal Strike* [Private correspondence].

Craddick-Adams, P. (2005) *The Home Front in World War One*. Available: http://www.bbc.co.uk/history/trail/wars_conflict/home_front/the_home_front_print.html. Accessed 1 April 2012.

Greenwood, A. (1911) *Juvenile Labour Exchanges and After-Care*. London: P.S. King and Son.

Greenwood, A. (1914) The Leeds Municipal Strike. *The Economic Journal*, 24: 93.

Jacks, L.P. (1920) *From Authority to Freedom: The Spiritual Pilgrimage of Charles Hargrove.* London: Williams and Norgate.

Jones, H.M.F. (2011) Darning, Doylies and Dancing: The Work of the Leeds Association of Girls' Clubs (1904–1913). *Women's History Review,* 20: 3, 369–88.

Kushner, T. and Knox, K. (1999) *Refugees in an Age of Genocide.* London: Routledge.

Mason, C. (1901) Our Work. *The Parents' Review,* 12, 68.

Sadler, M. (1914) Notes on Mr Greenwood's Article on the Leeds Municipal Strike. *The Economic Journal,* 24: 93, 138–52.

Schroeder, W.L. (1924) *Mill Hill Chapel 1674–1924.* Leeds: unpublished.

Scott, W.H. (1923) *Leeds in the Great War.* Leeds: Libraries and Arts Committee.

Sherbrooke, A.M. and Townsend, F.M. (1896) Working Girls' Clubs. *The Bristol Mercury and Daily Post,* Issue 14880, 20 January 1896.

Todd, S. (2005) *Young Women, Work, and Family in England 1918–1950.* Oxford: Oxford University Press.

Primary Sources

Annual Reports of LAGC.

Annual Reports of LDAGC.

Leeds Association of Girls' Clubs (LAGC) and Leeds and District Association of Girls' Clubs (LDAGC) Minute Books (incomplete).

The Bristol Mercury and Daily Post, 3 October 1896.

The Leeds Mercury, 16 April 1890.

The Times, 15 December 1913.

The Times, 16 December 1913.

The Times, 17 December 1913.

The Times, 18 December 1913.

The Times, 24 December 1913.

CHAPTER 2

'Fallen Women' and 'Artful Dodgers' – Historical Reflections on Youth Deviance

Naomi Stanton and Aniela Wenham

Distinct stereotypes regarding young 'deviants' existed during the nineteenth century and into the Edwardian era. One of these was the 'fallen woman', a label attributed to female members of the lowest strata. It was synonymous with 'prostitute' and meant a stigma of sexual immorality was automatically applied to women of the perceived criminal class. 'Artful dodger' was a second used with reference to young male criminals. This conjured up an image of arrogant, skilled thieves who engaged in pick-pocketing and other crimes to fund a life of promiscuity and alcoholism. Respectable society assumed that 'fallen women' and 'artful dodgers' congregated in gangs where they planned their wrong-doing and seduced others into joining them (Emsley, 2005).

Popular entertainment including cheap literature such as the 'penny dreadfuls' and the unlicensed theatres found in large cities were widely seen as both a cause and, in the case of the latter, a breeding ground that created a steady flow of young criminals (Springhall, 1999). Common Lodging Houses and the Rookeries were also classified as 'nurseries of crime' – places where prostitutes and young thieves congregated to orchestrate their criminal activities and spend their 'earnings' on debauched living. Aggressive consumerism was believed to be far more influential in luring the young into a criminal lifestyle than any need to survive within the harsh environment most 'fallen women' and artful dodgers' were born into. Middle and upper class 'Victorians gave little or no weight to the material circumstances of unemployment, wretched housing and poverty in their understanding of the crimes of the poor' (Pearson, 1983: 173). Rather, commentators overwhelmingly referred to a decline in religious and moral values among the lower classes as the reasons why they succumbed to the temptations of 'evil'.[1]

Class and gender in the nineteenth century

The widening gap between rich and poor in the Victorian era meant the lower orders often existed in a different 'reality' to that inhabited by the middle and upper classes. Urbanisation and subsequently suburbanisation led to heightened levels of segregation of the rich from the poor which in turn resulted in fears that the beneficial moral influence of the middle class upon the lower orders was being lost (Duckworth, 2002). It was an analysis that encouraged many to set aside the environmental factors of poor housing, poverty and unemployment as the cause of youth crime in favour of a belief that crime and disorder were symptoms of a moral crisis affecting the young working class. The working class were therefore frequently viewed by policy-makers as a problematic category. This Davidoff suggests led those in power to focus on the helplessness and 'polluting effects' of those beneath them (1983:18). The upper echelons were inhabited by men who considered themselves to be rational and intellectual in their behaviour and attitudes. They predominantly viewed the working class as being more 'physical', irrational and uncontrolled. It was an analysis that justified, and explained, existing gender divisions as much as it did those based upon income and class (Purvis, 1989: 49). The further down the hierarchy one descended, according to this ideology, the more closely people came to reflect nature, and their behaviour ever more approximated to that encountered within the animal kingdom. As a consequence animal imagery was readily applied to accounts of the behaviour and lifestyle of the lower orders (Davidoff, 1983: 21). Also these descriptions highlighted how the rational and educated middle classes, unlike the poor, kept the more 'natural' aspects of living to the private sphere, and the insanitary parts of life hidden. The gentility of the former it seemed was something that the latter were unable to accomplish; for them their natural desires, particularly sexual, seemed to so consume them that these were not confined to their private lives but came to devour all their energies. The working classes were perceived as constantly succumbing to the desires of their bodies. This meant for the good of society such behaviour and instincts needed to be controlled by the 'respectable' hence, as Davidoff (1983: 27) points out, the widespread use of corporal punishment by men to discipline servants, women and children. A practice that was both legal and socially acceptable well into the twentieth century.

Changing perceptions of childhood

From the 1800s onwards the child was increasingly viewed as dependent and in need of protection (Cunningham, 1995: 141). This change gradually resulted in an extension of childhood in response to the fears associated with working class young people. Legislative reform, during this period, was based to a great extent on the notion of the child as a victim of circumstances but it also flowed from a fear that the 'unrescued' posed a threat to social stability. Factory Acts incrementally made it more difficult to employ children whilst the rise of free schooling emphasised the need for them to be educated. As the dominant models of childhood came to emphasise dependency so the 'delinquent' were frequently those who refused protection, rejected dependency and sought independence (Hendrick, 1994: 27). The response to youth crime was accordingly adjusted over time notably with the emergence of reform schools, designed to help the wayward 'unlearn' delinquency and facilitate their submission to middle class values (Manton, 1976; Montague, 1904). These were institutions designed to teach their occupants what their parents had neglected to (Hendrick, 1994: 28). Equally Education Acts post-1832, which heralded the gradual imposition of compulsory schooling, were informed by the view that dependency was the desired state and that independence in children was an indicator of moral weakness. Changing perceptions of childhood rather than challenging the dominant middle-class morality served to enhance the notion that working class children and young people needed to be controlled. Given that Victorians overwhelmingly saw the poor as responsible for their own fate, their responses centred on 'changing behaviours rather than conditions' (Dyhouse, 1981: 79). Consequently education became the key to both preventing deviance and reforming the deviant. Indeed progressive reformers, in both Britain and elsewhere, vigorously campaigned for working class young people to secure access to free education and for their transition to independence to be 'delayed' (Addams, 1912; Platt, 1969).

The 'fallen woman'

The term 'fallen woman' emanates from the Biblical 'fall' wherein Eve ate the forbidden fruit before tempting Adam to follow suit. The widespread use of this metaphor tells us much about how the female criminal was viewed during the nineteenth century. Low rates of recorded female crime were considered by middle class Victorians as confirmation of woman's 'moral superiority' (Zedner, 1991; Duckworth, 2002), physical weakness and the importance of confining them to the private and domestic spheres of work (Emsley, 2005). The 'fallen woman' was seen as the exception and the antithesis to the 'natural woman'. A prostitute and associate of thieves who having rejected the roles of wife, mother, and homemaker now acted as a 'corrupter' of young men (Emsley, 2005). The 'fallen woman' features in much of the popular literature of the time but certainly the best remembered example of this demon is Dickens' teenage 'Nancy'. Her violent death, at the close of *Oliver Twist*, warns readers of the fate that must await those who choose to embark on that way of life.

The single mother

Gender stereotypes and the dominant ideology often combined to add to the difficulties of single working class mothers who needed waged work to survive. Some sympathy towards these women in the early Victorian period was to be found, for example, the artist Richard Redgrave represented the stress and over-work faced by single women through his art and poetry. However as Danahay (2005: 49) points out even this was at times double-edged; rather than invoking social support for these women, the image portrayed by Redgrave and others reinforced the label of females as the weaker sex. Also the frequently harsh and 'unsightly' representations of struggle tended to support the idea that women were naturally disposed to work of a private and domestic nature and that paid laborious work was more suited to men. Realities of working class life rarely conformed to this ideal not least because poverty created a necessity for so many women to work and earn, something that simply created a stigma of its own (Dyhouse, 1981: 80).

Many working class women had long worked from home but after indus-trialisation, home-based production was increasingly brought into factories, thereby exposing a growing number of working women to the public gaze. Gomersall (1997: 5) argues this growing presence in the workplace threatened patriarchal notions of family-life, and women's willingness to work for low pay brought a perceived instability in work and conditions for men. Therefore it can be argued that the introduction of formal schooling was, in part, designed to teach working class girls about their expected social roles and steer them away from paid employment. Certainly Dyhouse (1981: 175) argues mass schooling reinforced gender constraints and conceptions of 'femininity'.

The stigma attached to single working women was intensified with regards to those who were mothers of 'illegitimate' children (Pearson, 1983: 165). Middle class married women, thanks to the labour of female servants, had the option of carving out a role in the public sphere predominately via voluntary work (Vicinus, 1985). An essay published in 1849 showed how much more problematic this was for working class mothers. This article described how many had to administer opium to their child before going to work, then again during the lunch break, and once more at night so she could sleep. The child, it was widely assumed, would diffuse this dependency onto alcohol and be obliged as adulthood approached to turn to crime to fund the 'habit'.[2] Accounts such as these added to the growing fears that parental neglect and a lack of supervision, caused by women working, was increasingly responsible for youth crime and immorality.

Single mothers, although generally judged more salvageable than prostitutes, were often designated 'fallen women'. Such attitudes, along with the conditions for working women – long hours and hard labour often accompanied by a risk of physical violence – probably resulted in some single women and 'fallen' mothers entering into prostitution. For this may have appeared to be the only viable option open to many 'poor working women trying to survive in towns that offered them few employment opportunities and were hostile to young women living alone' (Walkowitz, 1980: 9).

Perceptions of prostitution

Prostitutes were not labelled as harshly across all social classes. Although they were considered 'public enemies, criminals, and outcasts' by the ruling classes, they were often treated by their immediate neighbours with tolerance (Walkowitz, 1980: 39: 29). Some also found companionship with peers in their shared lodgings. Legislation and dominant social attitudes meant prostitutes were condemned and treated more severely than their clients. A nineteenth century commentator justified this on the grounds that:

> . . . there is no comparison to be made between prostitutes and the men who consort with them. With the one sex the offence is committed as a matter of gain; with the other it is an irregular indulgence of a natural impulse.

> (cited in Emsley, 2005: 105)

This discriminating attitude was reflected in the Contagious Diseases Acts of 1864, 1866, and 1869. Each allowed women identified as prostitutes by the police to be subjected to regular, compulsory examinations for disease and if they were found to be infected incarcerated in 'lock hospitals' (Walkowitz, 1980: 1–2). No comparable constraints were imposed upon those men who regularly visited prostitutes. These Acts were designed to halt the spread of disease not to protect the women. Indeed it was widely held that syphilis was a deserved consequence for the actions of these women (Duckworth, 2002). These Acts were 'instrumental in crystallizing and shaping many of these social views' (Walkowitz, 1980: 5) about 'fallen women' but they also stirred into action a feminist movement, one anxious to campaign for their repeal (Manton, 1976; Jordan, 2001; Oldfield, 2008).

Respectable society embraced several flawed assumptions about prostitutes. For instance, the literature frequently referred to rising levels of child prostitution among girls as young as eight years.[3] This viewpoint may be mistaken for 'between 1849 and 1856 the proportion of female inmates under sixteen at the London Lock Hospital was only 6.5 percent' and 'this declined to 2.3 percent between 1857 and 1863' (Walkowitz, 1980: 17). Some organisations, such as the Rescue Society of London, which specialised in rescuing young girls and women, went so far as to deny 'the existence of child prostitutes under sixteen' (op cit.). Another commonplace of the Victorian era was that the 'fallen woman' was not easily reformed, once she became a 'hardened' offender it was to be expected she would live out her life in immorality and sexual deviance. For many women, however, prostitution was a 'temporary . . . solution to their immediate difficulties' (Walkowitz, 1980: 195). Finally the widespread belief that prostitutes were in collaboration with gangs and thieves and therefore involved in a wider network of criminal activity (Emsley, 2005: 96; Duckworth, 2002: 196) is also questionable. Most it seems were self-employed and generally independent who lived in lodging houses alongside other prostitutes. Only a minority ever resided in brothels' and even fewer lived in 'flash houses' seducing young men for criminal gangs (Walkowitz, 1980: 25).

The dominant Victorian viewpoint did not view the prostitute as needing material help rather it saw her as morally depraved, a corrupter of others through seduction into sex and crime. Often they were portrayed as the debauchers of middle class men and paradoxically a fire-wall protecting their middle-class sisters from the lustful urges and perverse fantasies of their husbands and suitors. Either way, they were an assemblage best hidden lest they expose the perceived natural desires of men or the antithesis of female respectability. According to this script the middle class and morally respectable wife was viewed as her husband's salvation, the prostitute as his downfall (Davidoff, 1983: 21). Josephine Butler and others were uncomfortable with this interpretation and in particular sought to portray a reality that recognised prostitutes as 'victims' rather than threats. Butler, as well as leading the campaign to repeal the Contagious Diseases Acts, sought to highlight the plight of women being trafficked between Britain and Europe (Jordan, 2001). Evangelistic missionaries and feminists such as Butler led the way in expressing sympathies towards 'fallen' girls. Though they usually focused their efforts on helping younger prostitutes and those deemed 'desirous of leaving their evil ways'.[4] Irrespective of their motives their work marked a significant development in that it demanded that wider society should begin to take a measure of responsibility for the welfare of young women.

Punishment of female criminals

Middle-class females who committed a felony rarely fitted the image of the 'fallen woman', therefore they were often assumed to be ill (e.g. kleptomania), feeble-minded (Whitlock, 2005) or in some way not responsible for their actions. The opinion that these felons might be controlled by husbands or fathers was so widespread that it manufactured the need for legislation allowing men to be tried for female crimes – 'feme covert' (Emsley, 2005: 94). Thus an examination of convictions between 1800 and 1900 shows middle-class females to be under-represented due both to bias in relation to the decision to prosecute and to the presence of 'feme covert'. Similar reluctance also existed regarding the use of sentences involving corporal punishment and the execution of women (Gatrell, 1994: 318). This contrasts with the situation encountered in the previous century when, although women were less likely than men to be convicted of a serious crime, those who were tended to be sentenced more harshly, and in the case of capital crimes their executions were less likely to be commuted to a life sentence or deportation (Walker, 2003: 136). Mary Carpenter, the penal reformer, believed that during the early to mid-nineteenth century, women in custody were treated more harshly than men. This probably reflects a widespread belief that they were morally superior and therefore they were only convicted with a certain measure of reluctance; but if guilty it meant they were less redeemable. Gender bias in the law during this period becomes apparent when examining the distinction between men and women accused of spouse murder. Until 1825 those accused of killing their husband were tried for 'petty treason'; whilst a man who killed his wife was merely charged with the lesser offence of murder (Walker, 2003).

The court's relative leniency towards middle class females contrasts with their treatment of working class 'fallen women', who even for minor offences faced punishments as severe as hard labour or transportation. Jackson provides an account of the variable treatment of those accused of infanticide that illustrates this (1994: 168). He explains how due to a long-standing reluctance to convict in cases of infanticide the law was strengthened in 1803. After which prosecutions and convictions increased. In the area covered by the 'Northern Circuit' three women were found guilty of concealment and sentenced to imprisonment between 1803 and 1810, and within the first two years of the new Act being introduced two women were executed for infanticide whereas in the previous 50 years no woman had been convicted (Jackson, 1994: 175). The new Act also meant a woman indicted for infanticide who had concealed a birth was no longer automatically guilty of murder, but a woman found 'not guilty' of infanticide could be sentenced for concealment of birth during the same trial even if not indicted for that offence (1994: 174). In no other circumstance could a person be convicted of a crime they were not indicted for.

The development of reform schools

Mary Carpenter, during the middle years of the century, was instrumental in setting-up reform schools for both young women and men as alternatives to prison (Manton, 1976). Regarding the former she believed provision was vital because 'left unreformed' they would 'be teachers of vice to the next generation' (Duckworth, 2002: 205). Other charitable refuges followed for young women not viewed as 'persistent' or hardened criminals (Duckworth, 2002: 207). Carpenter proposed a three-pronged programme to address the problem of juvenile crime comprising: free day schooling for children from deprived families; industrial day schools for 'vagrants and beggars' who were to be sent to them following a court order, which was to prevent parents colluding in their escape so they might work as beggars; and reformatory boarding schools for children convicted of crimes, which would be 'family homes' to encourage a 'true reformation of character' (Manton, 1976: 102). Carpenter oversaw the founding of a number of reform schools that served as alternatives to prison for young people convicted of an offence.[5] Besides being involved in penal reform Carpenter was actively involved in the 'ragged school' movement which sought to offer basic education and religious and moral instruction to the children of the 'dangerous classes'. Ragged schools emerged from the work of John Pound but the campaign for their implementation was largely mobilised by Carpenter during the 1840s. They embraced the notion that the lower classes needed salvation from 'poverty, ignorance and discontentment' in order to prevent them waging 'war' on the middle classes (Montague, 1904: vii, 8).

Carpenter's proposals influenced the contemporary debate as to whether prison or education was more appropriate for young criminals, which was only partially resolved with the passing of the Youthful Offenders Act in 1854, which introduced reformatory schools akin to those she had campaigned for (Mahood,

1995: 49). Even after the Act many magistrates held fast to earlier assumptions relating to the causations of juvenile delinquency, preferring to sentence young criminals to prison rather than send them to the new reformatories.[6] Prisons they believed would offer the discipline that alone might lead them away from the paths of depravity.

Private lives in the public gaze

Single women who had not fulfilled their roles as mother, wife and homemaker were categorised as either 'celibate spinsters' (something often associated with high levels of spirituality) or 'promiscuous prostitutes'. Davidoff (1983: 25) notes how public private distinctions between classes also existed in relation to the role of motherhood. Middle class mothers would be responsible for the moral and religious upbringing of their children but physical care was predominantly delegated to servants. This reflected the notion of the middle class woman as private and respectable, someone to be protected from such labours, indeed many never saw their children naked. Transferring responsibility for physical care to servants symbolised the Victorian view of the working class as more comfortable with regards to natural and bodily processes.

The 'artful dodger'

As noted earlier the label 'artful dodger' conjured up an image of a young male pick-pocket rehearsed and competent in his role, and belonging to a wider gang of thieves purposefully schooled in their criminal trade. It is questionable whether this is an accurate depiction of many juvenile offenders of the period. Although it bears a resemblance to certain Dickensian and other literary characters it may be misleading; especially when it is recalled that far more females than males were prosecuted for pick-pocketing in London between 1800 and 1850 (Emsley, 2005: 96). Nevertheless it is useful to consider the stereotype in relation to the idea that young people were 'seduced' into this lifestyle by more mature criminals. Contemporary literature often describes the work of criminals and prostitutes as an 'art' explaining in detail how they seduce others to join them.[7] This notion of the skilled and talented 'artful dodger' contradicts the perception of the 'idle thief' dominant for much of the previous century. Subsequent assumptions replaced this with a romanticised image, fuelled by contemporary literature and moral panics, of an arrogant and skilful thief; purposeful, successful and content with his chosen lifestyle. However, it is questionable whether the 'idle thief' was ever transformed into a skilled 'artful dodger'.

Moral panic about gangs

Published in 1818 the *Description of Juvenile Delinquency in London* describes 'Flash-houses' as venues where gangs of young thieves gathered to engage in 'debaucherous' activities such as drinking and promiscuity.[8] There are numerous references in the primary literature of the period to such places. However the name of these locales changed being variously called: 'nurseries of crime' (1831);[9] theatres and dance-halls (1833);[10] 'the den of the prostitute . . . the low beer and spirit shop . . . the resort of gamblers, thieves, and prostitutes . . . the focus of contagion – the low lodging house' (1840);[11] 'haunts of vice and schools of crime' (1853);[12] and 'penny-gaffs' (1858).[13] Whatever the appellation these are places where criminal gangs apparently gathered to engage in debauched behaviour and plot their crimes – 'Fagin's dens' where young people were enticed into and trained for a life of crime. The evidence of social reformers and philanthropists who surveyed and studied these dens or 'rookeries' is that they did exist.[14] However such focussed research may have led to an exaggerated idea of both their scale and impact (Emsley, 2005; Humphries, 1981; Springhall, 1999). Indeed subsequent analysis of the evidence and data by scholars, such as Humphries (1981) and Emsley (2005), suggests that pick-pocketing and street theft by young men was more often the result of 'opportunism', handkerchiefs poking carelessly out of a pocket or a tempting display outside a shop, than a pre-meditated act.

Certainly many, probably most, juvenile offenders did not proceed to become hardened, habitual criminals, rather most engaged in such activities as a temporary means of managing their poverty. Certainly statistical data confirms a correlation between poverty and criminal activity with crime levels rising during times of depression (Emsley, 2005: 38). In part, fears relating to adolescent crime and youthful gangs arose because 'juvenile lawlessness was believed to foreshadow the possibilities of political insurrection among the lower orders' (Pearson, 1983: 159). During the early Victorian period serious rioting and disorder took place linked to the rise of the Chartist Movement and labour unrest. However such events were not always perceived as a response to deep political and economic inequalities, or as one of the few routes of political expression available to those denied representation. Rather than acknowledge the class inequalities, much of the discussion regarding working class discontent focused upon the assumed moral corruption, greed and youthful irresponsibility of the participants. As Pearson notes:

> *The assumed connection between Chartism and juvenile lawlessness had been given some immediate encouragement by the observation*

that young people had been particularly active in some of the more riotous happenings in the summer of 1842.

(1983: 161–2)

Such perceptions inevitably contributed to generalisations about youthful gangs engaging in criminal activity as a manifestation of working class collective endeavour designed to address deep-seated political grievances.

Theatres and dance halls were long considered gatehouses to crime; horrid places where low dramas glorified the criminal character. Respectable society also believed much criminal activity was motivated by a desire on the part of young people to secure the money to gain entry to these places. Again these venues were perceived to be localities where older criminals preyed upon young men coaxing them into a criminal career. In response to such fears laws were introduced to control them. In 1839 the first of a number of Theatres Acts granted police the power to force entry. In 1843 a second forbade any spoken words in penny theatre performances in an attempt to curtail the glamorisation of criminals (Springhall, 1999).

Humphries (1981: 175) argues that the young male gang member was 'the symbolic folk devil of capitalist society' during the nineteenth century. Importantly he shows that gang violence was not as prevalent as it was perceived at the time and also that gang membership could for some be morally justified as a collective means of overcoming hunger and poverty (ibid. 1981: 177, 182).

Responses to youth crime

Rather than there being a network of 'Fagin's dens', the adult prisons of the first half of the nineteenth century, where young people were punished alongside more seasoned offenders, were the most significant institution for teaching petty offenders the 'arts' of criminality. Some public figures argued for prison reform and eventually succeeded in their campaign for a separate youth justice system with discrete courts, penal institutions and disposals.[15] Public campaigners in the nineteenth century blamed a diminishing significance of religion in the lives of the young for their descent into crime[16] and it was this perceived need for religious and moral instruction that influenced the responses to youth crime that emerged during this time. However a significant body of reformers looked beyond the 'moral failings' of the poor and advocated political and social reforms designed to improve the physical conditions endured by the working class. Carpenter, for example, spoke out regarding the disadvantages faced by working class children and the need for reforms to improve sanitation, housing and education (Montague, 1904).

Many of the key reformers of this period were women. Often they exemplified the acceptable voluntary helping roles that middle class women could take on within the public realm (Vicinus, 1985). Overall, charitable 'help' focused as much, perhaps more, on education as on altering the living conditions of the poor. This is not to downplay the role of ragged schools and reformatory schools in helping children and young people to change their material circumstances. However, it demonstrates how middle class help was largely provided for those who society judged to be the 'deserving poor'. A group whose existence of itself defined those who were designated to be 'undeserving' and therefore responsible for their own circumstances and plight.

Into the twentieth century – physical and moral degeneration

Pearson (1983) suggests the concept of the 'artful dodger' influenced the increasingly popular idea that criminality was hereditary and confined to the degenerate denizens of the lower classes. The arrival of compulsory free schooling made mass research far easier to undertake leading in particular to a discrete Child Study Movement that produced papers and articles in the UK and elsewhere which helped foster new anxieties about the perceived physical degeneration of young people (Hendrick, 1994: 34). Fears and attitudes concerning 'juvenile delinquency' as a consequence increasingly combined theories of both physical and moral degeneration, particularly as the Victorian era drew to a close. As Pearson explains:

> The sense of moral crisis and social discontinuity reflected here was deeply characteristic of late Victorian and Edwardian society and from the late 1890s until the First World War there was a flood of such accusations against the youth. 'A somewhat unlovely characteristic of the present day', Mrs Helen Bosanquet wrote in 1906, was that 'there is among the children a prevailing and increasing want of respect towards their elders, more especially, perhaps, towards their parents'. These typical judgements against dwindling authority formed part of a wider fabric of anxiety in this era and there were some quite delirious fears in circulation about a supposed deterioration – both physical and moral – among the British people which was believed to be producing new and unprecedented forms of violence and depravity. The wretched condition of so many recruits for the Boer War had brought this matter very forcibly into public attention, leading to the extraordinary fact-finding mission of the Inter Departmental Committee on Physical Deterioration

in 1904. And although the committee believed that the problem had been overstated, this did little to allay the anxieties.

(1983: 55–6)

These inflated fears about the physical and moral deterioration of young people reshaped many of the policy responses during the Edwardian era to youth deviance resulting in the focus shifting from the 'reclamation and reform of children' to 'attending to their bodily needs' (Hendrick, 1994: 41). The new awareness of environmental factors and the continuance of moral concerns arguably combined to inform policies that saw young people as both physically and morally dependent on middle class help.

The detailed research of Davies (2008) shows how the widespread presence of adolescent gangs in certain parts of the Manchester conurbation led to the formation of boys' clubs that sought to counter a perceived love of violence and physical deterioration amongst working class youth by creating healthier outlets for physical aggression. These 'Working Lads' Clubs' often acquired gymnasiums, playing fields and an ethos that reflected a belief that via games it was possible to improve the morals and physical well-being of members.

As the century progressed Victorian society began to take greater responsibility for the root causes of crime through the development of, first, 'ragged schools' and then reformatories, as well as changes in the court system. Included within this package of reforms were early alternatives to incarceration based upon supervision in the community. For example during the latter part of the century a 'Boys' Beadle' was employed in London to look after the welfare of young men on the streets.[17] Also evangelistic religious movements and philanthropists took some responsibility for outreach work by appointing court missionaries whilst boys' clubs and uniformed organisations such as the Scouts and Boys' Brigade sought to divert boys' energies into constructive and patriotic activities. However, even seemingly positive responses such as the Scouts stemmed from the perception of young men as being at risk through idleness and from the lure of casual, or even illegal, work and therefore in need of a more disciplined and committed lifestyle.

Contemporary notions of 'devious' youth

Reflecting on the pervasiveness of the discourses discussed in the preceding sections may help highlight the persistence of gender and class inequalities. Moreover through an exploration of contemporary moral panics about young people we can witness the legacy and resilience of earlier stereotypes.

Contemporary femininities

Within social policy much discussion still focuses upon young women deemed 'at risk' of social exclusion (Harris, 2004; McRobbie, 2000; Skeggs, 1997; Walkerdine et al., 2001). Popular representations of the 'at risk' girl remain couched in terms of their 'failure' to make a successful transition to adulthood, which leads to the manufacture of negative femininities/feminine identities. This typecasting of the 'at risk' girl is commonplace, and shares many similarities with the concept of the 'fallen woman'. Not least moral panics from both eras have been overly concerned with young women's sexuality, deviancy and criminality. What is particularly striking is how these have been predominantly tied to social class. With narratives consistently formulated within a vernacular of individual and group moral delinquency, rather than with reference to the material and structural conditions that shape their lives. Media outputs, especially tabloid headlines, describe an emerging 'ladette' culture (Jackson and Tinkler, 2007) in a way that echoes the Victorian notion that 'fallen women' were defying their femininity. Young women partaking in 'dangerous' behaviours such as substance and alcohol misuse, gang membership, risky sexual activities and behaviour leading to school exclusion have become the focus of contemporary moral panics – panics that yet again centre attention on the behaviour of working class young people.

Present day concerns relating to 'risky sexual behaviour' have strong moral undertones, and in recent years have been the focus of substantive policy interventions. The 'National Teenage Pregnancy Strategy' (TPS), introduced in 1999, is a prime example of this. Teenage pregnancy still invokes disapproval and disproportionate levels of intervention so that young mothers are made acutely aware of the 'dishonour' accompanying their status as 'teen mums'. Like the 'fallen women' of an earlier era young mothers frequently experience stigma in their daily lives (Arai, 2003; Carter and Coleman, 2006; Greene, 2003; Wenham, 2011). Increased concerns over the behaviour of the 'at risk' girl have led to greater regulation, surveillance and intervention. As Harris notes:

> . . . new times are characterised by a sense of danger and uncertainty about the world, and this is expressed in the management of public spaces . . . if they are not in education they must be in work, and if they are not in work they must be in an unemployment programme or training scheme.
>
> (2004: 100)

This provides an interesting contrast with earlier periods when women were criticised for undertaking paid work. It appears that, regarding some issues, feminism may have changed rather than alleviated the pressures working class women face.

Contemporary masculinities

While those 'at risk' have been the prime focus within the field of girl studies, the crisis of masculinity has dominated debates relating to the plight of young men growing up in late modernity (Frosh et al., 2002; Mac an Ghaill, 1994). In a similar vein to the 'artful dodger', the 'usual suspects' of young males drawn from economically deprived backgrounds are now the foci of media attention. The most recent of which was the moral panic created by the summer riots of August 2011. Heavily gendered this drew upon the underclass thesis (Welshman, 2006) and was linked to supposed or actual gang activity. In seeking to explain these events the Prime Minister placed emphasis on each of the above factors:

> *At the heart of all the violence sits the issue of the street gangs. Territorial, hierarchical and incredibly violent, they are mostly composed of young boys, mainly from dysfunctional homes. They earn money through crime, particularly drugs and are bound by an imposed loyalty to an authoritarian gang leader. They have blighted life on their estates with gang-on-gang murders and unprovoked attacks on innocent bystanders. In the last few days there is some evidence that they have been behind the coordination of the attacks on the police and the looting that has followed.*

> (Cameron, 2011)

The similarities with earlier stereotypes are striking. However, there is also a notable difference, namely the distinct challenges that late modernity presents for young people as a consequence of the uncertainty that surrounds the transition to adulthood (Furlong and Cartmel, 2007).

Leaving aside the social constructions of 'dangerous youth' over time, we now have a political climate in which young people are being abandoned to market forces, with only minimal state intervention. Spending cuts and the decimation of the statutory youth sector are the most recent measures in a long line of marginalising directives towards the young of this country. The young people who are already experiencing the worst, are indeed those already under the watchful gaze as being 'at risk', 'deficit' or 'underachieving'. The persistence of a discourse that blames inequalities on the 'deficiencies' of individuals or particular groups of young people has far-reaching consequences. By consistently demonising young people for particular behaviour or the circumstances in which they find themselves, whilst at the same time denying them the opportunities to fulfil their potential, we essentially set them up for failure (Coles, 2011). Increasingly they are being blamed for their 'failures', while public policy ignores the growing polarisation between those deemed 'successful' and those perceived to be 'failing' within the context of social structures which go a long way to explaining these different outcomes.

Conclusion

This chapter has focused not on the development of work with young people or communities but on the history of societal debates about them. In the current context of funded work with young people being often fear-driven and deficit-focused it is a useful reflection to make. Griffiths (2002: 34) suggests the concept of the 'juvenile delinquent' was 'legislated into existence' over a century ago when fears created by stereotypes of youth, class and gender caused the Victorians to focus on certain crimes that made them appear to be occurring at greater levels than was the case due to heightened publicity, new legislation and greater police attention. Certainly these stereotypes adversely influenced the attitudes of the magistracy towards sentencing (Emsley, 2005: 29). The biases and beliefs of Victorian culture were reflected in the language of fear employed in relation to young people. For example, juvenile offenders were described as 'a bane to society, which like an ulcer on the body, is continually enlarging, and distributing far and wide its noxious influence' (cited Pearson, 1983: 157). Too often it appeared the dominant assumption was that groups of young people were increasingly becoming morally degenerate.

Our analysis argues that anxieties regarding disaffected youth have long been a consistent feature in British history. An historical perspective can help us understand the central concerns of the present. There are, of course, different social and cultural possibilities open to young people in each era. However a dominant discourse that pathologises young people inhibits alternative ways of thinking and frequently results in the disempowerment of the most vulnerable amongst them – a disempowerment that has endured throughout the period under review.

Endnotes

1 For example: Walter Buchanan, 'Remarks on the Causes and State of Juvenile Crime in the Metropolis; with hints for preventing its increase' (London: Printed by Richard and John E. Taylor, Red Lion Court, Fleet Street 1846), pp. 3–10, 14–16, 18–19, 22, 24–25 (Crerar Lib.) 'Juvenile delinquency in London, 1846', p. 191.

2 Thomas Beggs, 'An Inquiry into the Extent and Causes of Juvenile Depravity' (London 1849), pp. 74–75, 84, 118, 121–22, 124, 149 (editor's lib.) in 'Prize Essay Contest to Prove That Intemperance Is the Major Cause of Crime and Juvenile Depravity, 1849', p. 220.

3 For example: Birmingham Society for the Protection of Young Females and Suppression of Juvenile Prostitution (Birmingham 1840) (Brit. Mus.) 'Juvenile prostitutes in Birmingham 1840', p. 165.

4 Female Mission in Connexion with the Reformatory and Refuge Union. 'Report of the Sub-committee' (London 1859) pp. 3, 7 (Brit. Mus.) 'Work of London City Missionaries with Fallen Girls, 1859–1867', p. 264.

5 Mary Carpenter, p. 228.

6 Rev. W. C. Osborn, 'The Cry of 10,000 Children; or, Cruelty towards the Young: being an Appeal to Legislature and Chaplain of the Bath Gaol, England, and author of The Preservation of Youth From Crime: A Nation's Duty' (1860); 'Not Guilty'; 'Prevention of Crime'; 'The Non-Imprisonment of Children'; etc. 'Ten Thousand Children Committed to Prison even after Passage of Reformatory Schools Act of 1854'.

7 Edward Gibbon Wakefield, 'Facts Relating to the Punishment of Death in the Metropolis' (London 1831), pp. v, viii, 16, 80–81, 88, 138, 140–41, 176 (Brit. Mus.) 'Wakefield describes Nurseries of Crime in London and shows how capital sentences imposed upon children are generally commuted, 1831', p. 144.

8 '[First] Report of the Committee of the Society for the Improvement of Prison Discipline, and for the Reformation of Juvenile Offenders' (London 1818), pp. 8, 13, 15, 17, 20, 32 (Brit. Mus.) 'Further description of juvenile delinquency in London, 1818', p. 110.

9 Edward Gibbon Wakefield, p. 141.

10 Anon., 'Old Bailey experience: Criminal jurisprudence and the actual writing of our Penal code of Laws. Also, an essay on Prison Discipline, to which is added a History of the Crimes Committed by Offenders in the present day' (London 1833), pp. 38, 72, 300, 302, 297–98, 312–13, 361, 363, 393–99, 290 (editor's lib.) 'Delinquent Children in the Eighteen-Thirties in London', p. 149.

11 William Beaver Neale, 'Juvenile Delinquency in Manchester: its causes and history, its consequences, and some suggestions concerning its cure' (Manchester 1840), pp. 7–8, 13–16, 46, 52–53, 40–41, 37 (editor's lib.) 'Juvenile Delinquency in Manchester, 1840', p. 167.

12 Rev. Micaiah Hill, and Miss C. F. Cornwallis, 'Two prize essays on juvenile delinquency', (London 1853), pp. lii–v, (UNC Lib.) 'Lady Noel Byron's Prize essay Contest on Juvenile Delinquency, 1851–1853', p. 232.

13 Samuel Philips Day, 'Juvenile Crime: Its Causes, Character and Cure' (London 1858), pp. 54–55, 168–69, 171, 176, 180, 185, 203, 208, 211 (UNC Lib.) '*Minor Theatres, Dancing Saloons, and Demoralizing Publications as Causes of Delinquency*', p. 259.

14 Thomas Beames, 'The Rookeries of London: Past, Present, and Prospective' (London 1850), pp. 95–96, 119, 122–24, 132 (Brit. Mus.) 'Rookeries as Nurseries of Felons, 1850'.

15 Mary Carpenter, 'Reformatory Schools, for the children of the perishing and dangerous classes, and for juvenile offenders' (London 1851) (editor's lib.) 'Miss Mary Carpenter Leads Movement to set up Industrial and Reformatory schools 1851–1853', p. 226.
16 Walter Buchanan, p. 191.
17 'Eleventh Annual Report of the Reformatory and Refuge Union' (London 1867), p. 11 (Brit. Mus.) 'William King Appointed First Boys' Beadle in London by the Reformatory and Refuge Union, October 1866', p. 269.

References

Addams, J. (1912) *A New Conscience and an Ancient Evil.* New York: Macmillan.

Arai, L. (2003) 'Low Expectations, Sexual Attitudes and Knowledge: Explaining Teenage Pregnancy and Fertility in English Communities. Insights from qualitative research'. *Sociological Review,* 51: 99–217.

Cameron, D. (2011) Speech on the Fight-back After the Riots. *New Statesman,* 15 August. Available at: http://www.newstatesman.com/politics/2011/08/society-fight-work-rights.

Carter, S. and Coleman, L. (2006) *'Planned' Teenage Pregnancy, Perspectives of Young Parents from Disadvantaged Backgrounds.* Bristol: Joseph Rowntree Foundation/Policy Press.

Coles, B. (2011) Youth. In Yeates, N. Haux, T. Jawad, R. and Kilkey, M. (Eds.) *In Defence of Welfare: The Impacts of The Spending Review.* Bristol: Social Policy Association.

Cunningham, H. (1995) *Children and Childhood in Western Society Since 1500.* Harlow: Longman.

Danahay, M.A. (2005) *Gender at Work in Victorian Culture.* Aldershot: Ashgate.

Davidoff, L. (1983) Class and Gender in Victorian England. In Newton, J.L., Ryan M.P. and Walkowitz, J.R. (Eds.) *Sex and Class in Women's History.* London: Routledge and Kegan Paul.

Davies, A. (2008) *The Gangs of Manchester.* Preston: Milo Books.

Duckworth, J. (2002) *Fagin's Children.* Continuum: London.

Dyhouse, C. (1981) *Girls Growing up in Late Victorian and Edwardian England.* London: Routledge and Kegan Paul.

Emsley, C. (2005) *Crime and Society in England 1750–1900.* Harlow: Pearson Education.

Frosh, S., Phoenix, A. and Pattman, R. (2002) *Young Masculinities.* Basingstoke: Palgrave.

Furlong, A. and Cartmel, F. (2007) *Young People and Social Change, New Perspectives.* Buckingham: Open University Press.

Gatrell, V. (1994) *The Hanging Tree.* Oxford: Oxford University Press.

Gomersall, M. (1997) *Working Class Girls in Nineteenth-Century England.* Basingstoke: Macmillan.

Greene, S. (2003) Deconstructing the 'Unplanned' Pregnancy: Social Exclusion and Sexual Health Strategies in Scotland. *Youth and Policy,* 82: 27–46.

Griffiths, P. (2002) Juvenile Delinquency in Time. In Cox, P. and Shore, H. (Eds.) *Becoming Delinquent: British and European Youth, 1650–1950.* Aldershot: Ashgate.

Harris, A. (2004) *Future Girl, Young Women in the Twenty-first Century.* New York: Routledge.

Hendrick, H. (1990) *Images of Youth.* Oxford: Clarendon Press.

Hendrick, H. (1994) *Child Welfare: England 1872–1989.* London: Routledge.

Humphries, S. (1981) *Hooligans or Rebels?* Oxford: Basil Blackwell.

Jackson, C. and Tinkler, P. (2007) 'Ladettes' and 'Modern Girls': 'Troublesome' Young Femininities. *The Sociological Review,* 55: 2, 251–72.

Jackson, M. (1994) *New-Born Child Murder: Women, Illegitimacy and the Courts in Eighteenth-century England.* Manchester: Manchester University Press.

Jordan, J. (2001) *Josephine Butler*. London: John Murray.

Mac an Ghaill, M. (1994) *The Making of Men*. Buckingham: Open University Press.

Mahood, L. (1995) *Policing Gender, Class and Family: Britain 1850–1940*. London: UCL Press.

Manton, J. (1976) *Mary Carpenter and the Children of the Streets*. London: Heinemann.

McRobbie, A. (2000) *Feminism and Youth Culture*. London: Macmillan.

Montague, C.J. (1904) *Sixty Years in Waifdom*. London: Woburn Press.

Oldfield, S. (2008) *Jeanie, an 'Army of One'*. Eastbourne: Sussex Academic Press.

Pearson, G. (1983) *Hooligan: A History of Respectable Fears*. Basingstoke: Macmillan.

Platt, A.M. (1969) *The Child Savers*. Chicago: University of Chicago Press.

Purvis, J. (1981) The Double Burden of Class and Gender in The Schooling of Working-Class Girls in Nineteenth Century England, 1800–1870. In Barton, L. and Walker, S. (Eds.) *Schools, Teachers and Teaching*. Lewes: Falmer Press.

Purvis, J. (1989) *Hard Lessons*. Minneapolis: University of Minnesota Press.

SEU (Social Exclusion Unit) (1999) *Teenage Pregnancy*. London: The Stationery Office.

Skeggs, B. (1997) *Formations of Class and Gender*. London: Sage.

Springhall, J. (1999) *Youth, Popular Culture and Moral Panics: Penny Gaffs to Gangsta-Rap, 1830–1996*. Basingstoke: Palgrave.

Vicinus, M. (1985) *Independent Women*. London: Virago Press.

Walker, G. (2003) *Crime, Gender and Social Order in Early Modern England*. Cambridge: Cambridge University Press.

Walkerdine, V., Lucey, H. and Melody, J. (2001) *Growing Up Girl, Psychosocial Explorations of Gender and Class*. Basingstoke: Palgrave.

Walkowitz, J.R. (1980) *Prostitution and Victorian Society: Women, Class and the State*. Cambridge: Cambridge University Press.

Welshman, J. (2006) *Underclass: A History of the Excluded 1880–2000*. London: Continuum.

Wenham, A. (2011) *Mothers in the Making: A Qualitative Longitudinal Study Exploring The Journey of Becoming and Being a Teenage Mother*. Unpublished PhD thesis, University of York.

Whitlock, T.C. (2005) *Crime, Gender and Consumer Culture in Nineteenth-Century England*. Aldershot: Ashgate.

Zedner, L. (1991) *Women, Crime and Custody in Victorian England*. Oxford: Oxford University Press.

Primary Sources

The documents listed in the endnotes are to be found in the bound volume held at York University library cited below:

Sanders, Wiley B. (1970) *Juvenile Offenders for a Thousand Years: Selected Readings from Anglo-Saxon Times to 1900*. Chapel Hill, NC: University of North Carolina Press, USA.

CHAPTER 3

'Doing Their Bit'; Girls' Clubs and the Great War

Tony Jeffs

Retrospectively, everything seemed so inevitable, so predictable. After all, the outbreak of war during August 1914 followed decades of mounting tension between the great powers of Europe, with Britain, France and Russia on one side and Germany, Austro-Hungary and eventually Turkey on the other. Yet when war came it took many unawares, not least some important youth leaders. Arthur Yapp, General Secretary of the English National Council of the YMCA, who between 1914 and 1919 administered the greatest ever mobilisation of voluntary effort and resources by a youth organisation, had planned to spend August attending the German YMCA Conference at Barmen-Elberfeld, then touring German YMCAs with his counterpart Herr Helbing. Family illness resulted in a last minute cancellation, so instead Yapp accompanied his wife on a two day holiday to Overstrand in Norfolk. Yapp's biography recalls that had he accepted the invitation he would 'probably have been interned' (1927: 59). Miss Yelf, Yapp's near equivalent at the YWCA, was less fortunate. Holidaying in Austria when war was declared she dashed across Germany to reach home only to be arrested as a spy upon her arrival at Hamburg. After a week languishing in a German prison the intervention of colleagues from the German YWCA and the British Foreign Office secured Yelf's release. Meanwhile her colleagues were arranging for young German and Austrian girls stranded in Britain to return home in 'protected parties' (YWCA Archive MSS 243/62/1-2).

Initially they may have been on the back-foot but with astonishing alacrity youth organisations swung into action during those early days and weeks. Scouts, in their tens of thousands, mobilised for emergency duty – guarding bridges against saboteurs, patrolling cliff-tops and shore-lines looking out for enemy incursions and spies sneaking ashore under cover of darkness. Across the country Scouts reported to recruitment offices and barracks to run errands and help out (Dimmock, 1937). Older Scouts, often led by their Scout-masters, and likewise senior members and leaders from boys' clubs during those early days marched to those same recruiting offices to 'sign-up' together so that they might serve in the same unit. For example 80 Scouts from the Toynbee Hall Troop marched behind their Scoutmaster T. S. Lukis to the local recruiting office to enlist as one (Briggs and Macartney, 1984: 79). In similar fashion 49 out of the 80 members of the Joe Walton Boys' Club in Middlesbrough along with a majority of the leaders did the same (Stephenson, 2006). Girl Guides exhibited similar zeal but Headquarters insisted their duties must be of a 'non-military' nature and that they must produce a letter giving parental consent for them to engage in 'war work' (Kerr, 1932). Soon they were helping in hospitals; serving at soup kitchens; and taking charge of children to release mothers for essential war work. Inevitably certain jobs were more glamorous than others. In September 1915 the Boy Scouts working as messengers at the MI5 headquarters were dismissed for being unreliable and troublesome and replaced by Girl Guides. For similar reasons they supplanted the Boy Scouts at the Postal Censorship Office. These Guides, aged 14 to 16 and paid ten shillings for a fifty hour week, proved so dependable that a contingent was taken as messengers by the British delegation to the Paris Peace Conference in June 1919 (Hampton, 2011: 13). Such was the proven worth of the Guides that in some workplaces where the need for safety or secrecy was paramount:

> *all the workers were Guides aged fourteen up. During their lunch hour they would assemble in the factory yard and remove their working overalls and caps to reveal their Guide uniforms and their hair in long, single plaits. Their Captain wore a long skirt, navy blouse and white kid gloves to go with her felt hat and lanyard . . . When the factory whistle went they would put their overalls and caps back on, and return to making armaments.*

(Hampton, 2011: 14)

Soup kitchens, child care and such seemed far too milk and watery for some young women so a rather improbable duo of Evelina Haverfield, a leading member of the radical wing of the Women's Social and Political Union, and Edith, Marchioness of Londonderry, founded the Women's Volunteer Reserve (WVR). Designed to offer 'girl workers roughly what the Boy Scouts movement had long been doing for their schoolboy brothers' (Churchill, 1916: 15) the WVR was highly disciplined and militaristic with girls 'posted' to battalions comprising eight companies. The leadership promptly awarded each other elevated military ranks, the aristocrat Londonderry becoming Colonel-in-Chief and the commoner Haverfield a Colonel. With Staff Officers dancing in attendance they ran the whole shebang from a headquarters in Baker Street. WVR girls were trained and drilled to become messengers, dispatch riders, signallers, first-aiders and, in the event of an air attack by Zeppelins or a sea-borne invasion, to take over the 'organisation of districts'. They were also taught fencing, shooting and camping skills. London and Birmingham proved fertile recruiting grounds. Haverfield signed up 700 members at the first public meeting she addressed in the latter. Before 1914 ended battalions also materialised in Guildford, Gateshead, Brighton and Worcester. Members paid a shilling to join and £2 to buy a uniform barely distinguishable from that of an infantryman. Joining costs plus the demands membership placed upon their free time meant relatively few working class girls joined the WVR. During 1915 Haverfield departed to serve in a field nursing unit in Serbia. Shortly afterwards Londonderry disbanded the WVR and urged members to join the newly formed Women's Legion. Divided into four divisions, Agriculture, Canteen, Cookery and Motor Transport, this quickly acquired 40,000 members each paid a wage of 35 shillings for a nominal working week of sixty plus hours (*The Motor*, 19 March 1918). In 1917 the Women's Legion itself disbanded and most members joined the War Office sponsored Women's Army Auxiliary Corps (WAAC).

Within 10 days of the commencement of hostilities, the YMCA had opened 250 recreation huts for servicemen; by 1916 the total exceeded 1,500 (Yapp, 1919; 1927). By 1918 YMCA Red Triangle huts and canteens were to be encountered in every theatre of war, at all ports and railway stations of any importance, in most military hospitals and in the central districts of all major towns and cities (Snape, 2009). Many YWCA members were amongst the 40,000 women who volunteered to work in YMCA rest-huts and canteens on the Western Front, and thousands more contributed to the YMCA's work at home. The YWCA also made its own unique contribution providing hundreds of rest-huts and canteens for the army of women mobilised to work in munitions and other war industries. By 1915 the YWCA had also opened 15 hostels for women who were either working in London or were there in transit (*The Times*, 6 November 1915). Then, after the formation of the WAAC and Women's Royal Navy Service in 1917, the YWCA opened Blue Triangle huts for women military personnel in Britain and abroad (McKenzie, 1918: 419–420). By the end of 1917, 42 Blue Triangle huts were operating in Belgium and France for WAACs and medical staff. Unlike most YMCA huts these ran mixed evenings and events to which women were encouraged to invite 'men friends'.

NOGC acts

Sophy Sanger, Secretary of the International Association for Labour Legislation and founding member of the NOGC (National Organisation of Girls' Clubs), was booked to address the first NOGC meeting after the 1914 summer break. The topic was 'Continuation Schools in Germany' (Min. Office Com., 4 March 1914). One suspects that, if the meeting proceeded, it would have demanded adroit handling by the chairwoman to keep the audience's attention focussed on the scheduled topic.

Like the Guides and YWCA, the NOGC reacted with commendable urgency. *Girls' Club News* carried a suitably patriotic, but far from jingoistic message from Louise Creighton, the NOGC's president. This urged members to help each other to 'keep up their spirits', be 'careful and economical with food' and refrain from spending money on 'drink and foolish pleasures'. Pointedly, at a time when shop-keepers with Germanic names found their windows smashed and those who owned of dogs with a Teutonic lineage were deemed unpatriotic, Creighton asked readers to befriend 'any Germans who have been left in England' (1914: 1). The same edition also carried an open letter to club girls from Mabel Lawrence asking them to remember that 'the ordinary people of Germany, like ourselves, do not want this war any more than you and I. It is a war of rulers, not of people' (Lawrence, 1914: 3). This tone did not alter as the conflict unfolded. Robert Graves noted how martial ardour seemed to increase with distance from the front achieving its maximum virulence in the home country. In particular he recalled a widely circulated tract containing a letter signed 'Little Mother' declaring 'There is only one temperature for women of the British race and that is white heat' (Graves, 1929: 188). To its everlasting credit such jingoism was, and remained, absent from the publications and pronouncements of the NOGC and other girls' organisations.

The NOGC's National Executive, then known as the Office Committee, rightly assumed that the onset of hostilities would generate unemployment amongst members employed at the luxury end of the 'rag trade'. After all, a widely distributed poster told women: 'TO DRESS EXTRAVAGANTLY IN WAR TIME IS WORSE THAN BAD FORM IT IS UNPATRIOTIC' – a, sentiment that encapsulated a widespread, but never quite universal, mood of patriotic austerity, that in tandem with the switch to war production fuelled job losses in certain niche trades. Edith Glover, the NOGC's Honorary Secretary, to help cushion the impact of this 'shake-out' of labour upon club members reported to the September Council Meeting that:

A scheme had been drawn up in two or three days with most earnest thought, after some financial assistance had been promised by friends. Notices were issued to Club Leaders stating that the Office premises would be opened on August 18th as a Temporary Relief Workroom. In consultation with Miss Montagu who was appointed to serve on the Central Committee on Women's Employment, the Scheme was revised to meet the immediate demands of the Central Committee. It soon became evident that larger premises would be needed to cope with the demand made by Club members, and Miss Montagu kindly placed her club premises at 31 Alfred Place, Store Street, at the disposal of the NOGC, as a relief workroom. The numbers had grown beyond expectation, and on the day of the meeting, Mrs Glover reported that 460 girls had been employed.

(Mins. Council Meeting 14 September 1914)

By mid October the anonymous gift of £800 that financed the workshop was spent and the scheme rundown. Fortunately closure did not create undue hardship as the demand for women to fill jobs vacated by enlisting men plus the torrent of new openings in war industries ensured female employment grew to unprecedented levels, unmatched until the late 1990s. To help overcome this excess of demand over supply, the government post-haste lowered the school-leaving age, releasing over 600,000 young people onto the labour market, a total augmented by thousands more who, although below the new statutory leaving-age, worked 'in total violation of the law' (Marwick, 1965: 125). Juveniles might undertake the work of absent men, however they rarely enjoyed comparable wages. Girls employed in engineering and shipbuilding, for example, automatically had deductions made from their piece rates of between 10 to 30 per cent (Drake, 1984). Yet the war undoubtedly bestowed a measure of prosperity for as a December 1914 survey of NOGC leaders reported 'young girls were taking the place of adults and were earning more than they hitherto had done'. But it was prosperity earned at a cost for these leaders, and others believed that 'on the whole' their working 'conditions were not satisfactory' (Mins. Council Meeting, 3 February 1915). They like many others, also expressed serious concerns with regards to the moral and physical dangers encountered by young women in 'masculine' occupations (see Churchill, 1916; Fraser, 1918; Thom, 2000; Woollacott, 1994).

These developments fostered within government circles, the press and amongst welfare practitioners fears regarding the risks wartime conditions posed to the moral well-being of young people. Regarding boys and young men

the primary focus was on the heightened dangers of delinquency; whilst in relation to young women it was fears concerning sexual promiscuity, 'war babies',
the spread of VD amongst troops, and public 'disorder' that predominated.
From the onset of mobilisation, according to Fraser, many girls were 'excited
by all that was happening' and felt 'that the greatest thing was to 'know the
soldiers and talk and walk with them, and consequently large numbers flocked
'around camps and barracks, being foolish and risking worse' (1918: 237). Such
anxieties generated a flurry of new initiatives. An early articulation of the need
to intervene came in a letter to *The Times* signed by Lady Jellicoe, wife of the
Commander-in-Chief of the Grand Fleet. Seemingly penned without consultation with any of the organisations already working in the field, Jellicoe called for
a crash programme to open clubs for girls in garrison towns. Her Ladyship's mis-
sive prompted a swift response from the NOGC and others, first because Lady
Jellicoe's social position gave her exceptional access to the upper echelons of
the military establishment, access that implied support for this scheme existed
at the highest of levels. If this was the case then the launch of a programme
along the lines she suggested might, it was feared, jeopardise the capacity of
organisations, such as the NOGC, to attract funding and volunteers. Both of
which would be siphoned off to sustain a seemingly more patriotic and pressing venture. Second because Jellicoe's proposal for the wholesale creation of
temporary clubs and refreshment rooms for young women and their 'invited'
servicemen friends threatened the raison d'etre of single sex work. Maude Stanley immediately responded to Lady Jellicoe via a letter to *The Times*. This called
for funds and volunteers to expand the number of 'club rooms for girls' provided
by existing organisations. Pointedly Stanley drew the attention of readers to the
situation in Portsmouth, the home of the Royal Navy, where 'the formation of
clubs has already been set in hand by a strong and efficient body of workers . . .
with an ardent love for girls' (*The Times*, 2 December 1914). Sadly this was the
final foray into the public arena of the *grande dame* of girls' work. Stanley died
a few months later aged 82. The NOGC was in no mood to gift Lady Jellicoe
a free rein. First Creighton dispatched a private letter to Lady Jellicoe explaining that 'existing clubs were being hampered by a lack of funds and should
not be harmed by new ventures' (Mins. Council Meeting, 2 December 1914).
It proceeded to request a meeting between Lily Montagu, the Honorary Chairman of the NOGC, and Lady Jellicoe. However it, and the others that quickly
followed, elicited no response. Creighton, sensing the NOGC was not exploiting
'the enthusiasm for temporary clubs', decided that despite these rebuffs they
must continue to 'seek involvement' (Mins. Office Com., 18 February 1915).
Eventually in March, three months after the preliminary approach, Montagu

and Glover secured an audience with Lady Jellicoe. They emerged unimpressed, reporting that 'any systematic co-operation would be most difficult' and that 'Jellicoe had no idea how many temporary clubs were operating, they had no rules or "systems of working"' (Mins. Office Com. 16 March 1915). Repulsed once more the NOGC tried a fresh tack. In response to a request from social workers who contacted the NOGC 'regarding urgent need for a club at Woolwich' (Mins. Office Com., 15 October 1915) the Honorary Officers approached Lady Jellicoe asking her to append her signature to a letter to be circulated to local and national papers appealing for funds to open in Woolwich a NOGC girls' club for munitions workers. Lady Jellicoe acquiesced and the club, located in a converted shop with an upstairs flat for the resident worker Rose Gardner, opened with an initial membership of 100. Shrewdly the NOGC invited Lady Jellicoe to 'cut the ribbon', which she did in the presence of the Commanding Officer of the Woolwich Garrison and leading members of the NOGC (Macrosty, 1914). The club, which ran throughout the war, opened daily between 12.30–14.00 and 18.00–22.00 (Mins. Council Meeting, 2 December 1914).

Overall it was the larger, wealthier YWCA, rather than the NOGC, who seized the initiative from Lady Jellicoe by establishing late in 1914 a *Committee for Work among Girls in Military Centres*. The YWCA then called a public appeal for funds to open and maintain centres which would offer:

> *a place for social intercourse under the best possible conditions for the girls and their men friends, supplying healthy influences to counteract the restless excitement of the present times, and to meet the needs of members and visitors.*
>
> (*The Times*, 25 March 1915)

The public appeal was launched at a mass meeting of women held at the Guildhall with Lady Jellicoe prominently in attendance. Lady Smith-Dorrien, herself married to a serving General, began by asking the audience to:

> *tell the women and girls that they can serve their country by leading quiet lives, thus setting an example of self-restraint and uprightness at home, which equally with the bravery of their dear ones in the war, is necessary to bring this country through this great national crisis with credit to those who have the good fortune to live under the Union Jack.*
>
> (quoted in Churchill, 1916: 17)

A committee to carry the work forward was elected by the gathering. Chaired by the Duchess of Hamilton it comprised 24 titled ladies including Lady French, wife of the Commander-in-Chief of the British Expeditionary Force then the senior British officer on the Western Front. The one commoner on the committee was the extravagantly wealthy Nancy Astor, who subsequently became a generous patron of clubs and settlement work (Popple, 2006). By January 1915, 20 Girls' Patriotic Clubs, as they were called, were operating in places such as Ripon, a town of 8,000 garrisoning 14,000 troops, that had 'no place for the young girls to go in the evenings'. In March 1915 Lady Jellicoe wisely decided to throw in her lot with the YWCA sponsored committee. Girls' Patriotic Clubs now regularly opened in the vicinity of barracks and camps located in towns and cities. They seemed popular, for example in Northampton where 'even young girls' were 'earning good money owing to the boom in the boot trade . . . the club attracted over 500 members within days of opening' (*The Times*, 4 March 1915). Seemingly they were also popular with the authorities:

> *While all engaged in social work in military centres agree that there has been a great improvement in the last two or three months, complaints are still received from some parts of the trouble caused by the thoughtless conduct of numbers of young girls whose open admiration for the recruits has been finding expression in undesirable ways. In some centres, it is stated, the excitement has caused numbers of girls to lose their heads, and in one district where many girls are employed the nuisance became so great that the military authorities had to consider the alternatives of moving troops or taking them on route marches from 8 o'clock until midnight.*
>
> *The YWCA has done valuable work by providing, as counter-attractions to the streets, clubs where girls are encouraged to show their admiration for the troops in a practical way by making shirts or knitting mufflers, socks, and mittens for the soldiers and sailors. At many of the clubs, sometimes by the desire of the Commanding Officer, girls are encouraged to take their soldier friends with them on certain evenings and entertainments are given.*
>
> (*The Times* 28 January 1915)

Mass mobilisation meant some NOGC clubs encountered difficulties owing to the 'influx of soldiers' or pressure from members to allow the young men 'in'. Initially the NOGC responded by recommending leaders invite a 'League of Honour representative to hold a meeting at the club' (Mins. Office Com., 19 November 1914). The League of Honour for Women and Girls' of the British Empire was founded in September 1914 by Mrs James Gow 'to band together the women and girls of the Empire, with the object of upholding the standard of women's duty and honour during the war'. Each girl who joined was asked to carry a card with her at all times bearing the member's pledge – 'I promise, by the help of God, to do all that is in my power to uphold the honour of our nation and its defenders in this time of war by prayer, purity, and temperance' (*Outlook* (YWCA); October 1914: 233). The League had no official connection with the NOGC, but one of its founders and vice-presidents was Louise Creighton, another was Maude Stanley, therefore it had to be accorded due respect by the NOGC leadership. Clubs affiliated to both the NOGC and YWCA were certainly put under some pressure to persuade members to enrol in the League. However the decision of the NOGC leadership to encourage clubs to invite the good ladies from the League to visit and counsel members as to the dangers attendant upon fraternisation was soon eclipsed by a need to help club members to adjust to the growth in demand for mixed clubs. For after the Girls' Patriotic Clubs, some of whom joined the NOGC and helped boost the levels of affiliation, breached the single-sex barrier making it increasingly difficult for others to hold the line. Generally where mixed activities were allowed they occurred on specific nights. For example a club opened in Coventry for munitions workers soon attracted so many members it was usually 'crowded to almost capacity'. Meeting in 'excellent rooms, well furnished, where girls could spend their time reading, writing, or playing quiet games' it also had an 'excellent canteen' and 'a large hall which is in constant use for dancing, physical exercises, and entertainment', these included a weekly dance to which members could invite men friends (*Midland Daily Telegraph*, 18 May 1918). By way of contrast, new girls' clubs were also located within places of work or the barrack-blocks adjacent to factories employing substantial numbers of young women. Some even operated within the perimeter fences of the camps established near Gretna, which housed almost 12,000 women munitions workers (Woollacott, 1994). These clubs generally eschewed mixed work, indeed in some instances this was impossible as the camps were guarded by women police employed to keep the women in and men out (Fraser, 1918). Some, like the one described below, were managed by a members' committee and served as social centres and somewhere members might access essentials such as washing facilities plus:

> a set of irons, a sewing machine, a piano (hired), there is a gas ring and they make tea or coffee whenever they like, supplying their own . . . The tone and standard are entirely in their hands and the Committee is responsible for all arrangements. There is room for about 10 couples to dance in an outer hall . . . The members have so far been busy getting together furniture, decorations, etc. Their plan is to have "Industrial"

mornings when their time off falls, and they have musical and social evenings alternate weeks.

(Imperial War Museum Women's Work Collection, Munitions 18.9/13, app. B)

Other clubs were free-standing but the *modus operandi* was usually determined by the working hours and shifts of the young women. Few accounts survive of these but we do have this one:

It had three open nights, plus evening classes on other nights in Class-Singing, Morris Dancing, Ambulance, Home-Nursing, French and Women's Volunteer Drill. Also open Saturday afternoon and evening and all day Sunday. Opens a few minutes after 9 a.m. and closed at 11 p.m. 'Difficulties and anxieties in a mixed club are inevitable – strenuous evenings and many wakeful hours after, but the committee and helpers who have seen the possibilities and who are keenly interested, as mine are, feel with me that it is well worth while. I think girls want showing that there can be friendly intercourse with men, without silly flirtation. When I watch friendships beginning and growing and I am told about the walks home and sometimes given letters to read, I feel that the club influence must surely be wholesome and the friendships surely of the right kind'.

(Lewarne, 1915: 63 see also Piercy, 1916)

Any decision to admit men to NOGC clubs was rarely unproblematic, and consequently the National Headquarters received frequent requests for advice. For example the leader of Redhill Girls' Club reported that permitting soldiers to join caused such difficulties 'she no longer allowed them admission' and therefore appealed to the NOGC for help in planning a programme of activities for her members now the men were excluded (Mins. Exec. Com., 18 May 1916). Concerns regarding the behaviour of some young women prompted requests that the NOGC intervene. For instance a Miss Potter asked the NOGC to open a club in the Strand and Piccadilly 'for young girls who visited those districts nightly in order to get them under good influence'. This was rejected on the grounds 'it would be inadvisable to open a club and draw girls to the district' (Mins. Exec. Com., 15 November 1917). A suggestion that met with more favour came from a Mrs Drury, a National Union of Women Workers (NUWW) patrol worker, who asked the NOGC to run 'week-end outings for munition and other working girls'. These, she suggested, could be Bicycle Clubs that would serve as 'a means of influencing . . . working girls' who would on these outings be 'accompanied by young ladies'. According to Mrs Drury both types of girls would benefit from the intercourse. Edith Glover agreed the scheme was a good idea and should go ahead. But being an experienced club worker Glover could not resist warning the novice that 'bicycles must remain the property of the Club' and that those in charge must be prepared for the very real possibility of 'girls leaving the parties and picking up undesirable acquaintances' (Mins. Exec. Com., 15 March 1917). Such fears meant the request from the YMCA for soldiers to use Bainbridge House, the NOGC's residential centre on the south coast, was unceremoniously refused as 'many difficulties would arise and possibly the good name of the Home would be marred if such arrangements were made' (Mins. Exec. Com., 10 October 1916). Mixed clubs yes, but the world was not yet ready for mixed residential centres.

Patrols and other initiatives

In October 1914, Creighton, by now President of both the NUWW and NOGC, launched the Women Patrol Scheme (WPS) under the auspices of the former and following encouragement to do so from the Chief Commissioner of the Metropolitan Police. The WPS was intended to better manage the behaviour of young women in public places. Within days funding was found to appoint a paid National Organiser, a Miss Carden, and 26 regional organisers. Amongst the tasks delegated to the latter was the training of volunteers who possessed the 'experience and knowledge of girls to patrol in the camp and barrack areas, and talk to girls who were behaving foolishly, and try to influence them for the good' (Fraser, 1918: 237). Upon completion of their training, the recruits undertook patrol work under the supervision of committees established in localities where significant numbers of troops were encamped. The WPS attracted widespread support and continued expanding until the close of 1918. Unlike most, if not all, of the street work previously undertaken, this was not 'rescue work' neither was it designed to proselytise a particular religious faith. Rather it was akin to what would now be labelled 'detached or street work'. Volunteers were required 'to make friends with the girls and gain their confidence, warn any girls seen speaking to men on duty or behaving in any way unsuitably' (Dewar, 1920: 93). Each WPS volunteer was supplied with an authorisation card signed by the local Chief Constable and when on duty wore an armband, but no uniform. They were expected to 'act quietly and without parade' and take with them handbills giving details of nearby NOGC clubs willing to accept girls recommended to them by the Patrols and provide 'places of pleasant resort for the girls and their men friends in winter evenings' (*The Times*, 31 December 1914). Edith Glover represented the NOGC on the London Women's Patrol

Committee (Mins. Office Com., 16 March 1915) and it was she who asked the London Patrols to co-operate as much as possible with the parents of girls 'in whom they were interested' (Mins. Council Meeting, 4 November 1914). Over-zealous engagement by some patrols did foster ill-feeling amongst young women and soldiers but this was the exception. Indeed their 'social work' slant meant Patrols were criticised by the more militaristic uniformed Women Police Volunteers (WPV) established in 1914 (Allen, 1925; Douglas, 1999). By the final year of the war certain WPV patrols, notably those operating in London parks, had been granted powers of arrest. However the WPV with a core membership of around 1,500 full-timers, a significant number of whom were on permanent duty 'guarding' the women at Gretna was dwarfed by the WPS which ran approximately 2,000 units (Levine, 1994; Jackson, 2006). Whereas the authorities in many population centres sought to keep the WPV at arm's length they were far more enthusiastic regarding the input of the Patrols 'whose great qualification was tact' and who exercised a 'considerable constraining restraining influence' on the streets (*The Times*, 28 January 1915). The NOGC was amongst a number of bodies who, on the basis of WPS's success, met with the Home Office in 1916 to plan the formation, in accordance with a suggestion made by the Criminal Law Amendment Committee, of a trained Women's Police Service (Mins. Office Com., 17 February 1916).

Underwriting much of this activity, as noted earlier, were fears that un-supervised fraternisation would cultivate unseemly behaviour resulting in pregnancy, illegitimacy and an epidemic of 'war babies'. Such misgivings promulgated a succession of moral panics of varying intensity towards which the NOGC, unlike many, retained a sense of proportion. Moreover to their credit the NOGC displayed a faith in the innate decency and integrity of the working girls that were the focus of these 'panics'. Glover, speaking on behalf of the NOGC at a Women's Imperial Health Conference on War Babies, bluntly informed the delegates the problem was 'grossly exaggerated' (Mins. Office Com., 15 May 1915). When the National Council for Combating Venereal Diseases (NCCVD) asked the NOGC to distribute warning cards 'amongst Girls at Stations' they were told it was 'not considered helpful in any way' to operate in this fashion and co-operation was withheld (Mins. Exec. Com., 15 March 1917). Shortly afterwards Sir Malcolm Morris, Vice President of the NCCVD, made allegations against shop and business girls concerning the spread of venereal diseases. Montagu set about Morris with a vengeance, and quickly extracted a public apology in which he regretted that 'any statements made by him should have caused friction' and a promise not to mention in future 'any special class of women or girls when speaking about Venereal Diseases' (Mins. Exec. Com., 19 May 1917).

Thankfully this fracas did not inhibit future collaboration and shortly afterwards the NOGC supported the NCCVD's campaign to outlaw unqualified persons offering treatment for sexually transmitted diseases, and the two bodies ran a series of well attended lectures on sexual health topics for club workers (Mins. Exec. Com. 15 February 1917). However the two were on opposing sides during the bitter controversy aroused by Regulation 40D of the 1917 Defence of the Realm Act which permitted the imprisonment of 'promiscuous' women to curtail the spread of venereal diseases amongst troops. The NOGC wrote to the Home Secretary asking instead for alternatives such as

> *Probationary Sentences, the establishment of suitable Homes before any legislation was introduced, the need to stimulate self-respect and independence into the girls when they entered these Homes, the necessity for taking into account the responsibility of both sexes in regard to solicitation, and the need for altering the wording of the Clause, so as to make it clear that girls and women were not at the mercy of individual Police Officers.*

(Mins. Exec. Com., 19 May 1917)

When finally it entered the Statute Book in 1918 the NOGC, much to the annoyance of Louise Creighton, joined with the Association for Moral and Social Hygiene in leading protests against the implementation of the Regulation (Mins. Exec. Com. 18 April 1918; Laite, 2008).

Government intervention

Concerns were expressed by politicians, the press and sections of the public regarding the behaviour of young men and young women during the war years. Not least the spotlight cast on young men relating to an apparent growth in delinquency which led to the Home Office creating in 1916 the Juvenile Organisation Committee (JOC). In effect this became the first governmental 'youth work department'. Simultaneously the Home Office asked local authorities to set up their own JOCs to assist in the co-ordination of services, particularly clubs for young people. By 1918 fewer than half of all LEAs had done so. The National JOC was chaired by Charles Russell, the Home Office's Chief Inspector of Reformatory and Industrial Schools. Russell had previously achieved some prominence as a leader at the Heyrod Street Lads' Club (Ancoats) and Boys' Brigade officer (Russell, 1905; 1914). A journalist by profession, Russell co-authored with Lillian Rigby *Lad's Clubs: Their History, Organisation and Management*, a pioneering youth work text. The National JOC included amongst its invited membership representatives of leading youth organisations. The NOGC sent Lily Montagu, who reported after its first meeting that its task appeared primarily to 'enquire into juvenile crime' (Mins. Exec. Com., 16 November 1916). After the second meeting, and clearly irritated at the turn taken by the Committee, Montagu concluded the women members 'felt themselves to be of little service, as the work suggested and discussed was largely dealing with boys' (Mins. Exec. Com., 18 January 1917). Shortly afterwards they hived themselves off to form a sub-committee comprising the JOC's women members. Chaired by Lady Frances Balfour, sister of Constance Lytton the suffragette, prison reformer and worker at the Esperance Girls' Club, it asked the NOGC to enquire as to how many girls belonged to clubs in 1915 and the proportion of these who subsequently allowed their membership to lapse (Mins. Council Meeting, 3 January 1917). Alas any data accrued via this research appears to have been mislaid, if it ever existed, for no mention arises in any NOGC documentation that the research was undertaken or a report submitted. Glover, who replaced Montagu on the JOC in 1918, the same year the Committee transferred to the Board of Education, reported after her initial meeting that nothing had changed – it still devoted 'most of the time . . . discussing the Boy Delinquent' (Mins. AGM, 6 March 1918). The Board of Education, upon acquiring responsibility, issued Circular 1137 requesting that LEAs consult with their local JOC concerning matters relating to the welfare of young people residing within their jurisdiction. Seventeen years after the Circular appeared the proportion lacking a JOC had barely altered (Board of Education, 1933). However their creation, albeit patchy, signalled the beginnings of local statutory youth services. Before the year was out St Pancras JOC had set up a Federation of Girls' Clubs that affiliated to the NOGC, thereby initiating the first formal link between a national voluntary organisation and the emerging statutory sector (Mins. Council Meeting, 2 October 1918).

Carrying on

Throughout the war years, despite the extra-tasks undertaken, most pre-existing NOGC programmes flourished. Apart from two months when troops were billeted there Bainbridge House thrived although the proportion accommodated as 'individuals' was higher than before. By 1917 the demand for places at Bainbridge was so great Windlesham Farm in Hertfordshire was booked for 178 leaders and girls. In addition free holidays were being arranged for girls at the homes of a Miss Stoehr at Hindhead and Lady Reid, a friend of Edith Glover, at Bath (Mins. Exec. Com., 20 Sept. 1917). Summer rambles thrived, and in 1917 alone the NOGC Office organised these for 1,751 girls and leaders; however leaders' conferences were discontinued due to poor attendance (Mins. Council Meeting 3 March 1915). Annual leaders' and members' meetings at Lady Swaythling's home remained popular, the one in 1916 attracting 270 workers and girls; as did the NUWW's three day conferences complete with its side meeting for club leaders, with over 200 attending the 1915 gathering which featured a talk jointly given by Montagu and Glover on 'The Joy of Life and the Disciplines of Life Promoted by Clubs' (Mins. Office Com. 16 September 1915). *Girls Club News* survived, despite paper shortages, under the editorship of Edith McCrosty who had managed it since its launch in 1912. McCrosty missed her first NOGC meeting in four years following the death of her son on the Western Front but returned within the month (Mins. Council Meeting 2 February 1916). The NOGC's Employment Bureau continued to interview potential leaders and put these in touch with clubs but the numbers coming forward declined; to a large extent as a result of the expansion in employment opportunities for women and the numbers recruited by the YWCA and YMCA.

Industrial work grew in line with the increase in the numbers of young women employed. NOGC leaders in many areas served as 'assessors' sitting on the Tribunals established by the 1915 Munitions Act to adjudicate in disputes between employers and employees. The NOGC also campaigned on behalf of young women entering employment within occupations from which they had previously been excluded. A typical example was the work undertaken on behalf of women tram conductors, many of whom due to early starts and late finishes were in urgent need of accommodation close by their depots; moreover few termini and depots had toilet facilities for women staff. In addition many lacked refreshment facilities so Glover, through her involvement with the non-profit Dining Centre's Company, organised for Coffee Stalls to be provided at many depots, whilst the NOGC created a register of suitable lodgings and arranged for Sanitary Inspectors to visit all the depots where women were employed (Mins. Office Com. 20 January 1916). The NOGC did not merely react to employment problems but sought to shape policy. For instance in 1916 the NOGC and the NUWW organised a conference on 'New Employments' to examine how to progress on issues relating to working conditions and the extension of the range of occupations open to women (Mins. Office Com. 26 March 1916). Seventeen months on, both were prominent in the formation of a committee that included representatives of the WIC, YWCA and the Suffrage Societies tasked with campaigning to protect from dismissal at the end of hostilities women employed by governmental Boards and Ministries (*The Times*, 21 September 1917).

Despite the burdens, new work was initiated during wartime. One example was the first national NOGC Club Members' Conference held in September

1916. The Manchester Union had organised in 1912 a local conference to which girls from all NOGC affiliated clubs were invited but this was the first centrally organised Club Members' Conference. Amongst the issues debated during the weekend the one that proved the most contentious was on 'Picture Palaces', a topic then prompting great concern amongst club workers, male and female; indeed Miss Lewis, on behalf of the NOGC, had recently joined a deputation of representatives from the leading juvenile organisations to the Home Office to express collective concerns regarding the damaging 'moral and physical effect of the pictures on girls and children' (Mins. Council Meeting, 5 June 1916). Few and far between at the turn of the century, by 1914 there were on average 22 Picture Houses in towns with a population over 100,000 (Cunningham, 1985). The outbreak of war did not curb growth. The Club Members' conference seems to have been a success and shortly afterwards the NOGC's Executive Committee recommended that where a Club Committee existed this should regularly meet with the Honorary Officers 'to discuss club developments and problems whereby a more corporate life may be obtained' (Mins. Exec. Com., 15 February 1917). A second noteworthy initiative was a joint enterprise with the Old Vic Theatre to establish Shakespeare Societies within NOGC clubs (Mins. Exec. Com., 15 November 1917). By 1918, 34 of these were functioning and the NOGC had recruited 6 specialist part-time teachers for what became known as Shakespeare classes (Mins. AGM, 6 March 1918). In the same year, the NOGC 'took over' the Old Vic for what might best be described as a performing arts day. The following year *The Times* reported on the second Old Vic gathering. The article recounts how after an address by Lady Runciman, the Chairman for the day, the audience was transformed into performers as the theatre:

> *was filled with eager girls from work-room, desk, and factory. They applauded each other with a certain critical good will that varied in volume and swelled to extra-ordinary strength when some outstanding "turn" held the boards. At the girls' own request Shakespeare figured largely in the bill. Some of the episodes presented, if they erred on the side of a too meticulous enunciation, had each some outstanding feature, and the lack of scenery seemed to worry neither performer nor audience. A curious choice was Act III, scene 2, of Twelfth Night by the Crossway Mission Club, but the acting was quite good. The trial scene of The Merchant of Venice was given by the Mitre Club. The West Central Girls' Club chose a scene from The Winter's Tale, the acting being remarkable. The St. Barnabas Club presented the second scene of Act III from King Henry V with considerable comprehension of its spirit and*

a good delivery of fine lines. There were physical exercises and danc-
ing, sight-singing and solos, recitations and eurythemics, skipping, and
some exceptionally good drilling – all representing the playtime hob-
bies of girls who work hard all day and only have the evening hours to
amuse themselves.

(The Times, 26 May 1919)

NOGC Shakespearian Societies in June 1919 were invited to contribute to the National Peace Procession involving thousands of allied troops. Specifically they were asked to perform extracts from a number of Shakespeare's plays in Regent's Park (*The Times*, 14 June 1919).

Training workers

By Christmas 1917 the YWCA had opened 18 additional clubs in London and 24 in garrison towns plus 213 factory based centres all of which needed staff-ing (YWCA Archive, MSS 243). Set besides the escalation in the number of community based girls' clubs plus the appearance of a network of Girls' Patri-otic Clubs and YWCA clubs for munitions and other workers, it is not difficult to explain why an acute shortage in the supply of suitable leaders developed post 1914. Predictably the NOGC encountered problems maintaining its level of provision. Especially when longstanding workers retired some clubs struggled to secure replacements. Sometimes this loss of a first generation worker precipi-tated the closure of once successful clubs. Amongst those disappearing in the early years of the war were some London clubs that had been in existence since the 1890s; notably the Hand-in-Hand Club, St Dunstan's Club and the Honor Club all three of which closed following the death or retirement of long-serving leaders (Mins. Exec. Com., 17 May 1917). The National Union of Suffrage Socie-ties being cognisant of the problem volunteered in 1915 to supply workers for NOGC affiliated clubs and help set-up new ones such as the Waterloo Road Patrol Club (Mins. Council Meeting, 3 March 1915). Some volunteers it sent were apparently disconcerted by the difficulties of communicating across the class divide with club members. A problem highlighted by one such volunteer, who recounted in the journal *Common Cause* that:

> *The girls were so easily satisfied, so hostile to innovation. They wanted*
> *dancing – their own sort of dancing, not ours; they wanted, also, to*
> *'do something for the soldiers', they did not wish for singing, apart*
> *from outbursts of impromptu ragtimes; they did not wish to learn new*
> *dances, nor songs, nor games, nor have to have anything read aloud*

while they sewed. They would unite in attacking or opposing anything or person they disliked, but they were slow to combine for purposes of pleasure or work.

(Weddell, 1917: 632)

One solution to the problem of securing and retaining staff was to initiate a training programme that prepared them for their labours. The YWCA, who ran a three month training programme for 'Hostel and Centre Workers' at its Hampstead Training College, was the first to pursue this route and in January 1915 it hosted a conference to launch a Scheme for Training Club Workers attended by Montagu on behalf of the NOGC (Mins. Office Com. 21 January 1915). A month later the first of their 12 day training courses for Club Workers commenced. The programme comprised morning prayers at 09.50, lectures from 10.00 to 18.30, with just 20 minutes for lunch, followed by evenings spent working in or visiting clubs. Amongst the lecturers were Lily Montagu and Mary Phillips both closely associated with the NOGC. The former lectured on 'Citizenship' and the latter, a Factory Inspector, on 'How our Industrial Laws help Working Girls' (YWCA Archive, MSS 243/32). Soon the NOGC decided, as a matter of urgency, to establish its own full-time three month course to train women as club leaders (Mins. Office Com. 15 April 1915). The YWCA and the Church Army expressed interest in this venture, the former asking if their Hampstead students might join elements of the programme. However the NOGC Office Committee stipulated they must have the right of veto regarding admissions (Mins. Office Com. 20 May 1915). In June Glover met with E.J. Urwick, the Director of the Department of Social Science and Administration at the LSE. Urwick, previously a sub-Warden at Toynbee Hall, had in 1904 edited the influential *Studies of Boy Life in Great Cities* which included Montagu's pioneering essay 'The girl in the background'. Glover and Urwick agreed that an inaugural course should commence in October 1915. Students would study Social Administration, Industrial Law and 'business training' at the LSE whilst Montagu took responsibility for the training of the students in the rudiments of 'actual club work' at an unrecorded second venue (Mins. Council Meeting 2 June 1915). Given the absence of any governmental support for those lacking private incomes if they were to be recruited in any numbers bursaries were needed. With her usual efficiency Glover secured six bursaries from the Ministry of Labour via the Training Schemes Sub-committee of its Central Committee on Women's Employment, fortuitously chaired by Irene Cox the YWCA representative on the NOGC's Executive Committee (Mins. Office Com. 15 April 1915). Bursaries were awarded to be solely at the discretion of the NOGC (Mins.

Office Com., 13th October 1915). On 8 October 1915 the course commenced when 30 students enrolled at the LSE. Thus began the first independent secular programme, the precursor of all subsequent university-based youth and community degree courses.

Conclusion

Compared to the embedded big battalions such as the YMCA, GFS and YWCA the diminutive NOGC had a low-key war. Essentially the organisation was too small and untried to do more than expand on a limited number of fronts. The good news for the NOGC was that by 1917 there were signs the state would play a more interventionist role with regards post-school leisure and educational provision once peace returned. High expectations regarding the potential benefits of greater engagement by local and central government with clubs were reflected in the topics chosen for the March 1917 NOGC's Leaders' Conference. Heading the agenda was 'How to get educational help from the LCC' followed by 'How to earn a Grant from the Board of Education' (Mins. Exec. Com., 15 February 1916). Optimism flowed from the top. Understandably so, for had not Russell himself argued that:

> *By some means or other, every boy of twelve or thirteen and upwards, should be made a member of the Boy Scouts, a Boys' Brigade or some other organisation which will provide for him healthy exercise, harmless amusement, fresh interest, discipline and most important of all, a religious motive.*
>
> (Russell, 1917)

It seemed possible that if the case for girls' clubs was diligently pressed then they also would secure in the near future vital governmental support and funding. Glover and Montagu were post-1916 engaged in a constant round of lobbying to ensure girls' clubs were included within the scope of Clause 17 of the 1918 (Fisher) Education Act. H.A.L. Fisher, who as President of the Board of Education, and ultimately responsible for much of the content of the 1918 Act, was an enthusiastic supporter of post-school education and Day Continuation Schools in particular. He also appointed the committee responsible for the 1919 Report on Adult Education, which was initially viewed as the prelude to the wholesale expansion of that sector. Initially the NOGC leadership had high hopes that Fisher would ensure that the 1918 Act fostered the development of club work. Fisher was not a typical politician, being a distinguished Oxford historian best remembered for his three volume *History of Europe*, long a standard university text. Killed in a road accident in 1940 he posthumously made a small but noteworthy contribution to the ultimate success of the D-Day Landings and the saving of many allied lives. For it was Fisher's underpants 'stolen' after his death from his college rooms by his academic adversary and rival J. C. Masterman, then in charge of the Twenty Committee responsible for running the network of double-agents, that were used on the body deposited in the Bay of Biscay as part of *Operation Mincemeat*. The corpse carried documents that helped convince the German High Command the main allied landings would not occur in Normandy. Amongst the tiny ensemble of spies who concocted *Operation Mincemeat* was Lily's notoriously obnoxious nephew Ewen Montagu (McIntyre, 2010: 67).

Lily eventually viewed Fisher as a sympathetic but vacillating figure, correctly predicting after one of their later meetings that he 'fully realised the valuable work done by clubs' but would not legislate for their direct support (Mins. Exec. Com., 20 December 1917). However she, and he, knew there existed within the Act a loophole for the NOGC to exploit and within a month of it entering the Statute Book seven girls' clubs had done so by setting up 'small scale' Day Continuation Schools (Mins. Exec. Com., 18 April 1918). Initially discussed in a document prepared for the Board of Education by Michael Sadler in 1907 and two years later in a report published by the same body (Acland, 1909; Thomas, 1975), they were intended to provide all school-leavers, apart from those training for a profession, with compulsory technical and liberal education for one day per week. The Fisher Act allowed employers, local authorities and crucially other agencies to individually or collectively establish Day Continuation Schools to be funded jointly by LEA and the Board of Education grant-aid (Thom, 1975). Grant-aid for Continuation Schools plus the potential of the JOCs to provide a conduit whereby girls' clubs received LEA funding gave justifiable grounds for optimism that the tenuous financial base upon which local clubs and national youth organisations resided might soon be substituted for something more solid. The buoyant temper of the times was captured in a 1917 *Girls' Club Journal* article entitled 'The Relation of Girls' Clubs to the Education Authority' which encouraged clubs to foster mutually beneficial relationships with their LEA. When these reforms are placed alongside the passing of the 1918 Representation of the People Act, which granted the suffrage to all women aged 28 and over, and the 1919 Sex Disqualification (Removal) Act, which not only gave women the right to hold all public offices, outside of the Church and military, but also prohibited bars against their entry into the professions, it is easy to comprehend the optimism then percolating through the girls' club movement. The promised raising of the school-leaving age and the passing of the

Trade Boards Act in 1918, which finally extended Board of Trade regulation to previously badly organised occupations, also seemed to signal that some longstanding and hard fought campaigns had been won: victories that might free-up the NOGC and others to move onto new and more luxuriant pastures wherein they might focus less on meeting acute social needs and more on providing liberal education, physical activities and leisure programmes as well as helping girls grasp the nettle of full citizenship. Although the proportion of the potential membership reached remained low it must have seemed to those pioneers that in the eight years since the founding of the NOGC they had made steady progress towards achieving the ambitions summarised by Ruth Lousada in 1912. Namely that: 'Every worker in a Girls' Club has two goals very much at heart. First, to improve the conditions of industrial work for girls; secondly, to make their lives a little happier' (Lousada, 1912: 4).

References

Acland, A.H.D. (1909) *Day Continuation Schools* (Cmnd. 4757), London: The Stationary Office.

Allen, M. (1925) *The Pioneer Police Woman.* London: Chatto and Windus.

Board of Education (1933) *The Work of Juvenile Organisations Committees. Educational Pamphlet No 98.* London: Stationery Office.

Churchill, J.R. (1916) *Women's War Work.* London: Pearson.

Creighton, L. (1914) Message to Club Girls. *Girls' Club News*, 31: 1.

Cunningham, H. (1985) Leisure. In Benson, J. (Ed.) *The Working Class in England 1875–1914.* London: Croom Helm.

Dewar, K. (1920) *The Girl.* London: G. Bell.

Dimmock, F. H. (1937) *Bare Knee Days.* London: Boriswood.

Douglas, R.M. (1999) *Feminist Freikorps: The British Voluntary Women Police 1914–1940.* Westport: Praeger.

Drake, B. (1984) *Women in Trade Unions.* London: Virago.

Fraser, H. (1918) *Women and War Work.* New York: G. Arnold Shaw & Co.

Girls' Club Journal (1917) The Relation of Girls' Clubs to the Education Authority. *Girls' Club Journal*, 9: 27, 58–60.

Graves, R. (1929) *Good-bye to All That: An Autobiography.* London; Jonathan Cape.

Hampton, J. (2010) *How the Girl Guides Won the War.* London: Harper Press.

Jackson, L.A. (2006) *Women Police, Gender, Welfare and Surveillance in the Twentieth Century.* Manchester: Manchester University Press.

Kerr, R. (1932) *The Story of the Girl Guides.* London: The Girl Guides Association.

Laite, J.A. (2008) The Association for Moral and Social Hygiene: Abolitionism and Prostitution Law in Britain 1915–1959. *Women's History Review*, 17: 2, 207–23.

Lawrence, M. (1914) An Open Letter to Club Girls. *Girls' Club News*, 31: 2–3.

Levine, P. (1994) Walking the Streets in a Way No Decent Woman Should: Women Police in World War 1. *The Journal of Modern History*, 66: 1, 34–78.

Lewarne, B.E. (1915) A Wartime Club. *Girls' Club Journal*, 7: 20, 62–3.

Lousada, R. (1912) Music in Girls' Clubs. *Girls' Club News*, 1, 3–4.

Macrosty, E.J. (1914) Woolwich Girls' Club. *Girls' Club News*, 34, 9.

Marwick, A. (1965) *The Deluge: British Society and the First World War*. Harmondsworth: Pelican.

Marwick, A. (1977) *Women at War 1914–1918*. London: Fontana.

Montagu, L. (1904) The Girl in the Background. In Urwick, E.J. (Ed.) *Studies of Boy Life in Our Cities*. London: J.M. Dent.

Popple, K. (2006) Plymouth, Paternalism and the Astors: The Origins of Virginia House Settlement. In Gilchrist, R., Jeffs, T. and Spence, J. (Eds.) *Drawing on the Past: Studies in the History of Community and Youth Work*. Leicester: Youth Work Press.

Russell, C.E.B. (1905) *Manchester Boy: Sketches of Manchester Lads at Work and Play*. Manchester: Manchester University Press.

Russell, C.E.B. (1914) *Social Problems of the North*. London: Mowbray.

Russell, C.E.B. (1917) Chief Inspector of Reformatories. *Sports Gazette*, 20 January.

Russell, C.E.B. and Rigby, L. (1908) *Working Lads' Clubs*. London: Macmillan.

Sadler, M.E. (1907) *Continuation Schools in England and Elsewhere*. Manchester: University of Manchester Press.

Snape, M. (2009) *The Back Parts of War: The YMCA Memoirs and Letters of Barclay Baron, 1915–1919*. London: Church of England Record Society.

Thom, D.W. (1975) The Emergence and Failure of the Day Continuation School Experiment. *History of Education*, 4: 1, 36–50.

Thom, D. (2000) *Nice Girls and Rude Girls: Women Workers in World War One*. London: I.B. Tauris.

Thomas, D.W. (1975) The Emergence and Failure of the Day Continuation School Experiment. *History of Education*, 4: 1 36–50.

Urwick, E.J. *Studies of Boy Life in Our Cities*. London: J.M. Dent.

Weddell, M. (1917) My Friend Sarah. *Common Cause*, 9 March.

Woollacott, A. (1994) *On Her Their Lives Depend: Munitions Workers in the Great War*. Berkeley, CA: University of California Press.

Yapp, A. (1919) *The Romance of the Red Triangle*. London: Hodder and Stoughton.

Yapp, A. (1927) *In the Service of Youth*. London: Nisbet.

Primary Sources

The documentation relating to the YWCA is located in their archives deposited with the University of Warwick. Material connected with the National Organisation of Girls' Club forms part of the UK Youth archive held by the University of Birmingham.

CHAPTER 4

Scouting in a Divided Society: Judge William Johnson and the 78th Belfast

Tom Wylie

One Sunday morning in the autumn of 1928 a young lawyer walking home from church in north Belfast fell into conversation with two boys who had been at the same service. The lawyer, who was also the Scout Commissioner for the area, asked them if they had ever considered becoming Boy Scouts. The two boys were Brian Rankin and Jack Braithwaite and they would eventually become scout leaders(WJ2). The young lawyer was William Johnson who would become a Judge but whose life's interest was Scouting, notably the 78th Belfast (Duncairn) Group which sprang from their conversation. This paper sets Johnson's development of this remarkable Group in the context of Belfast's – and Ireland's – social contours and political divisions.

William Johnson was born in April 1903, the second child of a solicitor. Growing up in Warrenpoint, Co.Down, and known as 'Willie' by his family, he was educated principally at Portora Royal School, Enniskillen (the alma mater of Oscar Wilde and Samuel Beckett) and thence at Trinity College, Dublin. An exceptional student, he graduated in 1924 with first class honours in Legal and Political Science and was called to the Bar of the recently established Irish Free State while still an undergraduate. In 1926 he was called to the Bar of Northern Ireland and for a number of years he combined legal practice with the post of private secretary to the Lord Chief Justice of Northern Ireland (WJ1).

Johnson's great interest, outside his profession, was Scouting. He joined a Scout troop near his home in 1915 (and volunteered to assist with the 'Scout Huts' set up in France as recreation centres for soldiers during World War 1:

Figure 2.1 William Johnson

since he was only 13, the authorities wisely declined his patriotic offer). While at Trinity Johnson continued his Scout interest, accompanying the Irish Free State contingent to the 1924 Imperial Jamboree in London. Moving to Belfast in 1925 he became District Commissioner for north Belfast, despite his youthful 22 years.

Scouting's beginnings in Ireland

Scouting had developed quickly in Ireland after Baden-Powell's experimental camp on Brownsea Island, Dorset in 1907 and the subsequent publication, in fortnightly parts, of his 'Scouting for Boys'. Initially, Baden-Powell had not planned to create a distinct organisation: he had hoped that his ideas would be taken up by existing youth bodies nationwide (Jeal, 1989). That, indeed, was the position in Belfast – Scout patrols were established in late 1907 and early 1908, first in the city's YMCA and in the locally strong Boys Brigade (Bell, M., 1985). But soon the demand grew across the country for such scout patrols to be developed into a separate national organisation. Baden-Powell's astute publisher encouraged him to take that road.

Baden-Powell's approach to establishing the nationwide infrastructure which would sustain the embryonic Boy Scout organisation followed a common pattern; he would enlist the local 'great and good' to give support, as co-ordinating bodies for Scouting were established in different areas and voluntary leaders were recruited ('commissioned') to run what was often viewed as a radical approach to working with young people (Jeal, 1989). By early 1909 Belfast had its own 'local association', soon chaired by the lord mayor, to develop scouting in the city while the Earl of Shaftesbury, appointed by Imperial Headquarters in London, became the Chief Commissioner for Ireland and Viscount Massereene and Ferrard the Commissioner for Ulster, one of Ireland's four provinces.

The political tensions surrounding the Liberal government's plans for Irish Home Rule were already evident as Scouting's structures in Ireland took shape. Baden-Powell, who had been briefly stationed in Cork and Belfast as a young soldier, visited in 1911 and reported back in London:

> *I need not say that the difficulties which present themselves over there are very much more varied and intense than anything that we meet with on this side of St George's Channel . . . We want the Movement in Ireland to run itself for Ireland. The scheme now being carried out is under an Irish Chief in Lord Shaftesbury, each Province will have its own Commissioner, with County Commissioners and local associations under them, the headquarters to be in Dublin.*

> (Bell, 1985: 9)

But Belfast increasingly saw itself as distinct from the rest of the island and as the capital of a strongly industrial and relatively prosperous region within the United Kingdom. Its civic architecture spoke of its enduring confidence in Imperial prosperity, even if those who worked in its linen mills or on its docks did not share equally in it (Golding, 1991). In such feverish times a proposal in 1912 to establish an Irish Boy Scouts Association with a Dublin HQ was resisted by the Belfast local association, and Baden-Powell thereafter concluded:

> *As to organisation, I do not think that a central executive body is feasible for Ireland. The most that seems possible is for each province to administer itself. This will require a particularly able Provincial Commissioner and one who will be acceptable in all parts of his Province. Possibly the best solution would be to have a leading man as Commissioner and a really efficient worker to assist him as 'Sub-Commissioner' for each Province.*

> (Bell, M., 1985: 9)

Here, as elsewhere, there was no suggestion that Scouting's hierarchy would be democratically elected, though the involvement of major landowners did bring the important benefit of easier Scout access to campsites.

Meanwhile, broader political developments hastened to their denouement. In summary, the implementation of Home Rule legislation was deferred to the end of World War 1. By then the 1916 Easter Rising in Dublin had been followed by Sinn Fein's success in the general election of 1918, the subsequent Government of Ireland Act, Anglo-Irish war and Treaty. In 1921 Ireland was partitioned with 26 counties seceding from the United Kingdom to form the Irish Free State, later the Irish Republic, and six north-eastern counties in the province of Ulster opting out of a united Ireland to remain inside the UK as Northern Ireland (Ferriter, 2005; Fitzgerald, 1998). These political developments had their implications for Scouting on the island. Scouting in Northern Ireland continued within the British system but in the South it came under the control of the Irish Free State Scout Council (much later, the Boy Scouts of Ireland). But, although open to all, this body's origins and imperial associations – moreover, one created by an English general – were impossible for some Irish nationalists to swallow. (A critique of Scouting's perceived role in fostering imperialism and militarism has not been confined to 1920s Ireland. See for example Springhall, 1977; Bell, D., 1990). In addition, and in common with broader cultural developments in the Irish Free State, many within the new jurisdiction also sought or accepted a considerable measure of Catholic Church control over the care and formation of the young (Elliott, 2009; Ferriter, 2005). In 1927 two priests in Dublin established a separate Catholic Boy Scouts of Ireland (CBSI). Both of these distinct Scout associations continued in the Irish Republic. Indeed a few CBSI groups also operated in Northern Ireland, unrecognised by World Scouting but encouraged by some Catholic clergy in order to extend the church's hegemony and possibly also to deter youthful attachment to a uniformed, paramilitary republican movement, Na Fianna Eireann, founded in 1909 by Constance Markievicz a leading light in Sinn Fein (Devlin, 2007). It would be another 60 years before the fault lines in Scouting would blur, South and North.

William Johnson's new scout troop opens

Meanwhile, slow progress had followed that brief Sunday morning conversation in north Belfast. Willie Johnson's hope had been that his own local Presbyterian church would sponsor the new scout troop – he had already persuaded two grammar schools to sponsor others in his district. But the church elders declined: they had enough youth organisations on site, notably a Boys' Brigade company. However, the original two boys had remained keen on Scouting and had been joined by eight other enthusiasts. They rejected Johnson's suggestion that they could join other local Scout troops. Caught by their enthusiasm and backed by their parents, he agreed to take on the formation and leadership of a new troop himself (WJ2).

A meeting place was found in a loft above a cobbler's shop, access was negotiated to the grounds of a nearby reservoir and the wooded spaces of one of Belfast's halo of hills were close at hand. In November 1929 the 78th Belfast (Duncairn) troop formally opened with the ten boys in two patrols. All boys dressed in a dark khaki shirt, heavy blue serge shorts, a dark green scarf or neckerchief which bore the troop's crest – a mounted knight above the motto 'Forward' – and wore the traditional Scout hat. In this garb, which cost £1.2s.0d, they could have come directly from the paintings of Ernest S. Carlos whose sentimental representation of Scouts were popular in the movement's early years. It was an 'Open' group, not sponsored by any institution such as a school or church – a feature which later contributed much to its ethos and development.

Johnson's commitment and enthusiasm were boundless: soon the fledgling troop was engaged in all manner of activities especially on the nearby Cave Hill. His enduring injunction was 'get out into the open air'. Competitions in the Scouting skills of mapwork and campcraft were entered and sometimes won. The first summer camp was held in 1930 in the Mourne Mountains and this would become a favoured venue. Additional leaders were recruited and the parents committed themselves to the Group acquiring its own premises. These enabled the opening of a Wolf Cub Pack and the enlargement of the Scout troop. Johnson's own role in Scouting was expanding and he was active in the wider local movement as well as busy in his legal work – he had taken on a lectureship in Law at Queens University, Belfast in 1935. By 1938 he was taking a back seat from direct leadership of the 78th troop and leaving this to other young men who were coming through the ranks of a successful enterprise: the Group now had 20 Cubs, 32 Scouts and 9 Senior Scouts (WJ2). Johnson's ability to encourage young people into leadership roles would prove to be one of the reasons for this group's longevity and success.

Belfast in the 1930s was not an easy place in which to grow up. Northern resistance to Irish Home Rule had not simply been one of national identity or religious persuasion, it also had an economic underpinning: Belfast was an industrial city with its manufacturing trades – shipbuilding, engineering, rope making, tobacco, linen – and consequent social structure having more in common with Glasgow and Liverpool than Dublin (Budge, 1973). These industries, taken with the city's Presbyterian sensibilities, did much to form its character – 'devout and profane and hard'. But the industries on which Belfast had grown and prospered, like those of Britain generally, were created in the nineteenth century. Most suffered during the years of world depression from the 1920s and especially after 1931. In the 30s, the number of unemployed in the city reached 45,000, a quarter of the working population, and Scouting began to offer training for the young unemployed. However, the 78th Scout Hall was located just off the Antrim Road edging into developing suburban north Belfast with traditional terraced housing giving way to semi-detached and detached villas (Bardon, 1982). This Scout Group thus had a catchment area which was middle class or skilled working class in nature, mainly Protestant in faith though also with a small Jewish community (Chaim Herzog, the sixth President of Israel was born in the area). This was a typical social zone for recruitment into Scouts (the membership subs were 10s a year and the annual camp £1.5s.0d: average industrial earnings were c £130 p.a.). At this time the district did not suffer from the sporadic riots or other disturbances which occurred in a city whose latent sectarianism was exposed by the pressure of unemployment (Golding, 1991). Soon, however, the attention of all its population was diverted from any parochial concerns by the outbreak of World War II.

Belfast was largely unprotected from air attack as it was considered to be out of reach of German bombing: this changed with the fall of France and thus the ability of the Luftwaffe to fly from its north-western airfields. Belfast's ship building yards, docks and aircraft factory were tempting targets and the under-defended city suffered two major bombing raids in the spring of 1941. With some 900 killed on Easter Tuesday, more lives were lost in a single night's bombing than in any other UK provincial city and there was substantial damage to housing especially in north Belfast (Bardon, 1982). Trivial by comparison to these losses, a landmine dropped in the first raid badly damaged the 78th f Hall and in a second raid a few weeks later its camping equipment was destroyed. Meanwhile, the evacuation of school children from the city had reduced the Scout troop to six members and the Wolf Club pack to nil. But the troop continued to function, meeting in other premises until its own hall was patched up, and continuing to camp each summer, apart from 1940 when the government had banned all camps. There was no conscription in Northern Ireland but over forty old members from the 78th volunteered for service against fascism and six were killed in action. Johnson joined the Royal Artillery within a week of war being declared. In his enlistment papers Johnson described his nationality as 'Irish' but, like others before and since, saw no contradiction between this and loyalty to the British crown (WJ1). Given his legal background, he was soon transferred to the Judge Advocate's department where he served for the duration, being mentioned in dispatches and attaining the rank of Colonel. His personal diaries for the latter stages of the war record his landing in Normandy shortly after D-Day and his horror at the sights of war's destructive power as, with the liberating 2nd British Army, he pushed up through Belgium and Holland and eventually across the Rhine (WJ1). He had visited some of these places in happier times as a young man in the 1920s and 30s and he would return to them again with Scouts, though without referring to his wartime experience in the area.

Post-war growth

When Johnson came back from the war he once more took up the leadership of 78th Scout Group. His legal career continued to flourish: he took silk in 1946 and was appointed county court judge for Tyrone in 1947, serving for a further thirty years. It is possible he accepted this role because it would give him greater opportunity for Scouting than private practice as a QC may have offered. He soon re-engaged also in the wider world of Scouting, taking on a variety of posts: helping particularly in the establishment of a major campsite at Crawfordsburn, just outside Belfast. He demonstrated his considerable organisational skills and indulged his taste for amateur dramatics through producing notable Scout pageants and 'Gang Shows', aided by his older sister Mabel, a useful pianist. In due course he became Chief Commissioner for Northern Ireland, serving from 1953 to 1963 and thus playing a part in the wider councils of UK Scouting through membership of its National Executive body. He was a sub-camp leader at the jubilee world jamboree in Sutton Coldfield in 1957 and also served on and chaired the Northern Ireland Youth Committee. When he laid down his national Scout post, the then Chief Scout, Lord Maclean wrote to him: 'what wonderful work you have done through so many stages of Scouting' (WJ1).

But his enduring love was for the Scout group he had founded – the 78th Belfast. The years following the war saw a considerable expansion in its membership. A Rover Crew, for those over 17 years, was established in 1949 and became a reservoir of adult leadership for other sections in the group and elsewhere. The whole Group developed rapidly and the wooden Scout Hall with its atmospheric fireplace, dusty floorboards and 'patrol corners' was extended and then, on the expiry of its lease, entirely replaced in 1965 with a modern brick building nearby (WJ2). Half the cost (£11,500 then; £165,000 in today's terms) was met by Government grant, the rest by parental fundraising: indeed Johnson's ability to secure the trust and backing of parents was a major contribution to the group's success. He achieved this in part by regular reports on the

Group's activities, noting the camps and badge work but also drawing attention to the formal educational achievement of its members, possibly to ward off parents' fears that Scouting interfered with schoolwork. Such reports also noted the running costs of the building (which had risen from £40 in 1937 to £400 by 1963) and commended the work of the Parents' Committee in running whist drives, jumble sales and the like to make ends meet and pay off the debt on the new hall (WJ1).

The new building was needed because the Group had grown rapidly. By 1969 it had a Scout troop of 55 boys, split into two sections meeting on different evenings: a cub scout pack totalling 60 members again in two sections; and a venture scout unit, for those aged 16–20, of 23 members (WJ2). What had caused this growth? The Group had a favourable reputation in the district, and well-structured programmes offered varied and purposeful activities attractive to boys of that era, many of whom were at grammar school. It provided individual recognition and hence self esteem through the skills encouraged and acknowledged in Scouting's badge system and posts of responsibility as (Wolf Cub) 'sixer' or (Scout) 'patrol leader'. The sense of belonging and the camaraderie of one's peers was an appealing alternative to a more constrained social life with the family gathered round a black and white television in front of a coal fire. The Group's strong ethos was partly encouraged by a 'grow your own' approach to securing adult leadership and the expectation that one would progress naturally through its age-related sections and hence be offered a continuity of supportive and challenging experiences from childhood through adolescence. Much of this ethos was due to the direct example of Willie Johnson. The bedrock to him lay in adhering to the traditional virtues, methods and code of Scouting, including the original Scout law which enjoined all members to brotherhood 'no matter to what country, class or creed the other may belong' – a telling injunction for Belfast Scouts. As with Robert Baden-Powell himself, Johnson perceived Scouting as a form of 'character factory' (Jeal, 1989) with turning out responsible citizens with resilience and determination being as important qualities as skills. His personal example represented a call to duty, honour, and service to others. Born into the mores of the Edwardian age, Johnson's whole life demonstrated his morally serious disposition: a man of his time and place, he turned his personal gifts into a particular form of social action. An accomplished public speaker given to the occasional morality tale, he was no theorist – for him, Scouting was experiential activity and outdoor adventure was a key component. His instructions to boys going off on planned hikes requested that they 'bring back notes on landmarks e.g. church buildings (with map references) and on the state of the crops in the fields' (WJ1). A particularly important feature was the annual summer camp. It was usual in the late 1950s and early 1960s for the 78th Scout troop to spend ten days every summer with over 50 boys under canvas, in peer-led patrols all cooking on open fires. The cost of camp in Borrowdale in 1964 was £6.10s.0d. including travel, with 10/- suggested as pocket money (WJ1). Though he had long retired from day-to-day leadership of the troop, Johnson usually attended summer camp to lend a hand by driving his small car to nearby towns to collect food supplies, to encourage adherence to high camping standards, and, not least, to offer his dramatic demonstration of various songs and yells at the evening campfires; performances viewed as melodramatic or magical according to taste. Perhaps reflecting his own experience as a student and young man, he had the imagination to encourage young people to look to new horizons. In alternate years the troop's annual camp was held in either the Lake District or Scotland; in the years between it was held in Ireland, north or south, but in such 'home' years an additional foreign experience was also offered. At a time before family package holidays became commonplace, the chance to travel as Scouts by boat and rail to Switzerland or Norway inspired many boys in the 78th to have a sense of being international citizens. The Belgium trip cost £25 in 1963 and included a night in London and a West End show.

The social and political structure of Belfast was little changed post-war but living standards were rising and the city's economy was diversifying from its declining heavy engineering staples into a service sector, in part created by the British welfare state's role in expanding health and education (Fitzgerald, 1998). The cost of Scouting – for its uniform and activities – was becoming less of a deterrent, at least for parents who were in the growing professional or white collar occupations.

The generally improving economic climate coupled with the 1960s optimism surrounding the approach of Northern Ireland's new, mildly reformist, prime minister was helping to erode community divisions and, though formal schooling remained divided on sectarian lines, the 78th was well-placed to capitalise on young people's leisure time. An 'open' body not affiliated to any church, it had in William Johnson a man of impeccable integrity, immaculate courtesy and obvious decency. Changes in the attitudes of local Roman Catholic clergy following Vatican Council II removed any previous injunction against joining the Scouts, though some nationalist parents may still have been reluctant to go along with the continuing markers of loyalty to the British Crown which Scouting invariably displayed and which might have been seen as attempting the cultural assimilation of those whose national allegiances lay elsewhere. In any event, by 1970, a third of the 78th membership of 180 was Catholic. But even to comment on the faith of its members, while understandable in a society like Ulster's, risks overemphasising one aspect of individual or group identity: as far as the 78th was concerned, the most important signifier was that all were Scouts. And, exceptionally, Scouting in this Group offered an open and shared space for social interaction, mutual understanding and friendship in what otherwise risked becoming parallel lives in separate communities. In Willie Johnson's 78th, promoting the universal values of Scouting took precedence over other identities.

The skies darken over Belfast

With this continued growth in membership there was discussion of the need to extend the building. Johnson had always been keen to win support for Scouting through displays and other public events. In May 1969 the then Prime Minister of Northern Ireland, Terence O'Neill, opened such a pageant marking the Group's 40th anniversary in the grounds of its recently constructed Scout hall. In retrospect, this expression of optimism marked a high water mark for the 78th Belfast. Within a few months the province would see the full onset of thirty years of 'the Troubles' fuelled by a long-standing sense of injustice at discrimination against Catholics in housing and employment. The Ulster socialist poet, John Hewitt, put his finger on the complacency which had been developing in the province, possibly even in Scouting.

In his poem, 'The coasters' (1969) Hewitt suggested that the middle classes had become too comfortable with their lives in larger, gadget-filled houses and at their weekend bungalows playing golf to notice that sectarianism continued to fester and that its infectious cloud might spill over the leafy suburbs.

By early 1970, life in the city, in the suburbs as well as in its traditional sites of communal conflict, was increasingly caught up in riots and subsequently by the sectarian murders and terrorist bombing which cost almost 4,000 lives and wreaked havoc on the economy and community. The arterial Antrim Road on which the 78th Scout hall was situated was now notably dangerous, in part because it was close to interface areas between working class Protestant and Catholic communities. Attitudes here had polarised following population migration into what people regarded as safer areas when inhabited by their co-religionists, albeit now with consequently sharper psychological boundaries between their respective territories. Unsurprisingly, parents were reluctant to let their children come out to Cubs or Scouts: numbers in the 78th, as elsewhere in Belfast Scouting, declined and the previously separate sections were combined. Nevertheless, brave voluntary leaders hazarded their own lives on dark nights in fearful streets to keep the Group functioning. Summer camps were shared with other troops and the concept of a continental expedition was re-instated. The Scout hall was regularly vandalised but survived. As 'The Troubles' gradually receded so the 78th Scout Group revived, and by 2011 its member-ship exceeded 60, male and female, and was now predominantly Catholic. The changed demography of the neighbourhood, the availability of other leisure opportunities for young people, and their changing attitudes, may mean that the Group is unlikely to regain the scale of membership it had known in the halcyon 1950s and 1960s but it continued to offer a distinctive contribution to successive generations of young people in north Belfast.

Johnson's legacy

Willie Johnson stood down from his role as the Group Scout Leader in 1971 – he had served the 78th for over 40 years – but continued to take a benign interest as Group President. His later years until his death in 1993 were overshadowed by the need for him to have round-the-clock armed police protection in view of his previous role as a Judge, from which he had retired in 1978. He told this author, visiting on one occasion: 'I don't care for the risk to myself, but I so hate that these young constables are being put in harm's way to protect me'. His ashes were scattered at his favourite campsite in the Mournes. His legacy is his influence, and that of the Scout approach to which he fervently subscribed, on so many who passed through the ranks of the 78th. 'Oft on a stilly night' they can still see in their mind's eye the inscription Willie Johnson had had carved over the scout hall's great fireplace: 'Here let the fires of friendship burn'.

References and Bibliography

Primary sources

WJ1: Papers of William Johnson, (PRONI D4022).
WJ2: 'Forty years of Scouting' (anonymous but probably written by W. Johnson, 1969).

Secondary sources

Bardon, J. (1982) *Belfast*. Belfast: Blackstaff Press.
Bell, D. (1990) *Acts of Union: Youth, Culture and Sectarianism in Northern Ireland*. Basingstoke: Macmillan.
Bell, M. (1985) *History of Scouting in Northern Ireland*. Belfast: Northern Ireland Scout Council.
Budge, I. and O'Leary, C. (1973) *Belfast; Approach to Crisis*. London: Macmillan.
Devlin, M. (2007) Services and Policy for Young People. In Lalor, K., de Roiste, A. and Devlin, M. (Eds.) *Young People in Contemporary Ireland*. Dublin: Gill and Macmillan.

Elliott, M. (2009) *When God Took Sides: Religion and Identity in Ireland.* Oxford: Oxford University Press.

Ferriter, D. (2005) *The Transformation of Ireland 1900–2000.* London: Profile Books.

Fitzpatrick, D. (1998) *The Two Irelands 1912–1939.* Oxford: Oxford University Press.

Goldring, M. (1991) *Belfast: From Loyalty to Rebellion.* London: Lawrence and Wishart.

Jeal, T. (1989) *Baden-Powell.* London: Hutchinson.

Springhall, J. (1971) The Boy Scouts, Class and Militarism in Relation to British Youth Movements 1908–30. *International Review of Social History,* 6: 125–58.

CHAPTER 5

Theories and Traditions Informing Finnish Youth Work

Juha Nieminen

Youth work is a practical field of rousing activities and strong personal opinions. Yet there has long existed an intention to construct theoretical foundations for youth work. The aim of this chapter is to give an overview of the historical development of the theory of youth work in Finland. What follows is divided into three parts. First, some meta-theoretical perspectives are discussed to call attention to the nature and the structure of the theories used to describe and analyse youth work. These sections highlight the changes and the continuities of the theoretical thinking about youth work. Second, the development of youth work theories will be described in the context of the history of Finnish youth work (Nieminen, 1995, 2012). In addition a general history of the country itself will be offered (Jutikkala and Pirinen, 1996), for theories relating to youth work arise from the prevailing social and historical conditions. Third, some conclusions about the theoretical foundations of youth work will be discussed.

The nature of the theory of youth work

Not every opinion or political manifesto concerning youth work represents a theory of youth work. Both in every day usage as well as in the philosophy of science, there are many different interpretations of the meaning of 'theory' (e.g. Niiniluoto, 1980: 60–80). In this chapter the term 'theory' is employed to mean the explicit unity of ideas or concepts which construct and systematise the principles of youth work. Generally, three different types of the theory have applications which relate to youth work.

The cognitive theory of youth work is based on the reality and truth of knowledge: knowledge is valued for its own sake. The aim of the cognitive theory is to explain, interpret or understand the phenomenon known as 'youth work'. Accordingly, research is undertaken to discover real and true information about youth work without immediate instrumental or explicit political aims. The resultant theory of youth work rests on the objectivity of the information. The cognitive theory is more of a calm, or disinterested, approach than one full of feelings. It helps a person build his or her view of the world. The cognitive theory tells us what youth work is and it compacts the storage of knowledge concerning youth work.

The normative theory of youth work is based on a behavioural and instrumental concept of knowledge: that is, knowledge is intended to lead to practical implementation. The aim of the normative theory is to shape and direct youth work while taking a clear, value-based stand on what good youth work is. Research is undertaken to acquire information that can be applied to youth work practice. This theory of youth work exploits such information. The normative theory, therefore, seeks to tell us what youth work should be and how youth work should be done.

The third type is the practical theory of youth work which is based on an individual's explicit or implicit idea of what youth work is. It represents a youth worker's subjective interpretation of the professional field and practices. The practical theory comes about through everyday experiences and professional education; it is a mixture of scientific knowledge, personal opinions, individual and societal values and intuition. The practical theory guides an individual's ways of working with young people.

Cognitive theory, normative theory and practical theory are ideal frameworks to be applied to a broader theory of youth work. They can be applied and mixed in many ways, but they direct our attention to the different meanings and forms of the theory. The idea of the practical theory also implies that everyone working in the field has their own theory of youth work whether she or he articulates it or reflects upon it systematically.

Elements of the theory of youth work

In addition to considering different theories, reflection across theories draws attention to the structure of the theory of youth work. Six important elements which constitute the ideal content of youth work must be included in any theory useful to the field. These elements include:

1. *A View of Society* – The idea of society can be an explicit conceptual theory: Marxism, functionalism and critical theory are well-known examples of theories of society. In the normative theory of youth work there is also an ideal goal

of what society should be like. Historically, youth workers have sought to help create, for example, liberal, capitalist, socialist, egalitarian and Nordic welfare societies. In the practical theory the idea of society can also be an everyman's view of how the society appears to be working.

2. *A View of the Idea of Man* – The idea of man (or humankind) in the theory of youth work can be grounded in philosophical or psychological theory. For example, Plato, E.H. Erikson, Robert Havighurst and existentialism have all had an impact on the Western ideas of man. In normative theory the ideal man is often a crucial part of the theory. In the pedagogical theories of youth work the ideal of man represents the desirable characteristics of humanity. Among other things, the self-educative human, free individual or active citizen have all been the ideals for humankind in youth work during past decades. The idea of humankind can also be an everyman's steadfast view of what a human being basically is.

3. *A View of Nature and the Ecology* – In the theory of youth work, there can also be an idea or an ideal of the relationship between a person and an environment. Youth work's understanding of the interaction between the individual and nature can be based on research and concepts of human ecology as well as on an individual's personal and emotional experiences from, say, the wilderness. The normative theory of youth work can take sides in questions like: 'Is man a master of Creation or a part of nature?'

4. *A View of the Function of Youth Work* – The function of youth work is an essential part of youth work theory. In cognitive theory the concern is for youth work's function in a society: it considers youth work's real purpose based on the evidence of research. In normative and practical theory the function can also incorporate a concept of youth work in relation to society: what is youth work's ideal function/purpose/role in achieving an ideal society or an ideal person?

5. *A View of Youth Work Methods* – The methods of youth work are not scattered stunts. Youth work's methods are derived in part from the fundamental theory and are informed by practice. Theories can include detailed views on how youth work is trying to perform its function and how to achieve the ideal society or man. The theory of youth work, therefore, lays a foundation for the practical methods employed.

6. *A View of Bedrock Values* – A fundamental element of a theory is the bedrock of values. In the cognitive approach, theory identifies the kind of values that are observable in contemporary youth work, whether or not the researcher or youth worker likes them. Objectivity is a traditional scientific requirement for

cognitive theory although there is an everlasting debate about the possibility/ reality of objectivity in scientific research and theory. In the normative theory the bedrock values indicate the desirable direction youth work should take and they form the ethical basis for work with young people.

In an ideal case, a theory of youth work addresses all six of these conceptual elements. They should also be logically connected to each other. In reality, different theories of youth work include, express, combine and ignore these elements in many ways. The cognitive theory of youth work can be a detailed explanation of current forms of youth work. The normative theory can be a guiding principle for the field of youth work. An individual youth worker validates her or his professional behaviour by adopting a personal practical theory. All in all, work with young people should always be studied, managed and done thoughtfully.

Traditions that shape theory

Many Finnish youth organisations and movements were born at the end of nineteenth and beginning of the twentieth centuries. The early history of Finnish youth work provides an insight into the influential traditions that shape youth work over time. By traditions I mean certain patterns and customs of thinking and practice which have existed over time (Smith, 1988: 48–64). The traditions also put together the essential features of the parallel ideas or strategies that were peculiar to anterior youth work. Certain socially constructed traditions are characteristic of the early youth organisations and activities. I suggest that four important traditions have shaped the history of Finnish youth work: the Christian, the national-idealistic, the political-corporative and the hobby-based.

Christian tradition

The practices of the Christian tradition of youth work were born at the beginning of the modern era during the years before 1809 when Finland was a part of Sweden. At first the confirmation class was part of Finnish popular education but became later the core of Lutheran youth work. Professional priests arranged the confirmation classes, but in the Sunday Schools laymen had an important role. Temporary Sunday Schools were arranged at the end of the 18th century, but in the 19th century the Lutheran Church adopted Sunday Schools as a method.

Early Christian youth work was characterised by a tension between a denominational Lutheran and a general Christian approach, on the one hand, and by the opposition of the Lutheran State Church to Free Church Christian youth organisations or the other. The worldwide YMCA movement arrived in Finland in the 1880s and became a leading Christian youth movement. Initially, the voluntary YMCAs were seen as competitors to the home and the parishes of the established church. Eventually the development of modern civil society legitimised religious youth organisations. At the beginning of the 20th Century the Finnish church lost its position in popular education to the secular power of the state and municipalities and so youth work became an important aspect of Christian education. The main aim of youth work within the Christian tradition was to guide young people to adopt a Christian outlook and mode of behaviour. A humble Christian was the ideal of man. In this tradition the development of society was interpreted as the intervention of Providence, and religious uniformity was an ideal.

National-idealistic tradition

From 1809 to 1917, Finland was an autonomous grand duchy of the Russian Empire. The Finnish national liberation movement gained strength throughout the 19th Century, and the national-idealistic tradition of youth work began to take shape at the beginning of the 20th Century. The aim of the nationalist ideology was to strengthen the national spirit and the feeling of togetherness through enlightenment and the Finnish language. The student movement played an active role in national liberation and this movement adopted an idealistic attitude towards the development of Finland. Young students interpreted the roots of Finland as a fatherland with a beautiful landscape and independent inhabitants. Students spread the national spirit among the common people, and leading nationalists saw youth as a 'hope of the future'.

The Finnish Youth Association Movement – which still exists – was a successful movement of rural youth. The first local association was founded in 1881, and the aim of it was 'to promote the education of young people through plays, writings, libraries and dances'. These nationalistically orientated youth associations connected local communities to regional and national centres. The Finnish Youth Association Movement defined the self-education of young people as the highest ideal, and the aim of the movement was to reform society through education and enlightenment. Three Anglo-American movements – the Scouts, the Girl Guides and the 4H (Young Farmers) – all adopted national features when they spread to Finland during the first quarter of the twentieth century. In all, the function of youth work in the national-idealistic tradition was to encourage young people in self-education and Finnish citizenship. A loyal Finn was an ideal of man. It was argued that the progress of the nation and the state could be achieved by the help of enlightenment and education. A Finnish nation-state would represent the ideal society.

Political-corporative tradition

The political-corporative tradition of youth work was born at the beginning of the 20th Century. The student movement had already become more radical and, after the general strike of 1905, Labour-orientated youth became active. The first openly political youth organisation, the Social Democratic Youth Federation, was founded in 1906. It saw socialist enlightenment as the function of youth work and pointed out that the class division had reached younger age groups and the class struggle was a part of its agenda. The League of Finnish School Youth was also founded in 1906 among secondary school students. The aim of the League was to develop a positive common spirit by means of school clubs. But the school authorities criticised the League because they thought pupils had no right to express their aims, and the League faded away. Youth later played a notable role in the Finnish trade union movement. In the political-corporative tradition young people constituted a new kind of pressure group united around a political ideal or a field of study. In the political-corporative tradition the function of youth work was to promote social and political citizenship thus raising the social and political consciousness of young people. The development of society was seen as a matter of power and political participation.

Hobby-based tradition

The growing political awareness, the class struggle, the Finnish civil war in 1918 and the ruin of the League of Finnish School Youth formed the background to the hobby-based tradition of youth work. Some adult authorities saw young people as unsuitable actors in the political arena and they wanted to channel the energy of school youth into more apolitical activities. Thus the League of Young Power was founded in the 1920s and its purpose was to promote young people's interests, abilities, skills and cultural activities. There were separate hobby clubs for technical interests, chemistry, composition, literature, acting, beekeeping, nature, sports, photography, stamp-collecting and so on. The work of the League had a considerable impact on shaping positive attitudes towards the individual interests of young people in Finland. Even though the original aim of the hobbies was to replace the collective political activity with more personal interests, many hobbies carried social intentions, not least poetry and literature. The hobby-based tradition saw the individual interest as a way to bring harmony to the virtues of personal interests in a way that also promoted national consensus.

While there was no comprehensive theory underlying the study and practice of youth work in this early phase, all non-profit organisations had value-based ideas of society and of human beings. Although there were notable differences between the traditions of Finnish youth work, youth organisations in all these traditions arranged many of the same kind of leisure-time activities in order to reach young people. Modes of thought and practice in these traditions laid the groundwork for more precise intellectual constructions of youth work.

Youth work as free youth education

Before the 1940s there was no central state or municipal administration of youth work in Finland. But some common interpretations of youth work did evolve between the First and Second World Wars. These public interpretations were focused on three aspects: distribution of welfare, unification of culture and education of citizens.

Finland became independent in 1917. In 1918 a Civil War between the right wing (the Whites) and people close to the Labour movement (the Reds) resulted in a deep chasm between the winners (Whites) and the losers (Reds), a rift that was also reflected in youth work. The great number of orphans created by the civil war, the significant class distinctions it produced and the bad living conditions in industrial cities all led to the development of child and youth welfare practices. Young people were often viewed as potential loafers and criminals, and this interpretation helped shape much child and youth welfare practice. The Child Welfare Law passed in 1936 belittled voluntary and preventive youth work done by youth organisations. Nevertheless, the Ministry of Social Affairs continued post-1936 to give small subsidies to the youth clubs of some youth organisations.

The question of national culture was important in the new nation. Youth work played an active role in the creation of a Finnish national culture. The emphasis of Christian youth work moved from voluntary youth organisations to the established Finnish Lutheran Church. Organisations of Finnish-speaking youth dominated and thus the movements of Swedish-speaking youth became a means to support this minority. In the name of guaranteeing the unity and existence of the nation, the state resorted to forms of coercion to prevent the development of a Communist youth movement. The aim of many youth activities was to infuse into the young people a common patriotism and a will to defend their country, these reasons they were supported by state authorities.

During the 1920s and 1930s some youth organisations and leaders criticised schools. They thought that schools were dominated by knowledge acquisition and competition instead of the character-building and civic education that marked the work undertaken by the youth organisations and which was seen to better accustom young people to the demands of Finnish citizenship. According to the view of the dominant culture, politics was not suitable for minors and young people were expected instead to arrive at political opinions after reaching majority. In the Labour youth movement there was a more positive attitude to the political activity of youth; nonetheless, the activities of non-political youth work were accepted as a useful means of acquiring the character-building and civic education required by the new nation and state.

In these social and political conditions the first Finnish comprehensive theory of youth work was introduced (Nieminen, 1998). It was presented by Guy von Weissenberg (1900–1984) who worked as a youth leader in the Finnish Settlement Movement and was also a Scout leader in the Swedish-speaking Boy Scout organisation of Finland. He introduced a comprehensive concept of 'Free Youth Education' that surpassed the intentions of separate youth organisations of the time. This was a synonym for the concepts of 'club work' and 'youth work' which he later adopted.

In his writings in the 1930s, Guy von Weissenberg outlined what would become the basic features of Finnish youth work through later decades, namely: youth organisations as the heart of youth work; a claim on state support and grants; a demand for a special law to help sustain youth work; and the need for a comprehensive formation of youth workers. Guy von Weissenberg thought that youth work should be a real profession of its own and that youth workers should earn their livelihood by doing youth work. He defined civic education as the main function of youth work, group work as a leading social form of youth work and he defended young people's right to be heard in youth work activities. He strongly criticised schooling which he argued concentrated too much on knowledge and individual competition, whilst youth work saw civic education and character-building as the most important functions. 'Free youth education' had to be based on the voluntary youth organisations that guaranteed the free nature and youthfulness of the education. He argued that 'free youth education' should be stabilised by laws that would guarantee state subsidies for voluntary youth organisations.

Guy von Weissenberg was a youth worker ahead of his time. However, the concept of freedom in his theory did not imply any radical or free education as such. It referred to the place to be given to the voice of young people and the priority accorded free youth organisations in Finnish youth work. His approach was also a counter-blast to the 'youth work' of the many communist and fascist regimes to be found in Europe at this time. After the Second World War von Weissenberg became a leading youth work expert in Finland. In the 1940s and 1950s he was Vice President of the Finnish State Youth Work Board and Chairman of its Executive Committee. He was also the President of the National Youth Council, the main editor of a national youth work magazine and a lecturer on youth education at the Civic College, later the University of Tampere.

Youth work as guidance of peer groups

In 1944 Finland withdrew from the Second World War. The re-creation of peacetime economic life, the settling of evacuees from the areas it had been obliged to cede in the post-war settlement and the re-arranging of internal and foreign policy were big challenges for a small nation. The baby boom after 1944 revolutionised the demographic structure of the Finnish population. Managing the care, schooling, employment and retirement of this generation would be one of the dominant policy issues throughout the post-war decades.

During the age of reconstruction (from 1944 to the beginning of the 1960s), Finland used youth work as a means of reconstruction, including calming down the post-war restlessness of youth and developing co-operation between different social circles. The core idea remained: youth had to learn civic ideals and practices in voluntary youth organisations. Youth work saw young people as future citizens, and in youth organisations they were expected to learn social and civic skills such as participation, co-operation, public spiritedness, the acquisition of positions of trust and how to work in a group without adult supervision. Young people's own organisations became more and more acceptable, but the open political activity of the young was still treated with public suspicion.

The whole system of youth work was based on citizenship education given by youth organisations, but it turned out that their activities were selective by nature. The youth survey (Allardt et al., 1958) carried out in 1955 indicated that 54 per cent of young people (10–29 years old) were members of at least one youth organisation. According to the study, members of organisations were also active in other parts of social life. Consequently, Finnish youth work was criticised for neglecting less active and more socially disadvantaged young people.

The most notable theory of youth work during the period of reconstruction was formulated by Rafael Helanko (1908–1986). He was a Scout leader in the Finnish Boy Scout movement, as well as a teacher and a scientist. In 1953 he published his sociological dissertation *The Boy Gangs of Turku during the Years 1944–1951* (Helanko, 1953). It was a noteworthy youth study dealing with the basic features of boys' peer groups. In his study Helanko found common features in the progress and structure of the boys' socialisation in their peer groups. The most important conclusion of the study was that peer groups are not always a source of anti-social or criminal behaviour, but are an essential agent in the overall process of socialisation.

Rafael Helanko built his theory of youth work on his own unique research work that lasted until the 1970s. Some of his findings were published in English (e.g. Helanko, 1978). Helanko, like Guy von Weissenberg, saw youth work primarily as a pedagogical institution: the main function of youth work was to guide, supervise and direct the natural peer groups of young people. Youth work had to adapt its activities to the regularities of the natural socialisation process Helanko had encountered in his research. These regularities dealt with the phases, rhythm, widening and continuity of the peer groups.

Rafael Helanko's theory of youth work offered foundations for group work in many youth organisations in spite of their ideological differences. Helanko himself had a view on socialisation which nowadays looks quite conservative. He had an ideal of conformity in society; he saw man as a social being ('zoon politikon') and thus supervising peer groups was a clear function of youth work.

Social theories' interpretations of youth work

The baby boom generation born into the 1940s and 1950s grew up in an agricultural Finland. Young people of this generation reached maturity in the 1960s and 1970s when Finland rapidly industrialised and urbanised. Many state-based welfare reforms were carried out during these years (e.g. study grants, comprehensive schooling, National Health Act). So the period from the 1960s to the beginning of 1990s is often viewed as the era of the welfare state. In the 1960s, old structures of society were seen as a part of 'the old power' and 'the old culture'. The pressure of the baby boom age group, international influences, elitist youth radicalism and the strengthening of youth cultures made room for the young themselves within many forms of youth work.

In the 1960s new youth policy thinking began to emerge. This gave rise to a holistic youth policy approach in which the aim was to improve young people's environment for growth and to enhance their influence. The political youth organisations and special-interest youth organisations were the key agents of youth policy and the political rights of the youth were emphasised. Youth policy was adopted as a comprehensive strategy within public administration. The basic idea was to influence the environment within which the young people matured through research, rational planning and local decision-making. This approach to policy-making and the emphasis on political activity met with difficulties. The Ministry of Education and the local Youth Boards could not effectively influence the environments which would shape young people's growth, nor the decisions of other administrative branches, let alone those of economic markets, business and industry.

As part of the era's state-based welfare reforms, the long-waited legislation on youth work was finally passed in the 1970s. It guaranteed state financial support for youth work. Under this legislation the youth work system was secured on the principles which had been formed in the course of the preceding decades. Municipal Youth Boards were established by law, and the legislation guaranteed the primacy of youth organisations within the field. The function of public administration was to support civil society organisations. Guy von Weissenberg's visions from the 1930s had eventually come to pass.

Youth policy approaches, the strengthening voice of the young people themselves and the legal base of the local Youth Boards led to the reconstruction of citizenship education in youth work. Young people were not only taught citizen skills, they were encouraged to carry them out in the youth organisations supported by the public youth work system. Young people were elected to the Youth Boards, different kind of 'youth elections' were arranged, the age limit of franchise was lowered and in the 1970s there was even a short-lived school democracy experiment. With the help of the youth policy strategy and through the operation of youth organisations and the Youth Boards, a cohort of young people emerged who actively tried to reform society and influence their environment.

During this period of the welfare state, social theories impacted on Finnish youth work. Social theories were instruments which sought to analyse youth work in a societal frame of reference. The main aim of the social theories was to look at society and youth work through explicit scientific concepts. Social theories helped to explain the role youth work was playing in society. There were two major sociological interpretations of youth work during this period: integration theory and conflict theory.

Youth work was interpreted by the theory and concepts of structural-functionalistic sociology. The key theorist was the American sociologist, Talcott Parsons. The functions of youth work were analysed with the help of his famous AGIL-scheme. According to Parsons, the existence of society was based on integration and solidarity. So, the function of the youth work 'institution' was to integrate young people into different sub-systems of society. The most widely known functionalistic analysis of Finnish youth work was provided by Ritva

Uusitalo, who used Parson's concepts in her sociological studies. According to her (Aalto, 1975), there was a disjuncture between the aims of youth work and the expectations of young people. The main functions of youth work were to integrate young people into the political and traditional value-systems of society. This according to Aalto conflicted with the expectations of young people who wanted youth work to help them deal with everyday problems concerning employment and schooling. The AGIL-scheme was still being used in Finnish parliamentary committee reports at the turn of 1970s and 1980s.

The second social theory approach to youth work was conflict theory. This was mainly based on Louis Althusser's, Ralf Dahrendorf's and Karl Marx's views of society and its institutions. The foremost interpretation of this in relation to youth work was introduced in the 1980s by Ehrnrooth (1985), much later than conflict theories were discussed in other areas of society. According to this view, society was characterised by the conflicts between different interest groups. Youth work was seen by those who adopted this analysis as an institution that tried to advance the interests of the ruling classes in a capitalistic society. In the social state, youth work had two functions: regeneration of the labour market and reproduction of the political system. In consequence, the idea of man in the theory was two-dimensional: young people were 'pre-citizens' and 'pre-wageworkers'.

Integration theory and conflict theory introduced quite different views of youth work from the classical theories suggested by Guy von Weissenberg and Rafael Helanko. These social theories looked at youth work from the standpoint of the society, and conflict theory in particular took a very critical view of youth work's role.

Back to the pedagogic theories

In the 1980s it emerged that the idea of creating a politically engaged youth which had underpinned the legislation had been overly optimistic. During the 1980s political youth organisations lost their position in young people's lives. Only an insignificant part of the youth wanted to be politically active in traditional ways. On the other hand, as a signal of late modern change, part of their social activity and participation was channeled into free youth movements, activism, youth cultures and consumption.

After the disappointment of this youth policy approach, youth work paid new attention to hobbies and education. The rise of the municipal 'youth houses' challenged the traditional voluntary youth organisations. During the 1980s there was a deepening tension between municipal youth work and youth organisations, because the latter saw the strengthening of the field work now being provided and managed by the municipalities as a threat to their own activities and subsidies.

The problems associated with the nature of the municipal youth houses led to the emergence of a theory of collective education. The background for this was the critique of the municipal youth houses: critical voices had called youth houses and clubs 'communal rain shelters' without serious aims and purposeful activities. Collective education was thus a way to activate young people and a means to bring democratic and participatory methods to the youth houses and open-door activities. Collective education was adopted as a means of citizenship education for non-organised youth in the 1980s. Such collective education was based on the classical reform pedagogy and on the collective pedagogy of the Soviet Union (e.g. Anton Makarenko and Vasily Suhomlinsky). Many implications of collective education – like youth house committees – are still in use and a part of the normal life of Finnish youth houses.

During the 1990s Finland experienced an economic recession which caused serious unemployment. The role of the state diminished and the independence of the individual and the responsibility of non-public institutions were emphasised. The social and administrative changes, including a curtailing of public spending, the idea of profit planning, new public management, neoliberalism and new balances of power led to a new strategy for Finnish youth work. According to the National Youth Work Strategy Report (Nuorisotyön Strategia, 1993) the basis of Finnish youth work was to be young people's right and responsibility to build their own future. Furthermore, youth work had to give young people possibilities to develop themselves, and youth work had to remove the obstacles in the way of young people's future plans. The Youth Work Law, which was reformed in 1995, defined the improving of young people's living conditions as an official function of Finnish youth work. During the 1990s the social citizenship of young people was threatened in many respects and youth work paid much attention to the problem of marginalisation.

Since the 1990s a strong aim has been to promote multi-professional networks in youth work instead of the previous sector-based youth work. The extension of the Youth Act in 2011 directs youth work towards multi-professional co-operation. It means that youth workers should work together with other professionalised social occupations – chiefly with social workers, teachers, psychologists and the police.

During the last 20 years there has been a debate on the shift from the welfare state to the welfare society. This means that beside the state, people and communities should also use time and money to promote welfare. The need for reflective youth work practice, the questions of youth work's identity in multi-professional networks, the strengthening professionalisation of youth work and international influences have been a background to a new wave of pedagogical theories. During the last twenty years at least four pedagogical theories have been launched in Finnish youth work.

From the end of 1980s, the ideas and practices of 'Erlebnispädagogik' and adventure pedagogy were brought to Finland. First came the German influence of 'Erlebnispädagogik', later came also an Anglo-American influence of outdoor education and adventure pedagogy. These offered a new kind of reflective thinking for Finnish youth work that already had a long experience of camping, hiking, playing and doing sports, arts and drama. At first, there were some tensions between those who related to the long tradition of nature-based Finnish youth work and the new professionals and entrepreneurs of adventure. Finally, however, the arrival of adventure pedagogy meant that growing and learning via one's own experiences gained a new respect within youth work. It is also important to note that methods that strengthened the surveillance of individuals with the help of the peer group became popular at the same time when society and lifestyles were individualising and the welfare-state was running into the troubles posed by the recession of the 1990s. Some modes of adventure pedagogy have also had explicit ideas about ecology.

The economic recession of the 1990s was one reason for the adaptation of social pedagogy in Finland. Some people and institutions were looking out for new approaches to handling social problems and the financial cutbacks in the Finnish welfare state. Social pedagogy was one solution: it offered an approach to support young people's growth and subjectivity in communities; an approach to strengthen political consciousness; and an approach which would promote voluntary work and self-help. Social pedagogy also gave value to educational activities outside schools. Social pedagogy was brought to Finland mainly from two sources: from Germany and from the Roman language area, but a Scandinavian trend was also noticed. As a normative theory of youth work, social pedagogy pays a lot of attention to the values of society and the good life.

From the 1990s non-formal education and learning as well as informal education and learning have been used as a theoretical framework for youth work. It came about for three reasons. First, non-formal education and informal learning came from the eternal nature of human species: men and women also grow and learn outside formal institutions. Now this essential characteristic of people can be described with specific concepts. Secondly, in administrative institutions, such as the Council of Europe and the European Union, youth work needed modes of thought to justify its existence, activities and resources when faced with the dominance of the formal education sectors. The framework of non-formal education and informal learning also gave tools to evaluate some outputs of youth work. Thirdly, these concepts help to describe and analyse those unique pedagogical processes that take place in everyday contexts of youth work (see Batsleer, 2008). Therefore, non-formal education and learning as well as informal education and learning are useful scientific, anthropological, political and practical concepts of education.

Finally, in the 2000s, the ideas of critical pedagogy have appeared in the discussion of Finnish youth work. By critical pedagogy I mean the Anglo-American theoretisation, not so much the classic Frankfurt school of critical theory. The aims of critical pedagogy, e.g. political consciousness and empowerment, have occurred particularly in those youth projects concerning participation, social problems and marginalisation of young people. Even if critical pedagogy has not much to offer for practical youth work, critical pedagogy provides a useful background for youth work's ethos of strengthening subjectivity and activity of young people. Critical pedagogy also offers views on contemporary issues in Finnish youth work, for example multicultural youth work, democratic participation and the prevention of exclusion.

Overall, the launching of 'Erlebnispädagogik' and adventure pedagogy, social pedagogy, non-formal education and informal learning and critical pedagogy has deepened the awareness of the educational character of youth work. In a recent textbook of more than 30 writers (Hoikkala and Sell, 2007) these new pedagogies were given an important role.

Conclusion

Most of the theories of youth work adopted in Finland have been normative by their nature. They include views of the ideal society, ideal man and good youth work. Many of the theories contain guidelines on how to do youth work. Those theories based on the social theories have been more cognitivistic by their nature: they have analysed and explained what youth work is in the context of explicit social theory. Guy von Weissenberg emphasised young people's right to be heard and Rafael Helanko proved the positive significance of the peer groups. Modern pedagogic theories put human growth, subjectivity and the needs of young people as a basis of the theory.

It is evident that the classical theories of Guy von Weissenberg and Rafael Helanko were important in their day. Almost every youth worker – there were very few of them – knew the theorists and their theories. Even integration theory and conflict theory received attention from academics and the authorities, but social theories did not have the same effect on practical youth work. Significantly, the new educational theories have been launched during the last decades, at the same time as the professional education of youth workers has developed. So youth workers have become more and more conscious of the different pedagogical theories and these have become – more or less – a part of youth workers' personal practical theories.

References

Aalto, R. (1975) *Nuorten sosiaalistuminen ja nuorisotyö*, Kansalaiskasvatuksen Keskuksen julkaisuja 25, Helsinki, Kansalaiskasvatuksen Keskus.

Allardt, E., Jartti, P., Jyrkilä, P., and Littunen, Y. (1958) *Nuorison harrastukset ja yhteisön rakenne*, Porvoo, WSOY.

Batsleer, J.R. (2008) *Informal Learning in Youth Work*, London: Sage.

Ehrnrooth, J. (1985) 'Nuorisotyön murros' in J. Ehrnrooth, V. Puuronen, T. Tammi and T. Tormulainen *Tarkasteluja nuorisotyön murroksesta ja nuorison asemasta Pohjois-Karjalassa*, Joensuun yliopiston Kasvatustieteiden tiedekunnan selosteita 10, Joensuu, Joensuun yliopisto.

Helanko, R. (1953) *Turun poikasakit*, Turun yliopiston julkaisuja, Sarja B osa XLVI, Turku, Turun yliopisto.

Helanko, R. (1978) *Pre-adolescent Culture in the Light of Yard-Games*, Department of Sociology and Political Research, Sociological Studies, Series A:2. Turku: University of Turku.

Hoikkala, T. and Sell, A. (Eds.) (2007) *Nuorisotyötä on tehtävä*, Nuorisotutkimusverkosto, Julkaisuja 76, Helsinki, Nuorisotutkimusseura.

Jutikkala E. and Pirinen K. (1996) *A History of Finland*, Porvoo, WSOY.

Nieminen, J. (1995) *Nuorisossa tulevaisuus, Suomalaisen nuorisotyön historia*, Jyväskylä, Lasten Keskus.

Nieminen J. (1998) *Guy von Weissenberg ja vapaan nuorisokasvatuksen idea* in Suomalaisia kasvattajia, Koulu ja menneisyys XXXVI, Helsinki, Suomen Kouluhistoriallinen seura, 199–220.

Nieminen, J. (2012) *A Finnish perspective: features of the history of modern youth work and youth organisations* in the conference report of the 1st European Conference on the History of Youth Work and Youth Policy, 2010, Gent, Belgium, forthcoming.

Niiniluoto, I. (1980) *Johdatus tieteenfilosofiaan*, Helsinki, Otava.

Nuorisotyön Strategia (1993) *Nuorisotyön strategia – Nuostra*, Allianssin julkaisuja 5, Helsinki, Suomen nuorisoyhteistyö Allianssi.

Smith, M. (1988) Developing Youth Work: informal education, mutual aid and popular practice, Milton Keynes: Open University Press.

CHAPTER 6

The Cambridgeshire Village College: Origin and Mutation, a Perspective

Robert McCloy

The focus of this chapter is the Cambridgeshire village college: a qualification to the accepted view as to its origin, and to a moment of its transformation, approximately 50 years after its 1920's invention. The latter scene is the 1960s, a period of upheaval spurred by population growth, a Labour government bent upon comprehensive education, and an initial re-casting of local government. Essentially, the article is an addendum to the admirable accounts of Ree (1973) and Jeffs (1998).

But first, a brief definition of *Village College* which some suppose is a fancy name for a school with premises available for adult education. This is not what it was, nor ever shall be: rather, it is a community centre within which there is a school, further education, and other statutory and voluntary provision, governed as a single enterprise: *strategic* in purpose, *institutional* in character, *territorial* in mission, *monocratic* in rule, and *democratic* in ambition (McCloy, 1974: 35). Nevertheless, confusion still exists, as it did in the beginning when a bad-tempered Prince of Wales returning from the opening of Sawston, the first village college, complained 'Nobody told me it was a bloody elementary school!'[1]

Initially two themes were uppermost: governance and premises. In respect of the former, the instrument of governance had to embrace the substance of the government's statutory requirements for secondary schools, albeit it proved possible to include governors from local parishes and the university. Arising from this, and the requirements of donors and auditors, the school and other functions were distinctively treated, as reflected in governors' meetings, possibly compromising, from the very start, the corporate approach that lay at the centre of the concept (McCloy, 1973: 300).

In the beginning

Three decisive agents were responsible for the creation of village colleges: a national concern advocating the reform of elementary education (Hadow, 1926); Cambridgeshire's character in the interwar years; and the arrival on the local scene, as the county's new education secretary, of Henry Morris. Their juxtaposition was surely essential for that exceptional institution to take wing, and may explain why its flight elsewhere rarely soared into the heavens. And of these three: Hadow, Cambridgeshire, and Morris, the greatest was Morris.

Hadow

The state system of education, operationally in the hands of the church and local government, had blossomed slowly from the 1870s. It was essentially a selective system wherein grammar schools provided places for a minority chosen on the basis of academic ability. For the rest, provision was made in elementary schools from whence the grammar school pupils were transferred usually at the age of eleven. The elementary schools varied in size, capacity and competence. By the 1920s it was realised that a re-ordering was necessary. Hadow confirmed that a differentiated curriculum was needed for the various age groups. The infant and junior provision, with boys and girls taught together invariably by women, witnessed the least reform. However, for the older children, who were not to be transferred to the grammar schools, a more structured regime was recommended. This would include specific lessons in science, woodwork [for boys], domestic science [for girls], and physical education. Segregation of boys and girls was deemed appropriate and, for the most part, the former would be taught by men, the latter by women. This necessitated staff redeployment and more premises in central locations.

Cambridgeshire

Cambridgeshire in the 1920s, as a jurisdiction, differed from that of earlier years and from what was to come. Momentarily the administrative county of Cambridgeshire consisted of the southern part of the historic county of Cambridgeshire, the northern part, The Isle of Ely, having been established as a separate administrative county. The administrative county of Cambridgeshire had a population of 140,001 of whom 66,803 lived in Cambridge, the only municipal borough (Census, 1921). Cambridge dominated the county, most principal roads fanning out from it into the rural hinterland, largely agricultural and lacking urban centres. While Cambridge was denied county borough status, which it most probably would have been granted had it been surrounded by a more populous county, it was a town of considerable civic energy, possessing its own police force and was an *excepted district*. An excepted district being a statutory arrangement whereby a borough, while not being independent of the county which was the local education authority, nevertheless enjoyed a wide measure of autonomy in the administration of services, most notably elementary education. Here was a constitutional arrangement possessing inherent tension. Within the town, the university was a significant political force which, until 1950, had its own parliamentary and council representation. As for the rural county, the elementary school population of 8,668 was accommodated in as many as 132 schools (Municipal Year Book, 1933: 261). Grammar school and further education provision was largely located in Cambridge. The town, in large measure sustained by the university, was economically more prosperous than the rural area, which shared with much of the country the general effects of the 1930s depression.

Henry Morris

In 1924 Morris, the county's recently-appointed education secretary, produced *The Memorandum* setting out a rationale and scheme for village colleges, which he distributed to members of the Cambridgeshire Education Authority (Morris, 1924). Its originality lay, in effect, in its union of a time-honoured model, the Oxbridge college, and a public education system at a point of flux. In one sense, the village college was a further example of creating an idealised or utopian construct, of which there were many, described, for example, in *Villages of Vision* (Darley, 2007). Morris's brilliance lay in the fact that he showed how a worthy, but for many an unexciting initiative – the development of a council's elementary education arrangements – could be economically transformed into something startlingly more valuable. Harry Ree, his biographer, presents a generally positive account of Morris from the perspective of personal knowledge implying that the village college sprang from Morris's imagination, though strongly influenced by Oxford and his Oxford supervisor Rashdall, and the Idealist Movement (Ree, 1973). The impact of Morris's earlier attendance at Saint David's College, Lampeter is played down. Morris largely disowned Lampeter which he left under a cloud (TSD, 1912). But surely it was there that we must locate the significant initial inspiration. It was at Lampeter where he first experienced the collegiate system (and attended compulsory lectures on Plato and encountered the philosopher king, the prototype for the warden!). While there he was but one of two students in the honours school of theology, which meant he was supervised by E. Tyrell Green who was also a specialist in church architecture (Green, 1911; TSD, 1904–8). Lampeter was a small and isolated university college, an Anglican foundation overtly modelled on Oxbridge, to which it was constitutionally related.[2] Lampeter, founded in 1822, was itself essentially an idealist picturesque institution, an Oxford college set artistically in the Cardiganshire countryside (Price, 1977: 189–200).

The village college differed in that it was not residential, although the warden and key staff lived in the college, and, of course, students, young and old, lived locally. They had in common the notion of a corporate institution set in the countryside where members slept, ate, worked and relaxed, no longer dependent upon distant locations. The word *college* implied a community sharing interests. Implicit, too, were the notions that members would be self-governing, be subject to unitary governance and occupy dedicated property. Ree, in his commentary upon *The Memorandum*, concedes:

> . . . *a surely half-conscious concern that the village colleges should offer the country people some taste of what Oxbridge offered their highly-privileged students.*

(Ree, 1984: 12)

But Ree claimed that the stimulus for Morris's enthusiasm for architecture was found in Oxford, where Rashdall was a particular inspiration, notwithstanding his prior sojourn at Lampeter (1973: 9). Rashdall's *The Universities of Europe in the Middle Ages* provided an account of diverse institutions, demonstrating that the collegiate system was more general than many had supposed and also challenged a contemporary notion that universities should reject 'vocational' study, showing that they had hitherto made no distinction between the abstract and practical (Rashdall, 1895). Morris, in crafting a curriculum for the village college, ardently advocated a similar holistic approach. Lampeter, where 80 per cent of the students, unlike Oxford, were engaged in vocational study, exemplified that tradition.

There was also a Tyrell Green-Rashdall link. Rashdall who looked to another Green, Thomas Hill the great Oxford leader of the Idealist Movement, as *his* principal mentor, had himself been on the staff of Lampeter where, in collaboration with Professor Tout, he had produced his initial publication on the theme of the medieval university (Matheson, 1928: 41). Rashdall had much in common with Lampeter's Tyrell Green, not least his priestly devotional life and deeply-committed respect for Anglicanism (Matheson, 1928). These were not traits found in Morris' later character. Indeed, Morris was subsequently aggressively hostile towards Anglicanism and its role in education (Ree, 1984: 36). Rashdall clearly did not share Morris' views concerning Lampeter, being a vigorous anti-disestablishmentarian and later maintaining his connection with the college as examiner and also a candidate for the principalship (Price, 1977: 148). Rashdall was strongly committed to the vocational purpose of Oxford's theology faculty and during Morris' brief period in Oxford was also a canon in residence at Hereford Cathedral. It seems probable that Morris would have been in Tyrell Green's company on more occasions, possibly daily in term time, and considerably less in Rashdall's, during his terms in Exeter College, although Morris subsequently stayed with Rashdall and always referred to him with the greatest respect (Ree, 1973: 9). Affection for Rashdall did not prompt maintenance of his academic study, vocation, or church loyalty, each of which Morris abandoned. As for architecture, Lampeter's inspiring character and Tyrell Green's *Towers and Spires*, must have been an initial prompt to Morris' subsequent interest in architecture. Morris's 'disowning' of Lampeter and his failure to accord Tyrell Green any gratitude for his support and inspiration must partly be explained by Morris's reinvention of himself as an Oxbridge man and his ignominious collision with Lampeter.[3]

Probably, the essence of the village college is to be found in the latter part of *The Memorandum*. Here, as Ree observes, Morris is at his most lyrical:

> *The village college . . . would not create something superfluous . . . It would take all the various but isolated activities in village life – the school, the village hall and reading room, the evening classes, the agricultural education courses, the Women's Institute, the British Legion, Boy Scouts and Girl Guides, the recreation ground, the branch of the county rural library, the athletic and recreation clubs, the work of village local government – and bringing them together into relation, create a new institution for the English countryside.*
>
> *It would create out of discrete elements an organic whole; the vitality and freedom of the constituent elements would be preserved . . . but the unity they would form would be a new thing. For, as in the case of all organic unities, the whole is greater than the mere sum of the parts. It would be a true social synthesis – it would take . . . live elements and bring them into a . . . unique relationship.*
>
> (Morris, 1925: xv)

Leaving little to doubt, Morris elaborated and came very close to the role to which the church had aspired and had, in many instances, practised:

As the community centre of the neighbourhood the village college would provide for the whole man, and abolish the duality of education and ordinary life. It would not only be the training ground for the art of living, but the place in which life is lived, the environment of a genuine corporate life . . . The village college would lie athwart the daily lives of the community it served; and in it the conditions would be realized under which education would be not an escape from reality but an enrichment and transformation of it. For education is committed to the view that the ideal order and the actual order can ultimately be made one.

(Morris, 1925: xv)

Lacunae in the Morris vision

Notwithstanding an unavoidable gap between vision and reality and without challenging the creativity of the concept, four reservations are merited: the restricted range of statutory and voluntary services envisaged; the notion that education for a rural community was distinctively different from that elsewhere; the acceptance that it would co-exist alongside a selective system of secondary education; and the absence of any obligation to evaluate performance.

Range of statutory and voluntary services

The Memorandum claimed that a comprehensive range of statutory and voluntary services should be accommodated. Specific reference was made to: primary, secondary and further education; the public library; agriculture classes; health and children's clinics; and youth employment services. These functions were within the scope of the education committee and education secretary. There were, however, other statutory services which could possibly have been associated with the village college. The county was a police authority and the inclusion of a police station for local constables might have featured. In a period of depression could there have been more overt reference to welfare work? There were also a range of registration and regulatory functions for which a 'one-stop shop' in the college could have been envisaged. Practical considerations may well have intervened but there may have been other factors. Though Morris's scheme vitally depended upon a single, inspiring warden co-ordinating activities and possessing exemplary team-building skills, this was not characteristic of Morris himself. Ree's biography offers evidence that many found Morris egotistical with an established reputation for not suffering fools gladly.

Edwards, Morris's successor, in castigating this writer's willingness to consult the county clerk on the application of section 13 of the 1944 Education Act, witheringly reminded him that Morris regarded the clerk as a 'tuppenny and a half country attorney'. Edwards who, in this respect, shared Morris's attitude towards inter-departmental co-operation, jealously guarded the then *de facto*, and partly, *de jure*, independence of the education service, and never came to terms with corporate management. A possible consequence is that Morris's fellow chief officers may well have responded negatively to any idea that staff for whom they were responsible should play any part in Morris's village college. There is also possibly an element of ambiguity about the village college's relationship to the voluntary sector. It is a contentious field possibly reflected in the fact, as noted by Ree, that some versions of *The Memorandum* do not include paragraph xiii treating with this subject and stressing that within the village college voluntary bodies would have an enhanced role. Ree's explanation is that it would be of interest to councillors (whose version of the text included the paragraph) but not to trusts, and government agencies and departments. However, individuals working in the statutory sector and voluntary world do not always relate well, each sometimes resenting the perceived incursions of the other. Morris's rhetoric was participatory, his practice was possibly paternalistic. The second factor that might have come into play, especially in respect of activities of a welfare character, was Morris's principal focus upon the aesthetic. Though his plan was egalitarian, much in its implementation put a premium upon enabling the community to 'rise' to a more fulfilling culture. There is little about a caring village college addressing, as priorities, hunger, social alienation, extreme poverty and want of recognition and love. The programme spoke of poetry, sculpture, painting, and much that was surely culturally enriching: little was said of day clubs for the housebound or soup kitchens.

Distinctive educational needs of the countryside

In the 1920s it was reasonable to see in the differences that then existed between the lives of the young in the town and the countryside a rationale for making distinctive education provision. For the majority of the latter social and employment prospects were limited. Such employment that was available would often have been related to the land. Some would find work in Cambridge and across the borders in contiguous, essentially agrarian, counties. As elsewhere in the United Kingdom, some would migrate to areas of greater prosperity in England, to the Home Counties and the midlands; and overseas. Those assessed able to benefit from a grammar school education would attend schools in Cambridge though some attended Soham Grammar School and Ely High School. For Morris a high priority was to provide in the countryside, for the countryman and countrywoman, an *appropriate* education. And here's the rub. Making localised provision comparable to the best that would be found in urban areas, was one matter; crafting it to the end that it would be, and remain so indefinitely, of a distinctive character, ostensibly to meet peculiar needs, was questionable.

Of course, Morris's concern had not simply been the young: it embraced the wider nature of community and the intrinsic deficit in leadership that characterised for him the rural area:

> *Without some such institution as the village college a rural community consisting largely of agricultural workers, small proprietors and small farmers will not be equal to the task of maintaining a worthy rural civilization.*

(Morris, 1925: xv)

There was, however, a flaw in the Morris thesis: the conditions in rural areas that had prompted the new system were already passing away in the 1920s and had largely disappeared by the time of the completion of the original colleges in the 1960s. In the aftermath of the first war there was a considerable development of road passenger transport facilitated by the mass availability of mechanically robust vehicles and trained mechanics, products of demobilisation. Rural isolation quickly ceased to be such a decisive factor. Cheap fares and regular services enabled all but the destitute and seriously infirm to travel beyond their parish boundaries for employment and recreation. Such travel, whilst liberating, was also contributing to a weakening of such community institutions as already existed (Zweig, 1948:109). While the bus was the principal agent of this change, the car had effectively challenged that role by the late 1950s. Cambridgeshire's flat terrain facilitated the provision of reasonable highways by the county council and Morris's colleague, the county surveyor. The irony of the situation was that Morris fully understood the transitory nature of conditions in the countryside as amply revealed in his address to the British Association in 1936 (Ree, 1984).

Continuation of selection

The sweeping prose of *The Memorandum* implies that the compass of the village college would be all-embracing. Nevertheless, academic selection took place but was not perceived to be at odds with the character of the village college. Morris took great pride in the grammar schools and there was much in his character of an elitist stamp. His advocacy of the village college stopped short of any notion that it should replace all other provision. There was the reality of the contemporary situation: the grammar schools existed and there were neither the resources nor the statutory means to accomplish their replacement. Morris, a pragmatist, accepted that situation. At a later stage it proved possible to complement provision at Sawston and Impington by adding grammar school streams. Ree reasonably observes that Morris:

> . . . was working in Cambridgeshire before the great educational reform of the post-war period had really got under way, and important though it was, the change to comprehensive education failed to take note of the need for curriculum reform and for the huge extension of education beyond the classroom and beyond the school. For a comprehensive school can remain a tightly closed institution and there are still areas of the country where the concept of community and the establishment of a community school are looked upon with suspicion and hostility.
>
> (Ree, 1973: xi)

Ree also draws attention to a paper Morris had presented to the Association of Chief Education Officers in which he had anticipated a considerable expansion of further education including county colleges, and the enriching of the general curriculum for those not accommodated in grammar schools. As for the latter, 'the arts should, like games, be free from discourse and examinations pressure'. Commenting upon another Morris paper addressing post primary education, he notes:

> Another distinction which was to become a major issue in the 1950s and 60s, the division between the experience of young people selected for grammar schools and those going to non-selective schools worried him much less. For he saw this distinction being overcome, not so much through the institution of comprehensive schools [this alone, as we now know, is not enough] but through the re-organization of teaching strategies, such as have been realized in the more selective comprehensive schools of the 1970s: that is through the introduction of individual learning, and through a great extension of library resources in schools.
>
> (Ree, 1973: 85)

In a sense, however, making the above reservations is to cavil over an inspiring initiative created at a moment of want and necessarily shaped by practical considerations. If it were possible to rid the mind of the disappointment that followed the establishment of the secondary modern school, with its claim that it would enjoy 'parity of esteem' with the grammar school, it would be easier now to recognise the exciting richness of what Morris was then advocating. As it was, in spite of many heroic efforts, rarely did that 'parity of esteem' exist in the minds of parents at large. All too often the challenge of staffing in the secondary modern school, generally requiring exceptionally gifted teachers to relate to pupils who were sometimes disaffected, was one to which it was harder to meet than in the grammar school. As for the latter, rarely did it lack teachers well able to accommodate the needs of their pupils who were, in any case, generally amenable. In the context of the village college, it need not be doubted that its distinctive mission, in a period prior to any general doubt about the secondary modern school, could have been the very place where true 'parity of esteem' could exist. The gifted staffing recruited to the village college augured well. Morris's faith in individual teaching strategies again places a premium upon the availability of teachers in appropriate numbers and with the necessary skills. Interestingly, Rashdall, Morris's mentor in so much, pointed out, in respect of higher education, that it was often the academically most well endowed who less needed well-organised and carefully calibrated structures. Morris, in putting so much faith in the individual's capacity to reach for the book of inspiration from a well-stocked library, possibly underestimated the demands of teachers coping with secondary modern classes often larger than those in grammar schools. Nevertheless, it is certainly possible to have imagined the development of the secondary modern school in a manner that ensured 'parity of esteem'. That would probably have required special incentives, in terms of recruitment, training, rewards and institutional promotion. The village college was constitutionally well placed to have fulfilled that role and for many it did.

Absence of evaluation

A later generation would be struck by *The Memorandum*'s confidence in postulating a structure that would be largely free of any need for subsequent renovation. In this it is truly an idealist vision. Morris was to be disappointed by some charged with leading the first village colleges. However, he never doubted the design's efficacy: its limited application was attributable to others. Nevertheless, the absence from the narrative of any mechanism or obligation to assess performance against goals, and as necessary to temper the course set, is a weakness. That said this is an indictment for general application until quite recent times.

All is flux: reorganisation of local government and education

By the late 1960s Morris had gone but his ghost still prowled the corridors of Shire Hall. Many there had served under Morris and newcomers, including this writer, were left in little doubt that his writ still held. Edwards, by now the chief, mercurial, and stylish in prose and appearance, was his own man but still fearlessly guarded Morris's legacy. The re-organisation of local government had resulted in the union of the administrative counties of Cambridgeshire and the Isle of Ely. Within the new unit Cambridge still remained an excepted district. Barely had the new order settled when the Labour government issued *Circular 10/65* (DES, 1965). The county's new character and the government's new circular now presaged a re-generation, or, depending upon one's viewpoint, a de-stabilising, of the village college.

The political colour of the new administrative county was bluish though many members served as independents. Party discipline, by the standards of a later age, was relaxed. Overall there was no enthusiasm for *Circular 10/65*. This general 'conservative' viewpoint was as characteristic of the Isle of Ely as it was of the rural area of old Cambridgeshire. The excepted district, vindicating its status, having a stronger contingent of Labour members and university representation, was more sympathetic to the comprehensive cause. *Circular10/65*, however, was employed to tip the balance in an argument with an ever frugal Establishment Committee in favour of recruiting two professional assistants to the chief education officer. Such assistants would bring experience of comprehensive education. Accordingly, the writer, attracted by the village colleges, came from Birmingham where he had taught in a comprehensive school while serving as a community centre warden. For him the village college was the embodiment in one institution of all that should characterise contemporary education. As intimated, however, this did not chime with the prevailing Shire Hall orthodoxy. Completing the original network of colleges had taken its toll. Selection was an accepted part of the terrain in which the grammar schools were cherished peaks. Though Shire Hall accepted the contemporary wisdom about the limitations beneath which small schools laboured, the establishment of Burwell and Gamlingay village colleges, to complete the original network, proceeded notwithstanding the limiting effect of their prospective two forms of entry, in the knowledge that they were not intended to serve the full ability range.

Making haste slowly

In spite of the government's commitment to comprehensive education, local accomplishment would be difficult. Opinion in the schools and colleges was divided. There were entrenched positions and though the authority could take the initiative it sought to proceed by consensus. Working parties, consisting of officers, heads and representatives of the professional associations, were established for each of the four areas into which the administrative county was partitioned: Wisbech, March, Ely, and Cambridge (including the surrounding rural area). Wisbech was relatively self-contained, March more diverse, and Ely straddled the border of the former administrative counties but included grammar schools from the two jurisdictions that had operated in tandem providing respectively for boys and girls. The fourth area was the largest, embracing most of the former administrative county plus Cambridge. Officers of the former Isle of Ely played no part in this exercise, and, from recollection, seemed well pleased to be out of it. The excepted district, on the other hand, tenaciously played a vigorous part throughout the protracted period of deliberation, an added complexity prolonging the process of arriving at acceptable solutions. Moreover, grammar school and further education provision was in the excepted district. Officers in Shire Hall, at the outset, presumed that the task of devising acceptable solutions would prove to be progressively more elusive from north to south, albeit each working party was at the starting block at the same time. That prognosis was accurate.

Preliminary meetings were amicable: courteous introductions and discussion of what might be entailed. Subsequent meetings revealed where dispute might arise when, on the basis of officers' reports doing little more than setting out estimated rolls and building capacities, comments were invited. There were few surprises: staff of grammar schools advocated the *status quo* or, if needs must, a carefully planned change that ensured the concentration of sixth form provision based upon grammar schools. Others were less reluctant to embrace change: some fully subscribing to the principle of comprehensive education, others less so, fearing its destabilising effects. Wardens and staff of village colleges, believing that comprehensive education was essentially at one with the village college, knew well that estimates of roll were insufficient in the case of most for the change to be made immediately. It was agreed that officers would produce further papers for discussion in the light of preliminary observations. Participants, hardly yet combatants, retired to their respective camps. *Circular 10/65* was statutory guidance: not the means by which an authority could be compelled into compliance. However, it was within the competence of ministers to authorise borrowing. Since significant building would be needed, for which the county would need to borrow money, compliance was presumed. Legislation compelling such compliance was possible but a change of government was also a possibility. Accordingly, haste was not the principal concern.

Progress was gingerly made. Plans in the two northerly areas, Wisbech and March, were first crafted. The former had two grammar schools and two secondary modern schools; the latter, likewise, two grammar schools but four secondary modern schools. Further, as well as adult, education would now be largely concentrated in the Isle of Ely College of Further Education and a further education centre in March. Location, capacities, a broad consensus that change had to take place, a recognition of the need to concentrate provision for older pupils and the academically more gifted, as well as ambivalence about comprehensive education, resulted in attention focusing upon 'guided parental transfer at 13 plus'. This was one of the circular's formulae offered as a temporary expedient if one of the others could not make a better fit. Nevertheless, it accommodated the muted enthusiasm for the comprehensive cause then prevailing. It was very much a compromise which, for the moment, was accepted with good grace. The secondary modern schools were recast as institutions for the 11 to 16 age range, two in Wisbech, and one each in Chatteris, March, and Whittlesey. The 13–18 age range was accommodated in upper schools based upon the grammar schools, one in Wisbech and one in March. The proposals were submitted to public meetings, the governing bodies, and professional associations, where they encountered no serious opposition. Major conflict had been avoided and, in due course, the education committee, council and ministry concurred in the proposals. Shire Hall focused its attention on implementation and what was earlier identified as a much more problematic set of conditions further south.

The Ely area possessed two grammar schools, three secondary modern schools, and a village college in Soham. The first village college had thus now moved into the frame. The process followed the established pattern. The disposition of properties and less ambivalence concerning comprehensive education amongst participants in the working party made it possible to develop more radical proposals (albeit this followed a less radical plan: unacceptable in Whitehall). There was the same commitment to concentrate provision for older pupils but now there would be no temporising: no 'guided parental choice' at 13 plus. There would be four establishments: Littleport, Witchford, Soham (the village college incorporating the grammar school buildings) and Ely (incorporating the secondary modern and grammar schools and adult education and youth centres), which would also accommodate the centralised sixth form centre. There would be two further twists giving the new arrangements a distinctive character: first, the constituent parts would be linked in *The Ely Federation of Village Colleges*, prompted by a concern that the sixth form centre could be handicapped were it not 'owned' by all the institutions and to guarantee equality of provision as between the colleges. The second development was spurred not simply because one of the establishments was already a village college but because the education committee 'arising from a discussion concerning community provision in the Arbury Estate in Cambridge, decided to give further consideration to the possibility of making more use of school buildings generally' (Cambridgeshire and Isle of Ely Education Committee, 1970). The first development had been warmly endorsed by the ministry, the second opportunely seized by officers. Other considerations were prayed in aid: the area's under-provision of further education, the premises' suitability, the opportunity presented by the basic needs building programme, and the benefit of enhanced status. What was now planned was generally greeted with greater enthusiasm than that which had occurred further north. Prompted by similar considerations the change to village college status was now retrospectively applied to Chatteris and Whittlesey in the March area. Because new ground was being broken it was agreed that the collaborative arrangements should be spelt out: a common basic curriculum, some joint staffing appointments, a policy on the transfer of pupils, a single governing body, and a joint planning board presided over by the Principal of the City of Ely College (Cambridgeshire and Isle of Ely Education Committee, 1970a).

This development was at once both a significant endorsement of, and a radical departure from, the original concept of the village college. There were the established notions of unitary governance and management, embracing a range of statutory and voluntary activities, and of placing school functions within the context of a larger whole. However, now set aside was the requirement to design and build premises especially dedicated to the re-defined purpose. Though the period was one of greater material prosperity than that of the 1920s and 1930s, when Morris had been so insistent upon the key role that specifically-designed buildings would play, a different attitude now prevailed. Even if not bespoke, accommodation was generous by the standards of an earlier age; neither the county nor government would be willing to sanction expenditure beyond 'basic' need; and there was no appetite, capacity, or willingness to raise capital by appeals to the voluntary or commercial sector. Some were less convinced about the necessity for extra spaces for the exclusive use of adults. Increasingly in later post-war years specialist accommodation, for example, for the separate sciences, physical education, and technical subjects, was being provided as a priority as was the provision of sixth form centres and youth centres with space for social as well as formal education. Such facilities, unlike the generality of small elementary schools invariably equipped with constricted metalled-framed desks in the inter-war years, could be used both by secondary school pupils and adults. The challenge was largely logistical, high-lighted by the fact that the Federation was equipped with its own fleet of three full-sized buses. A further factor was also being discreetly vectored into this development. Though Morris, loyally supported by Edwards, had distain for 'management' there were those present who saw some modest merit in the modern manager, with a commitment to clarity of aims, system and co-operative working.

Nomenclature

Morris had employed the labels *village college* and *warden*. There was now deliberation as to what would be the appropriate terms. Ely had long been a city and *city college* was mooted implying an institutional relationship with *village college*. Councillors and governors demurred: it should be *City of Ely College*. In vain was it suggested that this was inappropriate since that title indicated location rather institutional species. Officers backed off recognising that in all other respects they had been enthusiastic about what had been put forward and that, in any case, the point at issue was possibly rather arcane. In the cases of Chatteris and Whittlesey, other considerations would apply. These locations were neither cities nor villages. Whilst *town* might have been acceptable, *community* was adopted, for the first time in Cambridgeshire: a hostage to fortune since the term was subsequently used throughout the country as essentially a synonym for *county*, indicating public ownership, as opposed to voluntary foundation ownership.[4] The creation of institutions, distantly based upon the Morris model, in suburbs and conurbations, of course, could prompt further angst and momentarily, for a project still-born in Ealing, the term *metropolitan* was contemplated. In general, however, *community college* has prevailed. In the March area, the retention of the commemorative names seemed desirable and thus it was that the *Cromwell Community College* and the *Sir Harry Smith Community College* were established. The term *warden*, at this time, was widely accepted, albeit some questioned its use because of its association with the American prison service. However, its respectable antiquity, current use in the south of the county, basic meaning of a person caring for a range of community interests, and the fact that it chimed well with the co-operative leadership model being discreetly urged, now suggested its general adoption. Nevertheless, the need to underline the leadership role of the senior Ely appointment, relative to the other heads, suggested the use there of *principal*, a term, in any case, widely employed in local further education. Derivative of the Oxbridge influence, earlier considered, the titles *Adult Tutor*, and later, *Youth Tutor*, had been adopted for what in effect became distinct branches of responsibility.

Changes in the south

Meanwhile, the process of re-organisation in the southern part of the county was proving a more difficult task. As noted, Cambridge, the excepted district, was legally entitled to seek to settle matters within the city without concerning itself greatly with the rural area where its writ did not run. Nevertheless, at the outset, county and city accepted that they should seek to make progress jointly with the city's education office participating in the area's working party. Initially, matters in the working party proceeded as they had done elsewhere: courteous introductions, the presentation of raw material, requests for clarification, and the judicious exploration of the various positions being taken by participants. At first, there were no fissures to separate the authority from the excepted district: the same reluctance to embrace the comprehensive cause, commitment to the *status quo*, and general tardiness, were all in evidence. The range of opinion on the part of heads and staff replicated that of the other areas and in this there was no distinction between the city and county. However, contention could not be postponed indefinitely. An enquiring public, those firmly committed to the comprehensive cause, as well as the momentum prompted by the authority's proposals for the rest of the county, created a situation in which draft proposals had to be put forward. In the delicate footwork needed to respect the rights and dignities of the chief education officer and the city education officer, for each was ever poised to be offended by the other, there was much traffic between the offices. Duly a hybrid scheme was crafted which provided a three tier scheme in the city and an 11 to 16 arrangement with centralised sixth form provision for the rural area. The city office was especially attracted by the Plowden Report's advocacy of the three tier formula and momentarily believed that this would most appropriately fit the city's accommodation (Plowden Report, 1967). This compromise solution hardly met with general approval. Apart from the criticism attaching to any proposal upsetting the established order, there was concern that what was now envisaged were separate plans for city and rural area. Be that as it may, it did appear that a three tier arrangement could work in the city whilst it was obvious that it ill-fitted the village colleges. With grudging assent from those consulted in public meetings, governing bodies and professional associations, the authority, at the city's prompting, duly dispatched the proposals to the secretary of state. It was hardly a surprise that the plan was found wanting in Whitehall. So it was back to the drawing board.

There was now a new sense of realism. Possibilities had been tested and more was known of the likely reaction of key players. The experience of what had hitherto taken place in the other areas was brought to bear and there was a greater determination to see the task through to implementation. Many wished to be rid of the debilitating effect of an unknown future. The process of drafting, with the two offices co-operating, was now actually much easier: ground rules had been clarified. In substance, there would be a uniform transfer of all pupils at 11 plus, and a concentration of sixth form provision. In the light of the favourable reaction to the development of the community college concept elsewhere it was possible to bring that idea into the frame.

The question of post 16 provision loomed large. In a context where many of the secondary schools had yet to develop well-resourced courses up to 16, few considered that they could also provide for the post 16 age group. The phenomenon of the sixth form college was largely untested and locally unknown. Such post 16 school provision there was existed in the well-established grammar schools and Impington Village College. Under further education dispensations there existed the Cambridgeshire College of Arts and Technology, increasingly also providing advanced further education, and the Young Street and York Street Further Education Centres, in Cambridge, largely providing technical further education. The notion that the village colleges could be the place where joint pupil and adult provision could be made, thereby mitigating the problem of small uneconomic classes and enriching the learning experience, received little traction. Many would have been daunted by the constitutional and cultural barriers separating school and adult education. Similarly, there was no strongly articulated case made for exploring the feasibility of supplementing provision by distance learning and individual teaching approaches.

Views divided about the future; some believed that the sixth form colleges would prevail, others that sixth forms would develop at institutions primarily cast for the 11–16 age range. The scheme sought to accommodate this division of opinion by providing a mixed economy of two sixth form colleges, two sixth form centres attached to 11 to 16 establishments, one in the city, Netherhall (incorporating the Grammar School for Boys), and one in the rural area, Impington Village College, and supplementary non A-level provision at 11 to 16 establishments. Additional sixth form centres attached to the 11 to 16 establishments could be subsequently considered, namely: Bassingbourne, Comberton, Cottenham, Linton, Melbourne, Sawston, and Swavesey Village

Colleges; Coleridge, Chesterton, and Manor Secondary Schools, St Bede's and Parkside Community College, in the city. As in the case of the Ely area there was the need to avoid costly duplication and to ensure equitable arrangements for transfer at 16 plus. Here the chosen instrument would be a *Collegiate Board* consisting of the heads of establishments providing sixth forms, assisted by an *Administrative Secretary* (Cambridgeshire and Isle of Ely Education Committee, 1972). The smallness of the 11 plus age group at Burwell and Gamlingay village colleges was such that, reluctantly, they could not be brought into this scheme. Their schools were to be re-constituted as middle schools with pupils transferring thereafter to upper schools respectively maintained by neighbouring authorities, West Suffolk in the former case, and Bedfordshire in the latter. A feature of the new arrangements was that those with form-entries below six were to be eligible for additional staffing, beyond that available by application of a general pupil/teacher ratio, to safeguard a general uniformity of provision (Cambridgeshire and Isle of Ely Education Committee, 1972).

The fate of the Grammar School for Girls necessitated much discussion. Various formulae were advanced each attracting its share of obloquy. In due time, a consensus settled for the novel development of its re-establishment as Parkside Community College embracing a four form-entry 11 to 16 mixed comprehensive school. This was the first time the concept, although substantially recast, had been introduced into the City. As in the north, part of the rationale was that community college status could enhance its position. Set in the middle of the city the community it would serve would be more diverse than that of a village college. In this respect, a defining characteristic, its territorial mission, was set aside. It was predicted that it would become a popular institution, its adult education and voluntary activities complementing its comprehensive school. The character of this initiative prompted a text detailing the duties of principal with due emphasis upon surveying community needs and aspirations (Cambridgeshire and Isle of Ely Education Committee, 1973). The village college concept had hitherto been much taken for granted and the critical reference points tended to be those of a building accommodating a range of activities, corporately managed. Little was written as to the means by which these activities were selected or to any evaluation of their utility.

Contemporaneously with the national drive for comprehensive education, a further reform affecting local government was taking place. The Seebohm Report (1968) had advocated a fundamental re-casting of the children's education welfare, health, and general welfare services. Much more was involved than a mere re-grouping into a new major local government function: an emphasis would be placed upon generic social work. Under the new arrangements sectional specialisms would be subordinated to having a professional team approach which focussed upon clients in their family and living environment. At one level, apart from its purpose in strengthening the professional competence of local government in meeting the needs of the most vulnerable, it was a further manifestation of a belief in corporate management, of the serious need to promote team working. Though proposed, there was no willingness to contemplate basing the new generic social worker teams in the village colleges. The same departmental insularity which had been noted in Morris's day still prevailed.

As the curtains descended in the early seventies, on the eve of implementation, questions were posed, some more cautiously than others, concerning what would happen.

- Would the village college indeed flourish with the introduction of comprehensive education or would it be seriously compromised? Would the quest to provide comprehensive education for the full ability range be so demanding that the 'wider' community role would necessarily shrink in relative terms?
- Would 16 plus provision develop in further establishments or become increasingly concentrated in colleges exclusively organised for the post 16 age group, and, as a supplementary consideration, would the mechanisms put in place to regulate transfer in the interests of students and equitable provision, be sufficient?
- Would the *de facto* separate class and tuition provided for school pupils and for adults remain largely inviolate in spite of the then anticipated advances in technology and teaching methodology?
- What arrangements would be devised to ensure that the village college responded to the needs of the community it sought to serve and overtly to assess its performance?

Time would play its part in providing answers to these questions and, indeed, others not then posed.

Endnotes

1 George Edwards, deputy to Morris and his successor, recounted this incident to the writer.
2 Ree incorrectly described Lampeter as a theological college: this it had never been though in later years it included Burgess Hall, which was a theological hall specialising on training ordinands. In that Burgess had intended the institution to provide a broadly-based education for his ordinands and until the 1960s the majority of undergraduates were aspiring to Holy Orders, the misconception is understandable.

3   The writer, who had likewise been a student at both Lampeter and Oxford, suggested as much to Ree who dismissed the idea.
4   When the writer, then director of education and recreation of the Royal Borough of Kingston upon Thames, proposed the establishment of *Chessington Community College*, there was concern on the part of some councillors that *community* offensively smacked of communism. Notwithstanding, the term was employed.
5   Concern that it would be handicapped by its small size relative to other Cambridge comprehensive schools prompted an arrangement whereby it was linked to Coleridge School pending an eventual full union.

References

Cambridgeshire and Isle of Ely Education Committee (1970) *The Community School.*

Cambridgeshire and Isle of Ely Education Committee (1970) *The Re-organization of Schools in the Ely and Soham Area.*

Cambridgeshire and Isle of Ely Education Committee (1972) *The Re-organization of Schools in the Cambridge Area.*

Cambridgeshire and Isle of Ely Education Committee (1973) *Parkside Community College, Appointment of Principal.*

DES (1965) *Circular 10/65: Re-organization of Secondary Education.* London: HMSO.

Darley, G. (2007) *Villages of Vision: a Study of Strange Utopias.* Nottingham: Five Leaves.

Hadow Report (1926) *Report of the Consultative Committee on the Education of Adolescents,* Chairman, Sir W.H.Hadow. London: Board of Education, HMSO.

Jeffs, T. (1998) *Henry Morris: Village Colleges, Community Education and the Ideal Order.* Nottingham: Educational Heretics Press.

Matheson, P.E. (1928) *The Life of Hastings Rashdall.* Oxford: Oxford University Press.

McCloy, R.J. (1974) 'Community Colleges: Their First 50 Years and the Corporate Ideal.' *Local Government Studies.* June/October.

McCloy, R.J. (1973) *Local Government Corporate Management and the Community College: An Examination of the Relationship of these concepts in the context of Cambridgeshire 1965–71.* Unpublished M. SocSc thesis. Institute of Local Government Studies, Faculty of Commerce and Social Science, Birmingham University.

Morris, H. (1924) *The Village College: Being a Memorandum on the Provision of Education and Social Facilities for the Countryside, with Special reference to Cambridgeshire.* Cambridge: Cambridgeshire County Council [Reprinted in Ree, 1984].

Morris, H. (1925) *The Village College: Being a Memorandum on the Provision of Education and Social Facilities for the Countryside, with Special Reference to Cambridgeshire.* Cambridge: Cambridge University Press [Reprinted in Ree, 1973].

Plowden Report (1967) *DES, Children and their Primary Schools (Report to the Central Advisory Council for Education, No. 1).* London: HMSO.

Price, D.T.W. (1977) *A History of Saint David's College Lampeter, Volume 1: to 1898.* Cardiff: University of Wales Press.

Rashdall, H. (1895) *The Universities of Europe in the Middle Ages.* Oxford: University of Oxford Press.

Redcliffe-Maud Report (1969) *Royal Commission of Local Government in England 1966–69.* London: HMSO.

Ree, H.E. (1973) *Henry Morris, Educator Extraordinary: The Life and Achievement of Henry Morris*. London: Longmans.

Ree, H.E. (1984) *The Henry Morris Collection*. Cambridge: Cambridge University Press.

Seebohm Report (1968) *Report of the Committee on Local Government Personal Social Services (Cmnd. 3703)*. London: HMSO.

The Municipal Year Book: 1933. London: The Municipal Journal.

Tyrell, Green, E. (1908) *Towers and Spires*. London: Wells, Gardner, Darton and Co.

Zweig, F. (1969) *Men in the Pits*. London: Heinemann.

Primary Sources

TSD, 1912, Trinity St David University Archives, Lampeter.

TSD, 1912, Board Minutes, U/C/1/7.

TSD, 1912, Newspaper cuttings, 27 May, 1, 3, 5, 8, 11, 22, and 26 June.

TSD, 1912, St David's College Magazine, vol.x, no.4, 225.

TSD, 1904–8, St David's College Magazine, *Annual Reports of the Architectural Department*. Architectural Department.

CHAPTER 7

History Illuminates the Challenges of Youth Work Professionalisation

Judith Metz

The professionalisation of youth work is currently high on the political and social agenda in the Netherlands. Although Youth work has been a preventive provision for centuries, the shift of the central policy focus away from reducing problems to preventing them has the consequence that more is expected of youth work. It is currently expected to correct behaviour, raise awareness of social norms, point the way to school and paid work and prevent trouble and criminality. It is essential that youth work occupies a place in the chain of youth provision whether to prevent young people from dropping out (of education, the economy or civil society) or to restrict the demand for expensive youth care. The government has brought about cooperation between the relevant sectors such as education, youth care, the police, and youth healthcare. Within this integrated system there is criticism of the quality and effectiveness of youth work. The arrival of New Public Management in the public sector in the mid-eighties has the consequence that the public sector has a greater market orientation (Metz, 2011). For youth work this means that more than ever it is accountable for the output and outcome of its projects and activities (Noorda et al., 2002).

Youth work in the Netherlands has almost 3,000 paid youth workers, reaches 161,991 young people and is solely financed by the municipalities (Noorda et al., 2009). Dutch youth work has only had a professional association for five years, and there is no registration of youth workers although a professional code is in development. After various abandoned attempts, there is still no independent study route within higher education and research at an academic level is only slowly emerging (Metz, 2011). Youth work in the Netherlands thus has a long way to go to meet the new requirements for professionalisation.

Within the Netherlands there is an ongoing debate regarding the status of the youth work field and the professionalisation of youth workers. While there is general consensus on the necessity of the work and the relevance of professionalisation, opinions differ on the strategies needed to build professional capacity, assure accountability and quality, and elevate the status of youth work in society. One of the ways to think about the possibilities, chances, and traps of professionalisation is to look back at youth work in history. The lessons from the past provide insights into youth work's professionalism to date and offer points of departure for its continuation.

The 140 years that youth work in the Netherlands has existed can be divided into six distinct social and political periods, each distinguished by different visions for youth work, anticipated outcomes, realities of policy and community expectations, and the capacity of youth workers to respond. This chapter reflects on each period beginning with a brief sketch of the development of youth work as well as the trends, challenges and lessons to be learned from the period. The final discussion focuses on how history can enlighten current issues and help us work toward solutions in the current debate about the education, training and expertise necessary to assure a professional workforce for the future. The chapter is based on literature research into the history of youth work.

Origins of youth work, 1870–1915

The roots of youth work go back to the industrialisation of Dutch society at the end of the nineteenth century. The Dutch migrated in mass to the larger cities and primarily ended up in slums where ties with their old surroundings were severed (Nijenhuis, 1987). The labour movement was manifesting itself (Nijenhuis, 1987; Neij and Hueting, 1989). The growth of the Dutch Reformed Church and the emancipation of the Catholics resulted in controversy over the funding of schools (Neij and Hueting, 1989). Although the practical implementation of social work including material help was still a matter of private initiative, the intervention from national government steadily increased. Legislation was enacted to deal with exploitative situations. In 1889 the Factory Act was passed (and revised in 1911), followed by child welfare legislation in 1898 and 1911 which gave the government the power to take action to protect neglected and mistreated young people and to enforce compulsory education (Nijenhuis, 1987).

The new labour relationships and changes in family life resulted in the realisation that being a child is a specific phase of life that requires special attention (parenting and education) and materials (toys) (Selten et al., 1996; Meilof, 1999;

Bijlsma and Janssen, 2008). Young people were growing up in a society which differed from that which the previous generations had known and many of them threatened to affiliate themselves with the various social movements of the time (Harmsen, 1961; Bijlsma and Janssen, 2008). In an attempt to prevent this perceived radicalisation among young people, separate leisure facilities were developed by the various socio-political groups (socialists, progressive liberals, Catholics and Protestants) for working class boys and girls. None of these socio-political groups had a pedagogical vision of how to organise this leisure provision for young people. They themselves provided the means for organising the leisure facilities. The work was carried out by paid workers who were untrained. This marks the birth of professional youth work (Metz, 2011).

In 1899 progressive liberals in Amsterdam set up one of the first schools of social work in the world. That they were the first is the direct consequence of their conviction 'that the task to alleviate social distress cannot only be fulfilled from a sense of justice and devotion, but that social work also requires expertise' (Hueting and Schneiders, 1999: 7). The need for education in social work was endorsed by the growing class awareness of workers who rejected the patronising charity of the upper classes (Hueting and Schneiders, 1999). The first twenty years of the existence of the Amsterdam School of Social Work made little impression on the professional quality of youth work as far as its collective expertise was concerned. The training programme needed time to develop its curriculum and content (Neij and Hueting, 1989).

In this period, youth work in the Netherlands was positioned in the third domain (leisure time), next to the first domain (family) and the second domain (school and work). The legitimacy of youth work's role lay in how it supported youth growing up *as part of* society. Youth work originated in civil society: neither national nor local government contributed to its coming into existence, not even through funding. In these early days no attention was paid to professionalisation despite the fact that the work was being carried out by paid workers. Both within the School of Social Work as well as in youth work practice, there was no consideration of what specific expertise was required for working with young people.

Importance of youth work, 1914–1945

The First World War caused an increase in the attention paid to young people. The rise in unemployment and the closing of primary schools resulted in children and young people 'hanging out' on the streets. In 1917 the national government set up a State Commission for Conducting Research into the Development of Young People of 13–18 years old (Nijenhuis, 1987). The conclusion of this research was that six years of compulsory education was not adequate for preparing young people to become adults. It was also observed that, in addition to the child protection interventions in dysfunctional families, preventative work was also required (Jansen et al., 1989). The solution recommended by the report was to expand 'free youth education' (the current term for youth work) and provide 'a whole range of means for youth education outside family, church and school' in which participation would be voluntary (Gerhard, cited in Nijenhuis, 1987: 114).[1]

The report by the State commission signified recognition of youth work as having its foundations within civil society (Metz, 2011). The national government made funding available for these developments in youth work, albeit only symbolic in amount (Jansen et al., 1989). This had the consequence of strengthening efforts by civil society (Metz, 2011).

After the First World War the realisation also occurred in religious circles that its social work should be extended beyond the realm of charitable work and that professional training was necessary. From 1921 the national government subsidised domestic, science and technical education, paving the way for the first Catholic and Christian schools for social work opened in 1920, the RC School for Social Work in Sittard, and in 1926 the Central Institute for Christian Social Work in Amsterdam (Hueting and Schneiders, 1999).

Youth work was still carried out by paid workers who had not undergone specific training. In the debates about youth work, the concept emerged that the personality of the workers was central to their contact with young people. Also it was important that the activities offered matched the needs and aspirations of the young people involved. There was still no question of collective ways of working being developed in the field (Nijenhuis, 1987).

At that point youth work practice was confronted with a new problem: it proved difficult to find sufficient professional workers (Nijenhuis, 1987; Jansen et al., 1989). Various explanations account for this. First, it was work that required specific skills, which not everyone had at their disposal. Secondly, the irregular working times (evenings and weekends) proved to be a hindrance. Thirdly, youth work had a bad image in professional circles: 'All that playing around with children and young people was looked down upon' (Nijenhuis, 1987: 91). To solve the lack of youth leaders, amongst other issues, some individual youth work organisations started to organise themselves in umbrella organisations (Heuting and Schneiders, 1999; Jansen et al., 1989).

Meanwhile within youth work organisations, criticism grew of the study programmes of the schools of social work. The curriculum was not in keeping with what was required in the actual practice of youth work (Nijenhuis, 1987). Two umbrella organisations started their own youth leader training programme with the intention of bridging the knowledge gap between the realities of youth work practice and the graduates from the school for social work (Nijenhuis, 1987; Oudenaarden, 1995).

The period between the First and Second World Wars can be characterised as fragile professionalisation. For the first time research appeared that recognised the societal relevance of youth work. Also it became broadly acknowledged that welfare work needed professional expertise. Within youth work practice, preliminary ideas of what specific youth work expertise might be, emerged. Disappointingly, the curricula of the schools of social work did not take youth work into account. When the severe criticism of the schools of social work inspired no results, some youth work organisations started to cooperate in umbrella organisations designed to educate youth workers for themselves.

Youth work in the welfare state, 1945–1960

After the Second World War there was considerable anxiety about the corruption and rowdiness of young people (Du Bois-Reymond and Meijers, 1987). This anxiety was fuelled by particular concerns about social change. Large parts of the cities and infrastructure were destroyed by the war, affecting business and economic activities. Social and moral problems were huge. For young people there seemed to be no future. In response to these concerns, the national government set up the Directorate for General Extracurricular Education (VNG, 1957).[2] Three priorities were identified for the allocation of government subsidies for leisure-time youth provision.

The first funding priority was for general youth work for which national youth organisations and umbrella organisations of youth work could apply (VNG, 1957; Nijenhuis, 1987). A second priority was for cooperating bodies having a religious, philosophical or general ideology to access the funding. This subsidy was allocated to relevant umbrella organisations so that the national government no longer had to negotiate with a jumble of mostly small church and private organisations that were concerned with youth work. The financial benefits were intended for national organisations, the training of youth leaders, maintaining salaried officials in the departments and for extra support for the local departments if necessary. The third important priority for this funding was for subsidising the schools of social work (VNG, 1957).

The extensive subsidy regulations had the consequence that, within all civil society organisations, a provision for youth work was developed. The target group for youth work was youth in general and the objective was to counter-act lawlessness and moral degeneration. In the first instance the civil society organisations differed in their religious leanings. As the 1950s progressed and secularisation increased, the religious or philosophical identity became less significant (te Poel, 1997). The essence of youth work was the organisation of activities, often in their own accommodation, where children and young people could contribute to their own development through their contact with paid workers and with each other. Youth work responded to a range of material and developmental needs (Metz, 2011).[3]

Because the financing of youth work was coordinated through the umbrella organisations and money was available for forming these, all providers of youth work started to organise themselves (VNG, 1957; de Haan and Duyvendak, 2002). The umbrella organisations thus developed into organisations with a support function. Their working activities varied from administrative coordination, consultancy services, collective promotion of interests, guidance for member organisations and the acquisition and distribution of state subsidies (Nijenhuis, 1987). The umbrella organisations were also concerned with the advancement of expertise. They periodically published information so that people could keep abreast of professional developments (Nijenhuis, 1987).

The subsidy which was provided for social study programmes resulted in an increase in the schools for social work. For example, the number of Catholic schools increased from five to eleven within five years (Hueting and Schneiders, 1999). Half way through the 1950s a job-based delineation came to exist between social work and cultural work. Cultural work was understood to be:

> all activities geared to the flourishing (formation and development) of the human personality, as individuals and as members of a family and the community. Social work is described as the systematic involvement with people, families or groups of the population with the objective of providing for existing social needs or to prevent threatening social needs.
>
> (Neij, 1989, cited in Neij and Hueting, 1989: 250)[4]

It lasted until 1958 before a course for youth leaders was created at the schools for social work. Because youth work still did not have a clear methodology, group work theory from the United States formed the methodological underpinnings for this training.[5] But this group work theory was not applicable to the dilemmas which the youth workers faced in practice. The theory did not strengthen youth workers' capacity to develop activities which were relevant to the interests of the young people who attended the youth centres. Moreover, the concept of the youth leader was explored from the perspective of psychoanalytical theory as an identification figure or role model who, through a balanced use of his or her personality, attempts to gain insight into the relationships within the group. This was at odds with the reality of working in the youth centres in which the leaders were primarily required to have organisational capabilities (te Poel, 1987). Contrariwise, in the eyes of the scholars, the youth work approach in practice had serious shortcomings. From their perspective, the practice was trailing behind what they were taught at school (Neij and Hueting, 1989). As a result tension between youth work practice and the social work schools increased again.

The training programme set up by the youth work organisations themselves did not appear to have been viable either. The other umbrella organisations for youth work regarded themselves as being insufficiently acknowledged within the programme's profile and refused to participate in it. Lack of students and funding forced the youth work programme to merge with the social pedagogy programme of the Middelloo School of Social Work into a broader training programme for youth work, youth care and child protection. Because this programme had to be in line with general training for social work, the specific focus on youth work disappeared.

The development of the welfare state provided considerable impetus in the professionalisation of youth work. Extensive subsidies for the work resulted in the growth of youth work provision. With the new scope and funding for developing umbrella organisations and study programmes, for the first time youth work could position itself more strongly with its own area of expertise. Unfortunately, youth work in the Netherlands still lacked its own body of knowledge. Instead group work theory became the basis of youth work education. Because this taught theory did not match the questions and dilemmas of youth work practice, further professionalisation was stifled.

Being young together, 1960–1980

For the Netherlands 'flower power' is synonymous with the sixties and seventies. Social relationships were in a state of change (Koopmans, 1992). A hierarchical society with prescribed relationships and ways of operating was replaced by a new individualised and autonomous culture. Parents were no longer stood in authority over their children, but their side. The regimented household gave way to the negotiation household (Brinkgreve and de Regt, 1990). The sixties also left its traces in welfare policy. The emphasis shifted from prosperity to well-being: it expressed a person's right to be occupied creatively, or in the words of state secretary of social work, Klompe: 'it is not possessions which make us free, but play' (cited in de Haan and Duyvendak, 2002). The alarmist cries about the degradation and moral corruption of youth in the fifties gave way to opinions in which children and young people were considered to be the bearers of social innovation.

'Being young together' became the basis of pedagogical ideology instead of the former 'not yet an adult' mentality (te Poel, 1997). Mutual relationships between young people and adults were central to this process. The didactic relationship was consigned to the past. It was not appropriate to approach young people with either a specific intention or to intervene in the development of a child (Hazekamp and van der Zande, 1992). Dialogue became the most important methodological concept and resource in the pedagogical relationship within the youth centres. This notion of dialogue rapidly acquired the objective of independent nurturing: that young people have to be educated to have the preparedness and the capacity to communicate (te Poel, 1997). The youth worker acquired the role of facilitator and the task of creating a supportive environment. The concept of the youth service made its debut (Hazekamp and van der Zande, 1992). In actual practice youth workers were unsure about their role. How could they support and supervise young people, without influencing them? Should youth work even have a pedagogical function? Many youth workers were unconcerned with any pedagogical theory that might underpin practice and were committed completely to offering practical support and organisation (te Poel, 1997).

The social criticism of the time came to a head in the schools of social work where both education and welfare work were accused of merely having the objective of getting the individual to adapt to the capitalist society (Neij and Heuting, 1989). At the Amsterdam School of Social Work the study programme for cultural work, which came about as a result of a great deal of effort and following heavy pressure from the field, came to a complete standstill. Students entered a five-year conflict both about the content of the curriculum as well as the way in which it was managed (Neij and Heuting, 1989). Indirectly the standstill at the schools of social work stimulated national cooperation towards youth work professionalisation. The umbrella organisations came together to advance the expertise of head youth leaders (Nijenhuis, 1987). This cooperation also involved national government. The Ministry for Culture, Recreation and Social Work (CRM) was tired of having to deal with the many national umbrella organisations and in 1969 set up the Cooperative National Central Body for District, Neighbourhood and Club House Work (SALCO) (Nijenhuis 1987; van der Zant, 2003).

The ideology of flower power left deep marks in Dutch society and youth work. Due to societal change, youth work had to redefine its role, pedagogical assignment, field of expertise and ways of working. Paradoxically, the uncertainty of the time about the position of youth work and its purpose, as well as the stalling of the development of training programmes, became a catalyst for the stakeholder organisations to join together and define the field. Through the dialogical approach, the field found, for the first time in its existence, a methodology which was in keeping with the practice of youth work. None-the-less a lot of youth workers were not comfortable with this need for innovation. They retreated into their youth centres and became caretakers.

New public management 1980–1995

The oil crisis in 1973 revealed the costs of the welfare state in the Netherlands. The explosive growth of social work, secularisation and the democratisation of Dutch society placed the organisation of social work further under pressure (Hueting, 1989). The appearance of *The Market of Well-being and Happiness* by Hans Achterhuis (1979) marks the definitive end of the development ideal of the sixties and seventies (de Haan and Duyvendak, 2002). New Public Management (NPM) became the central management form. Effectiveness, expediency and efficiency became the leading concepts. Because development is not easily measured, the welfare policy shifted to focus more on provision for concrete problems (de Haan and Duyvendak, 2002). The national government introduced the State Contribution and Regulation of Social-Cultural Work in 1980. Youth work became combined with community work, and was decentralised to the provinces and later to the local authorities (Hueting, 1989; de Haan and Duyvendak, 2002).

For the first time since 1918, therefore, youth work was no longer a separate national policy category and this had major consequences. It was no longer possible to organise one lobby for the interest of youth work. Instead, this lobby has to find its shape in each municipality, and youth work has to compete for money with other kinds of welfare work. Cutbacks followed. Professionals with higher vocational education were replaced by less expensive workers with secondary vocational education (Hazekamp and van der Zande, 1992).

Youth work, just like all welfare work, was considered to be primarily intended to solve problems. Special groups of children and young people became the target of state policy; these included school drop-outs, young people with an addiction, those who were long-term unemployed and young people from ethnic minorities (Hazekamp and van der Zande, 1992; Tilanus, 1997; de Haan and Duyvendak, 2002). These new objectives and new target groups in youth work required the redefinition of the role of youth work, its pedagogical assignment, field of expertise and the development of new working methods.

The umbrella organisations and study programmes which had been set up by youth work organisations to play a role in the necessary development and transfer of knowledge were so occupied with their own survival that they did not have the time or resources to continue to develop youth work as a profession. Parallel to this, the subsidy to 35 national support organisations was stopped. In their place the Netherlands Institute for Care and Welfare (NIZW) was set up, a broad organisation with a support function for all social professions. For youth work this meant the loss of its specialised support (van der Zant, 2003).

The schools of social work also faced various waves of cutbacks which resulted in a large-scale reorganisation of the education system. The many individual higher professional education institutes merged into larger ones which compared in size and organisational structure with universities (Neij and Heuting, 1989). The great diversity of social work study programmes, including youth work, were reduced to four (social work; social-cultural work; social pedagogical service provision; and personnel and labour). The argument for this was that social work was subject to such a degree of change that this bundling together of forces would lead to better quality education (Noorda and Vosskuhler, 1986; Neij and Hueting, 1989). For youth work it had the consequence that, for the umpteenth time, a study programme which had not been easy to establish now disappeared.

The connection between educational provision and the actual needs of the field became a problem again. An attempt was made to bridge the gap between the study programmes and the field by creating consultation structures between higher professional education sectors and fieldwork organisations and through working with more instrumental professional qualifications. The Centre for Professional and Educational Issues (part of NIZW) supported this exchange with the development of a profession structure that served four to seven key professions (Neij and Hueting, 1989). Unfortunately for youth work, it was not included in this structure. This omission was only rectified in 2007.

Social pedagogy, the academic subject which until this point had paid the most attention to issues in youth work, was also in crisis. Under the influence of postmodern criticism of enlightenment ideas concerning the extent to which social change can be effected by government policies, the autonomy of the individual and the existence of truth, fundamental doubts emerged about the legitimacy of social pedagogy (te Poel, 1997). Within social pedagogy the realisation was dawning that there existed no universal, unequivocal, and normative guidelines for the supervision of young people on their passage to adulthood (Gilligan, 1982; de Waal, 1989; Sansone, 1991; Naber, 1992). Internal reorganisations sealed its fate and social pedagogy disappeared as an academic subject (Mathijs, 1993).

The economic crisis combined with the loss of welfare ideals led to altered social priorities. Youth work had to look for new working methods. The institutes which were set up by youth work organisations to take the lead in the development of specific expertise and working methods had lost their relevance for youth work because of their increase in scale. The consequence was that youth work was left to its own devices to secure its professionalisation.

Pedagogical offensive, 1995–

The economic boom, neo-liberalism and their 'risk society' marked the nineties and the start of the twenty-first century. These changes led to greater social division (van Houten, 1999; Sennet, 2003). The social professions regained significance due to their potential role in stemming these increasing divisions. Youth policy acquired a two-pronged approach: (1) the advancement of opportunities and (2) the prevention of drop-outs (Gilsing, 2005). The new public management style which had started in the eighties was maintained (WRR, 2006). European legislation enabled the contracting out of welfare work. This time the local government demanded insight into how public resources were being spent and what the outcomes were.

In implementing such policy, youth work mirrored two objectives: the development of talent and the prevention of nuisance and criminality. Once again youth work had to look for new working methods and also assure accountability and guarantee quality. In situations in which youth work organisations were not able to deliver the work or accountability, or both, the tasks of youth work were contracted out (Fabri, 2006).

At the end of the last century, the professionalisation of youth work was on the agenda for the first time. There were multiple reasons for this. First, hardly any new youth workers were graduating from higher and secondary vocational education because the schools of social work had ended youth work study programmes in the 1980s. In addition the status of youth work was low; new generations of social professionals preferred to work in related professions such as youth care, social work and sports rather than in youth work itself (Noorda et al., 2002; Spierings and Steketee, 2004). Third, the current practice in youth work was of insufficient quality and quantity to meet the new demands set by the governments (van Griensven and Smeets, 2003; Spierings and Steketee,

2004). Finally, the relationship between youth work and local authorities was blurred as a result of the new public management. Local authorities sought greater effectiveness of youth work while youth workers faced problems with the lack of a clear vision of youth policy and deficient directing of their work by local authorities (Fabri, 2006).

To professionalise and raise the status of youth work the NIZW set up the National Development Project called Youth Work, Innovation and Quality Improvement (LOJIK). Concrete results from LOJIK were the starting up of study programmes in youth work at secondary vocational schools (Fabri, 2009); research into youth work (Fabri, 2007); a national network of quality circles in which youth workers would come together to exchange ideas and input into the development of methodology; and the appearance of the publication *Youth Work: The State of Affairs and Perspective* (Fabri, 2006 see also LOJIK, 2004, 2005). In addition, under the auspices of LOJIK, a powerful lobby was set up for youth work which, in 2004, resulted in the establishment of a professional association for youth work, BV Jong, and the late appearance of youth work in the profession structure (van Dam and Zwikker, 2008).

The demand for professionalisation in youth work continued to increase despite the enormous efforts of youth work practice to face the raised challenges. The development of evidence-based practice in youth care led to the expectation of evidence-based practice *of youth work*. Within the field of youth work this led to a debate about which form of professionalisation would do the most justice to the character of youth work. Spierts (2005: 18) indicated that the diversity of manifestation and practice in the social-cultural professions was at odds with an 'all-encompassing professionalisation strategy'. At the same time youth work could not ignore the move towards evidence-based practice. The schools of social work indicated a need to be knowledgeable about young people and youth work methodologies in order to educate youth workers well (Metz, 2012).

This time the youth work organisations sought collaboration with the local authorities, schools of social work and regional training programmes. In Amsterdam youth work organisations and study programmes joined forces and set up Youth Spot, the research and practice centre for youth work (Youth Spot, 2007). In Maastricht the comprehensive welfare organisation Trajekt has taken the lead in developing innovative projects such as Droomjongeren, a combined approach for learning and working to prevent dropping out of school and youth unemployment. In Rotterdam the city centre authorities, together with youth work organisations, directed the setting up and implementation of qualitative and quantitative evaluation of youth work. The future will tell whether Dutch youth work is capable of meeting the high expectations for expertise, professional quality, accountability and, most important of all, has the ambition to contribute to the positive development of the young.

Conclusion

Youth work is a separate profession with a clear position within society. It is positioned in the third domain and has the legitimacy to support young people in growing up *as part of* society. Youth work is primarily focussed on young people of low socio-economic backgrounds and marginalised youth. The goal of youth work is full participation in society. Its starting point is the life worlds of the young. The exact content and target groups differ according to societal developments and trends in the needs and lifestyles of young people.

That youth work is a separate profession underlines the need for specific expertise. By the beginning of the twentieth century it was already beyond dispute in the Netherlands that the professional supervision of young people required specific expertise, and that the education of future youth workers was necessary. People who did not have the skills were not able to work effectively with young people. General social work approaches such as group work did not fit with the dynamics and challenges of youth work practice. The same situation appeared in the eighties and today, since there is a shortage of skilled youth workers due to the lack of specific youth work education at the schools of social work.

Still the question remains as to what exactly is the expertise and skills of the youth worker. Until now youth work in the Netherlands has had a small body of knowledge with an even more limited theoretical or empirical foundation. Most of the knowledge is experience-based: both from being a professional youth worker and as having been a member of the target-group. Achieving a separate body of knowledge has been difficult because youth work is a relatively small subject area; there is thus a tension between having sufficient scope to offer the necessary quality while at the same time having to be specialist enough to be in step with specific professional practice. The recent development of evidence-based practice in youth care, which led to the expectation (and ambition by some youth work organisations) of an evidence-based practice *of youth work*, finally forces youth work practice to invest seriously in the development of its own, specific body of knowledge.

What does history teach us about the expertise and the skills of youth work? History shows that for youth work, innovation is a permanent process. Both society and young people are in continuous development. Social developments and trends amongst young people – negotiated through governmental policy – lead to changing tasks for youth work. In consequence, youth work has to constantly develop new working methods and approaches. It is this dynamic character of youth work that hinders the development of a specific body of knowledge. Does this mean that there is no fundamental underpinning for youth work expertise and skills? The practice of youth work is defined by its position in society at a particular time, its societal legitimacy and its goals. The exact content differs according to societal developments and trends in the needs and lifestyles of young people.

That permanent innovation lies at the heart of youth work has consequences for its future professionalisation. This limited historic overview suggests an agenda with three points of attention. The first priority has been the development of a specific body of knowledge for youth work. The demands of this domain of expertise are that it corresponds with the dilemmas and challenges of youth work practice and provides the academic foundation needed for the development of evidence based practice. It is important that accountability of output and outcome are taken into account. Second, an urgency is needed by both youth workers and their organisations about the need to further develop contemporary youth work practice. Youth work in the Netherlands has the choice between becoming a full profession with a specific body of knowledge or reframing itself in the also important and needed realm of volunteer work with young people. A redefinition of the role, skills and expertise of the youth worker is inevitable if it is to continue to professionalise. Future youth workers need to understand the relevance of research and be able to incorporate new insights into their practice. In their interaction with the young, youth workers need to be transparent about their role and the output of the work. From youth workers this requires, besides the skills of working with young people, an entrepreneurial, reflective, open and learning attitude. Finally, regular training is neccesary in order to keep abreast of changes.

Endnotes

1   Gerhard, A.H. (1919–1920). About the more mature adolescents. Brief summary of the above-mentioned report. In *Volksontwikkeling* I (developments in the working class), pp. 233–234. Source: Nijenhuis 1987, p. 114.

2   VNG stands for Verenigde Nederlandse Gemeenten, which can be translated as Cooperation of Dutch Municipalities.

3   In this period social work took care of both the material as well as the immaterial assistance. The many specialisations that we have today did not yet exist.

4 Neij, R. (1989). *De organisatie van het maatschappelijk werk*. Zutphen, Walburg Pers. In: Neij and Heuting, (1989): 250.
5 Hendriks was head of the department of research and social community work at the former Ministry for Social Work (de Haan and Duyvendak, 2002).

References

Bijlsma, J. and Janssen, H. (2008) *Sociaal werk in Nederland*, Bussum: Coutinho.

Brinkgreve, C. and de Regt, A. (1990) 'Het verdwijnen van de vanzelfsprekendheid' *Jeugd en Samenleving*, 11 pp. 324–333.

de Haan, I. and Duyvendak, J.W. (2002) *In het hart van de verzorgingsstaat: het Ministerie van het Maatschappelijk Werk en zijn opvolgers (CRM, WVC en VWS), 1952–2002*, Zutphen: Walburg Pers.

de Waal, M. (1989) *Meisjes, een wereld apart*, Amsterdam: Boom.

Du Bois-Reymond, M. and Meijers, F. (1987) 'Inleiding. Een orientatie' in F. Meijers and M. Du Bois-Reymond(eds.) *Op zoek naar een moderne pedagogische norm. Beeldvorming over de jeugd in de jaren vijftig: het massajeugdonderzoek (1948–1952)*.

Fabri, W. (2006) *Jongerenwerk. Stand van zaken en perspectief*, Amsterdam/Utrecht: SWP/NJi.

Fabri, W. (2007) *Hoe houden jongerenwerkers hun vak bij. Onderzoek naar de professionalisering van jongerenwerkers*, Utrecht: NJi.

Fabri, W. (2009) Jongerenwerker moet voldoen aan steeds hogere eisen. Professionalisering van het jongerenwerk. *JeugdenCo Kennis*, 01, 2009.

Gilligan, C. (1982) *In a different voice. Psychological theory and women's voice*, Cambridge: Harvard University Press.

Gilsing, R. (2005) *Bestuur aan banden. Lokaal jeugdbeleid in de greep van nationaal beleid*, Den Haag: SCP.

Harmsen, G. (1961) *Blauwe en rode jeugd. Ontstaan, ontwikkeling en teruggang van de Nederlandse jeugdbeweging tussen 1853–1940*, Assen: Van Gorcum.

Hazekamp, J. L. and van der Zande, I. (1992) *Het jongerenwerk in hoofdlijnen*, Amsterdam: Uitgeverij Balans.

Hueting, E. (1989) De permanente herstructurering in het welzijnswerk. Zutphen: Walburg Pers.

Hueting, E. and Schneiders, P. (1999) *Van Sint Marta tot Fontys. 60 jaar sociaal-agogisch onderwijs*, Tilburg: Fontys Hogescholen.

Jansen, P. P., Lunenberg, M. and Vossen, H. (1989) *Van beschermelingen tot actief deelnemende jongeren: continue vernieuwing in jeugdzorg en vormingswerk in Maastricht (1915) 1935–1955*, Letterenwinkel Utrecht and Geschiedeniswinkel Groningen.

Koopmans, R. (1992) 'Van provo tot rara. Nieuwe sociale bewegingen en het Nederlandse politieke systeem' in Duyvendak, J.W. e.a. (eds.) *Tussen verbeelding en macht. 25 jaar nieuwe sociale bewegingen in Nederland*, Amsterdam: SUA.

LOJIK (2004) Terugblik 2003 en concept werkprogramma 2004. Utrecht.

LOJIK (2005) Terugblik 2004 en concept werkprogramma 2005. Utrecht.

Mathijs, M. (1993) *Mythe van de jeugd 2. Beleid en interventie*, Groningen: Wolters-Noordhof.

Meilof, J. (1999) *Een wereld licht en vrij. Het culturele werk van de AJC 1918–1959*, Amsterdam: IISG.

Metz, J. (2009) 'Over burgerparticipatie, welzijnsbeleid en de Wmo. Historiografie van de werksoort maatschappelijk activeringswerk' *Journal of Social Intervention*, 18 (2) pp. 61–83.

Metz, J. (2011) Kleine stappen, grote overwinningen. *Jongerenwerk historisch beroep met perspectief*, Amsterdam: SWP.

Metz, J. (2012) 'Jongerenwerk als werkplaats voor professionalisering' *Journal of Social Intervention*, 21, 18–36.

Naber, P. (1992) *Vriendschap onder jonge vrouwen*, Amersfoort: Acco.

Neij, R. and Hueting, E. (1989) *De opbouw van een sociaal-agogische beroepsopleiding 1899–1989*, Zutphen: Walburg pers.

Nijenhuis, H. (1987) *Werk in de schaduw. Club en buurthuizen in Nederland, 1892–1970*, Amsterdam: IISG.

Noorda, J. and Vosskuhler, D. (1986) 'Een opleiding voOor jongerenwerkers' in R. Veenbaas, (ed.) *Jongeren op straat. Jongerenwerk in de jaren tachtig*, Den Haag: VUGA.

Noorda, J., van Schijndel, M. and Spies, H. (2002) 'Jongerenwerk: Hobbyisme of professie' in E. A. Hortulanus (ed) *Sociaal Debat deel 8, Ontmoeting, ontspanning en ontplooiing*, Utrecht: Elsevier.

Noorda en Co (2009) De staat van professioneel jeugd en jongerenwerk in Nederland anno 2009, Utrecht: MO groep.

Oudenaarden, J. (1995) *Met brede vleugelslagen: de geschiedenis van 75 jaar Instituut voor de Rijpere jeugd en zijn clubhuizen 'De Arend' en 'De Zeemeeuw', 1920–1995*, Rotterdam: Phoenix and Den Oudsten Uitgevers.

Sansone, L. (1991) *Schitteren in de schaduw. Overlevingsstrategieen, subcultuur en etniciteit van Creoolse jongeren uit de lagere klasse in Amsterdam 1981–1990*, Amsterdam: Het Spinhuis.

Selten, P., Adriaanse, C. and Becker, B. (1996) *Af en toe met pa en moe – De speeltuinbeweging in Nederland 1900–1995*, Utrecht: De Tijdstroom.

Sennet, R. (2003) *Respect in a World of Inequality*, Norton: New York.

Spierts, M. (2005) 'Een "derde" weg voor de sociaal-culturele professies' *Sociale Interventie*, 1 pp. 13–21.

Spierings, F. and Steketee, M. (2004) 'Jongerenwerk op het spoor van nieuwe groepen' *Tijdschrift voor Sociale Interventie* 13 (1) pp. 31–44.

te Poel, Y. (1997) *De volwassenheid voorbij. Professionalisering van het jeugdwerk en de crisis in de pedagogische verhouding 1945–1975*, Leiden: DSWO Press.

te Poel, Y. (1987) 'Jeugdleiders tussen massajeugd en moeilijk opvoedbaren. De onmogelijke pedagogiek in het clubhuiswerk' in F. Meijers and M. Du Bois-Reymond (eds.) *Op zoek naar een moderne pedagogische norm. Beeldvorming over de jeugd in de jaren vijftig: het massajeugdonderzoek (1948–1952).*

Tilanus, C.P.G. (1997) *Jeugdbeleid.* Amsterdam: SWP.

van Dam, C. and Zwikker, N. (2008) *Jongerenwerker*, Utrecht: Movisie.

van Griensven, R. and Smeets, K. (2003) *Jeugd en jongerenwerk in Nederland, huidige stand van zaken vanuit gemeentelijk perspectief*, Den Haag: VNG.

van Houten, D.J. (1999) *De standaard mens voorbij*, Utrecht: De Tijdstroom.

van der Zant, P. (2003) *Van bondgenoot naar professioneel adviseur. Meer dan vijftig jaar begeleiding en advisering van het sociaal-cultureel werk*, Utrecht: Vereniging steunfuncties welzijn.

VNG (1957) De gemeente en het jeugdwerk. Overzicht van de verschillende vormen van het jeugdwerk en de mogelijkheden tot subsidiering daarvan door de gemeenten.

Youth Spot (2007) *Bedrijfsplan 2008–2010*, Amsterdam: Hogeschool van Amsterdam.

CHAPTER 8

Reconsidering the Emergence and Establishment of Community Development in the UK: the 1950s and 1960s

Keith Popple

The 1950s and 1960s were important decades in the emergence and establishment of community development in the United Kingdom. Such factors as the substantial physical damage incurred in the UK during the Second World War, the subsequent extensive peacetime rebuilding programmes and the establishment of the welfare state paved the way for a more affluent and critical population. UK citizens enjoyed the benefits of new material goods but some also came to question the impact of the drive to sustain an increasingly higher standard of living. Critics pointed to mounting private affluence at the same time as many valuable public services were considered to be inadequately funded.

One conduit for dissent, for those who wanted to create a more balanced society was involvement in community action work and community development efforts. These strategies provided a way to engage neighbourhoods that were considered to be left behind in the drive for the 'New Jerusalem'. At the same time community development methods were deployed by post-war governments to manage poverty and disadvantaged communities. This chapter re-considers these community action and development efforts and charts the emergence of UK community development against the changing national and international political, economic, social and cultural milieu.

Post-war Britain discovers peace and debt

The Second World War proved to be a pivotal turning point in the development of modern Britain. Prior to 1939 Britain was a major international power which maintained the world's largest navy and exerted enormous economic influence over a sprawling empire that ranged from India and the Far East to large parts of Africa and the Caribbean (Morgan, 1992). After the war, the country's internal capacities as well as its relationship with its remaining colonies were damaged; by the end of fighting in 1945, it had become the largest debtor nation in the world. Although Britain was a wealthy country in the late 1930s it could not realistically sustain the financial burden of a prolonged and expensive war. In consequence the British government had secured a massive loan from the United States in order to prevent financial insolvency. Britain paid a high price for securing American financial assistance not only in terms of staged interest attached to fiscal repayments but in requirements to provide unequivocal support for US foreign policy as well as to allow the location of American forces in the UK. For many it seemed a contradiction that Britain entered the Second World War in September 1939 to protect its independence and way of life when five years later it had become increasingly dependent on the US.

Labour Party in power 1945–1951

During the war the powerful German Luftwaffe damaged or destroyed millions of homes, factories, schools and other structures in British cities and towns. The food, clothing and fuel rationing imposed during the war continued in peace-time as Britain struggled to rebuild itself with major re-construction programmes. At the same time, the post-war Labour Government led by Clement Attlee established the modern welfare state including the National Health Service and universal free education promised for everyone to the age of 16. At the 1945 general election, a tired and war-shattered electorate found the Labour Party best captured their imagination for a possible 'New Jerusalem'. Labour seemed to offer the possibility of a country fit for heroes with an expansion of jobs, the introduction of free education and health services, and the building of new homes and public institutions. It was no real surprise that the outcome of the election was a Labour majority of 146 seats in the House of Commons (Butler and Sloman, 1976). This allowed Attlee to lead what is generally considered to be the most far-reaching, reforming government in British history. For example, as well as establishing the modern welfare state, the Labour government nationalised the Bank of England, fuel, power and inland transport industries. These developments demanded major undertakings and the crea-tion of new types of citizen-government relationships as Britain tried again to make its way in the world (Sked and Cook, 1993).

Whilst Britain was coming to terms with newly created national public organ-isations and bodies and newly built homes and municipal buildings, it was also adjusting to a changing relationship with countries that had lived under its imperial rule. In due course most colonies moved towards independence and many expatriates returned to the UK. Amongst the latter were community development practitioners who returned and helped shape the advance of this activity in the UK; a trend we will consider later.

'Age of austerity'

Immediately after the war the British public saw the glimmer of the 'New Jeru-salem', however by the end of the decade they were required to accept new levels of material self-denial as the government both led a drive to increase exports and restrict imports as well as pay for the Korean War (Marwick, 2000). In 1949, four years after it had been elected, the Labour government devalued the pound sterling in order to make exporting goods and services cheaper. The outcome was an increase in the cost of imported goods. Along with cuts in public expenditure, living standards were lowered and hard-pressed British citizens experienced a poor reward for living through a brutal and difficult war. During the 1950s both the Labour and subsequent Conservative administrations discovered that while it was possible to manage the substantial programmes to re-build the UK infrastructure, it was much more difficult to control the economy when spending on imported goods exceeded what was earned from exports (Kynaston, 2007).

Critique of the new affluence

By the mid 1950s Britain felt and looked a different country than it had been twenty years earlier. The damaging and conspicuous social divisions of the 1930s, the difficulties of shortages and rationing, and the austerity of war time were replaced by a booming economy, low unemployment and increasing con-sumer choice. Newly built towns and reconstructed town centres together with new schools, hospitals, council housing and public buildings were public sym-bols of a new Britain. In addition average weekly earnings were outstripping the rise in the cost of living and individual and family spending was going on an increasing range of goods and services, this meant most people could relate to

Harold Macmillan's 1957 reply to a heckler in Bedford that they had 'never had it so good' (Morgan, 1990).

However, by the late 1950s criticism of the new-found affluence in both the USA and the UK was growing. The critique appeared not only as economic analysis, but in the form of research on local communities, theatre productions, films and popular writing. Many of the papers on local communities were written by the growing number of community development practitioners returning to the UK after working within outposts of the British Empire.

One influential critic, the American economist J.K. Galbraith, published his seminal book *The Affluent Society* in1958 which identified the income disparities perpetuated as a consequence of the USA's private sector growth in wealth and underfunding of public services. Galbraith's views found resonance in the UK. While it had a better funded public sector than the USA, the UK was similarly seeing the growth of an increasingly affluent middle class at the same time that members of the working class in some regions of the country were suffering from long-term unemployment and growing poverty. This dichotomy was documented in the following decade by a number of social scientists who demonstrated that poverty, which many thought had disappeared, was prevalent and on the increase in several areas in the UK (Abel-Smith and Townsend, 1965; Coates and Silburn, 1970; Hobsbawn, 1968). The Institute of Community Studies in particular helped document the impact of the social and economic changes on community life during this period and its influential reports demonstrated the importance of family networks in the neighbourhoods studied (Young and Wilmott, 1957). An example of similar work was Dennis et al. (1956) who described and analysed the strength of working class neighbourhoods in Featherstone in West Yorkshire where the coal industry was predominant.

The Labour Party, who had been out of government since 1951, was also now engaged in highlighting the need for policies to tackle increasing inequality. One of the leading thinkers in this area was the Oxford academic and Labour MP Anthony Crosland. Although criticised by those on the left of the party, Crosland's book *The Future of Socialism* (1956) nevertheless became highly influential. In particular Crosland's case for the need to re-balance public spending and individual consumption came to shape much of the policy making of subsequent Labour governments.

Other criticism came from a new wave of talented writers and playwrights such as John Osborne, John Braine and Colin Wilson (often described as the 'angry young men') who argued that the British Establishment including the monarchy and Tory Party represented a privileged class and an era that had

had its time. These new writers advocated a society based less on class and unearned wealth and more on ability and hard work.

The return of community development practitioners to the UK, from newly independent colonies kick-started the practice of community development here. In particular the work of Reg Batten (1957, 1962, and 1967 with M. Batten), who had been engaged in community development in Nigeria from 1927 to 1949, led to a construction of a distinct body of community development literature in Britain. Batten was critical of the way community development was used to perpetuate colonial domination (1967: v) and instead advocated a more liberating form of practice known as the 'non-directive approach' wherein:

> *The worker who uses the non-directive approach does not attempt to decide for people, or to lead, guide, or persuade them to accept any of his own conclusions about what is good for them. He tries to get them to decide for themselves what their needs are: what, if anything, they are willing to do to meet them; and how they can best organise, plan, and act to carry their project through. Thus he aims at stimulating a process of self-determination and self-help, and he values it for all the potential learning experiences which participation in this process provides. He aims to encourage people to develop themselves, and it is by thinking and acting for themselves, he believes, that they are most likely to do so. Moreover, the outcome will usually be a project designed to produce some change for the better in people's lives.*
>
> (Batten with Batten, 1967: 11–12)

The majority of the community development literature during this time emanated from the US and Canada (Biddle and Biddle, 1965) and perhaps the most influential book of this period was written by Murray Ross (1955). Smith (1979: 65) suggests that the work by Ross:

> *captured the imagination of staff in councils of social service because it suggested there was a theoretical basis for their work, and set about community work as neighbourhood work . . . and . . . as interagency work.*

The bulk of community development practice in the 1950s took place in the voluntary sector with much of it concerned with youth, leisure and education. At the end of the decade the influential Younghusband Report (1959) argued that community development was the third method of social work (alongside case work and group work). As Thomas suggests this was quite remarkable given that so much of community development in the inter-war and post-war years 'had not been at all connected with social work' (1983: 18). Nevertheless Kuenstler (1960) was to develop Younghusband's idea of community development as a method of social work.

Consumer society in the 1960s

In the early 1960s with workers' incomes rising faster than price inflation, those in work (and in particular the young) were able to spend their surplus cash on a variety of consumer products and services including vinyl records, cinema going, fashion, magazines and alcohol, thereby fuelling growth in the industries that manufactured them. The 1960s was a period when people were encouraged to achieve self-fulfilment. Amongst journalists and academics terms such as the 'the autonomous self', 'the contemplative self', and 'integrity of self' were used to describe a new way of viewing the individual. The advertising and marketing departments of companies employed psychologists to help them develop approaches to selling that emphasised, to the potential consumer, the benefits of buying their goods and services in order to achieve 'personal fulfilment'.

Increasing consumerism and the prevailing view that material goods provided individuals with personal fulfilment was countered in the US by the emerging 'hippie' subculture. Growing numbers of young people argued that experiencing individual reflection and achieving personal growth was not dependent on accumulating more possessions. They rejected consumerism and advocated a mixture of Eastern philosophy, spiritual concepts and drug use in order to explore altered states of consciousness (Donnelly, 2005). The ideals of the hippie subculture spread to other countries including the UK and found a home among those young people who were attracted to collective and shared living. In some cases due to a housing shortage in some localities people occupied or 'squatted' in abandoned or empty buildings and this led to what became known as the squatting movement (Radford, 1970).

Two opposing views of these changing circumstances were at play in Britain. Those who had lived through the Second World War felt that the rising material wealth and social stability for the majority were just rewards for the hardships and difficulties experienced during the conflict and the austerity encountered in the immediate post-war period. Young people, with no experience of the war highlighted the negatives of the pursuit of material possessions and contrasted the wealth of the majority with the plight of those, who through no fault of their own were living in poverty. Some young people joined left-wing groups such as the International Marxist Group and the Socialist Workers Party as well as the Labour Party Young Socialists. These groups, together with the ideas and literature of the New Left, provided a critical analysis and opposition to the status quo. Nonetheless, it is debatable how much of the drive for the deployment of community development at the neighbourhood level was due to practitioner involvement in radical left-wing politics. As Waddington has remarked, the analysis of the majority of community workers was 'basically reflected in a gut reaction against bureaucracy and a rather unspecific idealism which owed more to the ideals of the "alternative society" than to the thinking of the New Left' (1983: 42).

Changes at community level

Anxiety about rising juvenile crime rates and the subsequent moral panics (Cohen, 1972) were juxtaposed with the fact that young people were enjoying leisure pursuits and free time unavailable to their parents' generation. Contrary to the concern that young people with increased leisure time could engage in criminal activity, the majority of this new generation of teenagers were not involved in anti-social behaviour.

The labour shortage in key industries and services led the government to encourage immigration from the Afro-Caribbean islands and the Indian sub-continent. The influx of migrants was to have an impact on already changing neighbourhoods in large towns and cities, in a manner that had not been anticipated or planned for. The experiences of recently settled West Indians in Brixton, south London including attacks from white residents is well described by Sheila Patterson (1965). Patterson argued that the creation of 'ghettos' and 'zones' of settlement by the newcomers, which she considers to be negative features, delay the assimilation of immigrants into communities. She further stated that ghettos could 'perpetuate minority group values and traits, to limit social and cultural contacts between newcomers and local people, to reinforce local views on the "alienness" of the newcomers, and so to retard ultimate integration or assimilation' (Patterson, 1965: 195).

Published two years after Patterson's work, the study by Rex and Moore (1967) examines the connection between 'race', community life and disadvantage in Sparkbrook, Birmingham, home to a population of around 18,000 including English, Irish, West Indians and Pakistanis, and some Arabs, Cypriots, Indians and Poles. This study found that Birmingham City Council's housing policy, together with the private housing market, discriminated against different ethnic groups. Rex and Moore described Sparkbrook as a 'zone of transition' with many of its residents having little control over their housing situation. The work of Patterson and the study by Rex and Moore reveal that migrants in the 1960s were likely to be victims in the labour and housing markets and were often exploited due to their lack of social networks and knowledge of procedures, practices and laws.

International and national social and political change

Internationally and nationally the 1960s was a decade of significant social and political change. In the USA the black civil rights movement was inspired by Rosa Parks who refused to vacate her bus seat for a white passenger in 1955 and Martin Luther King's stirring 'I have a dream' speech of 1963 that contained a vision of an equal and united America. The Civil Rights Movement and the growth of feminism in the USA presented a concerted challenge to the white male domination of politics and power. Meanwhile US foreign policy in Vietnam and Cambodia came under increasing public scrutiny.

> *Later in the decade, the certainties of the post-war period were to be further challenged by unrest and struggle in many major cities throughout the world, with student riots in Paris and the rise of the new left in Europe challenging capitalism, and the brief but iconic 'Prague Spring' in Czechoslovakia challenging the Soviet regime.*
>
> (Craig et al., 2011: 26)

In the UK new waves of dissent emanated from the late 1950s onwards with for example the foundation of the Campaign for Nuclear Disarmament and Amnesty International. In the 1960s a range of organisations emerged advocating on behalf of the poor and disadvantaged, and action groups were set up aimed at protecting the environment. These included the Child Poverty Action Group, Friends of the Earth, Women's Aid and Shelter. The change to traditional ways of doing things was reflected at the party political level with the Labour Party defeating the Tory Party at the 1964 general election.

The growing influence of community development

The 1960s was characterised by a growing official appreciation that economic and social change was leading to the fragmentation and isolation of local communities. This led to the publication of a number of reports that exposed the failure of the welfare state to eradicate the problems associated with poverty and disadvantage:

- The Ingleby Report (Home Office, 1960) advocated an increase in state-funded schemes to help prevent vulnerable children and young people coming before the courts.
- The Plowden Report (DES, 1967) focused on primary education and the transition to secondary education.
- The Seebohm Report (1968) argued the need to reorganise social work.
- The Skeffington Report (HMSO, 1969) highlighted the need to increase public participation in planning.
- The Fairbairn-Milson Report (DES, 1969) addressed issues of youth work and education.

The Seebohm Report is particularly significant in the growth of community development as it recommended that the latter should become a key element in the delivery of social work. Further, the Fairbairn-Milson Report examined the relationship between the youth service, community schools and the role of community development in rejuvenating and developing neighbourhood groups.

The role Batten was to play in the creation of a British community development literature has already been noted. A number of his contemporaries similarly contributed to this development including Peter du Sautoy who was previously Director of Social Welfare and Community Development in Ghana. On his return to the UK in 1960 du Sautoy took up the post of lecturer in Fundamental Education and Community Development at the University of Manchester. He, like Batten, was alarmed to see that community development was still in its infancy in the UK and wanted to apply the experience of work overseas to the country's neighbourhood problems. Both he and Batten argued that the casework approach that was dominant in social services departments was clinical in nature and demanded a high degree of detachment on the part of the practitioner. Du Sautoy was instrumental with other practitioners returning from the colonies in launching in 1966 the *Community Development Journal* of which he was the first editor (Popple, 2006). The *Community Development Journal* asserted that it would offer readers in the UK, and elsewhere, a new community development literature. In the same year the Association of Community Workers was launched and engaged community development workers in establishing a clearer identity for themselves and helped to add to the activity's knowledge base.

The establishment of UK community development as a consensus rather than a radical activity received a boost with the publication by the Calouste Gulbenkian Foundation (1968) which reported on an investigation into the role and purpose of the activity. The research was funded by the Calouste Gulbenkian Foundation, a wealthy international charitable foundation with cultural, educational social and scientific interests that was based in Lisbon, Paris and London. Eileen Younghusband, the chair of the report committee had a social work background and helped establish the first generic social work training course that perceived community development as a form of social work and which wanted the activity to remain within the social work field. Although there were ideological disputes within the working party (Jones, 1983) the final report argued that community development should be seen as 'part of the professional practice of teachers, social workers, the clergy, health workers, architects, planners, administrators and others' (Calouste Gulbenkian Foundation, 1968: 149). The report's conclusion disappointed those who saw community development making strong links with community action and political activity. Rather its view was that community development had an important role in assisting the state to better approach problems in disaffected communities.

The Urban Programme

The Urban Programme emerged as a response by the Labour government to Enoch Powell's 'Rivers of Blood' speech given in Birmingham in April 1968. A Tory front bencher, Powell predicted racial tension in British cities similar to those witnessed in the US (Powell, 1968: 99). Although Powell was sacked from his position as a front bencher by the Conservative Party leader Edward Heath for this inflammatory speech, his views received wide publicity and much popular support. Fearing increasing racial tension the government moved with speed to introduce the Urban Programme which provided money from both central and local government to address social problems in those areas considered to be experiencing deprivation.

With unemployment now increasing in certain UK regions in the early 1960s, both Conservative and Labour governments began a practice of restricting immigration from the developing world whilst attempting to further integrate those immigrants already settled here. The 1962 and 1968 Commonwealth Immigration Acts restricted immigration, while the Race Relation Acts of 1965 and 1968 outlawed racial discrimination and established the Community Relations Commission. The Labour government introduced the 1966 Local Government Act Section 11 which provided funds to educational and welfare projects in localities where two per cent or more of the local population were from the New Commonwealth. The Urban Programme was therefore a further effort to contain the 'problem' of immigrants living in urban areas. However the reality was that few of the thousands of projects and organisations financed wholly or partly by the Urban Programme actually did fund work with immigrants as the basis for granting financial assistance was broad. In fact, the Urban Programme was not restricted to areas experiencing racial tension partly for 'fear of provoking accusations of favoured treatment for immigrants' (Loney, 1983: 34) and according to Demuth (1977) the Urban Programme proved ineffective at reaching minority ethnic groups. Nevertheless the Urban Programme was to have a long life as a scheme for funding projects and, over time, distributed millions of pounds to community development projects. Taylor and Presley (1987) claim that in 1987 the Urban Programme was supporting 4,000 voluntary and community development projects although by the mid-1980s the resources in real terms were declining (Whitting et al., 1986). Importantly according to Benyon and Solomos (1987) the reduction in the Urban Programme was 'dwarfed' by the financial cuts applied to inner-city local authorities.

National Community Development Project

The other major development of state-sponsored community development during the late 1960s was the National Community Development Project (NCDP). Like the Urban Programme it was launched in 1968 and was part of a wider initiative to address social disharmony and concerns that certain sections of the population were failing to successfully respond to the changing social and economic circumstances. Informed by the American 'War on Poverty' Programme the NCDP was developed by the Home Office to improve the delivery of social services and to co-ordinate the work of already established projects and identify where other services could be introduced. A total of 12 projects in areas of populations varying from 3,000–15,000 were established to address significant social need (1983: 42). Community Development Projects (CDPs) were funded by a combination of local and central government finance and were expected to operate for a five year period.

The NCDP was to prove to be one of the most important and defining initiatives in the evolution of British community development. Although the local CDPs were state funded and were directed through the Home Office, those employed by the projects went on to create a way of working and of analysing their practice that was at odds with conventional Whitehall thinking. The government's analysis in relation to CDPs was based on four key assumptions. These were:

1. Poverty was predominately caused by individuals.
2. 'Deviant' family structures caused poverty rather than poverty causing 'deviant' family structures.
3. 'Poverty bred poverty' and an 'underprivileged' individual or family had an increased possibility of remaining poor.
4. Collecting intelligence and data from the 12 communities would prove valuable in identifying trends and changes that related to the transmission of poverty.

The NCDPs focus was on the micro rather than the macro-level. Loney (1983) has argued that it was the Children's Department in the Home Office that conceived the CDPs and it was traditional social work theories and practice rooted in individual, family and community pathologies that were dominant in shaping their brief. For example, the key indicators used to assess the effectiveness of local projects included reducing rates of disease, debt, the number of children taken into care, juvenile delinquency and marital breakup (Greve, 1969). However within four years of the projects being rolled out into communities, CDP personnel, who included practitioners, researchers and academics, were articulating their disquiet with the initial key assumptions. They argued that

> . . . *problems of multi-deprivation have to be defined and reinterpreted in terms of structural constraint rather than psychological motivations, external rather than internal factors . . . even where social 'malaise' is apparent it does not seem best explained principally in terms of personal deficiencies so much as the product of external pressures in the wider environment.*

(CDP IIU, 1974)

Divided lines of accountability between local projects and local and central government, together with the sudden death of Derek Morell, the senior civil servant in the Home Office responsible for the projects, and then further central management personnel changes weakened control over the NCDP. It led to 'local projects having increased room for manoeuvre and enabled the workers to develop and exercise their radical approaches' (Popple, 2011: 4).

One key lesson that can be learnt from the work of these practitioners and researchers and the extensive literature they published at the time is that it is impossible to have a detailed understanding of local issues and therefore the role community development can play without an appreciation of the wider forces shaping events. This approach to community development has resonated through the decades since the 1960s and has come to influence our understanding of both the potential for and the limits of the practice. While there is understandable criticism of the CDP's literature of the period for its failure to represent or articulate the issues facing women and ethnic minorities, the writings and research do highlight the increasing impact international capitalism was having on communities. This radical critique of the CDPs is now seen as more mainstream as we struggle with the effects of globalisation and neoliberal economics on localities in the UK and elsewhere. Today it is not possible to successfully understand or consider approaches to tackle rising individualism and declining social capital and the accompanying diminishing trust and solidarity without taking account of increasing inequality, the emergence of powerful global power structures and the role media organisations play in shaping ideas, cultures and opinions. In this sense the CDPs were well ahead of their time in analysing the role of capital and the state in advancing economic and social disadvantage whilst intervening at community and neighbourhood level to try to contain and mobilise people to solve their own problems.

Conclusion

By the end of the 1960s the UK was a very different country compared with the end of the 1940s. Although trade unions grew in strength during the 1960s and were able to influence Labour Party policy and hence government policy as well as achieving real wage increases for their members, the solidarity of the population that was evident during the war, and in the immediate post-war period, gave way to individualism and in particular to rising consumer demand for goods and services.

Community development was in its infancy in the 1950s but with the efforts of those previously involved in colonial enterprises it became possible to establish in Britain roots for the activity and to observe the beginnings of an identifiable literature. By the 1960s community development was being used by the state to intervene in areas of social and economic stress. Practitioners recognised this contradiction and were able to use projects to develop imaginative and more radical ways of working and in particular, through the research produced by the NCDP, were able to demonstrate that local problems could be linked with major shifts in the increasingly global economy.

The 1950s and 1960s proved to be a period when community development was firmly established in the UK and for many young people and community development workers there was a belief that the world could be changed for the better. The period was generally one of optimism and concern to establish a more humane society. Whilst the attack on poverty was considered important so was the need to tackle deprivation of opportunity and choice both individually and collectively. Community development played an important part in this ideology as it gave practitioners, organisations and local authorities 'permission' to intervene in localities and to experiment with different approaches. Community development was seen as a benign and creative activity that could both deliver government programmes and act as a platform for people to argue for improvements in their life chances.

This optimistic approach was a key driving force in the 1950s and 1960s but appeared to run out of steam during the following decade when a sense of disillusionment was evident as the world struggled with an international recession and increasing conflict within and between nations. In the UK the economy came under considerable pressure with significant increases in unemployment and inflation and, unlike the 1960s when many community development workers critically attacked the workings of the welfare state, the 1970s was a decade when practitioners moved to one of defensive struggle as the ground was laid for the ideas of the New Right which were to influence the 1979 Conservative Government of Margaret Thatcher.

References

Abel-Smith, B. and Townsend, P. (1965) *The Poor and the Poorest*, London: Bell.

Batten, T.R. (1957) *Communities and their Development*, London: Oxford University Press.

Batten, T.R. (1962) *Training for Community Development: A Critical Study of Method*, London: Oxford University Press.

Batten, T.R. with Batten, M. (1967) *The Non-directive Approach to Group and Community Work*, London: Oxford University Press.

Benyon, J. and Solomos, J. (1987) *The Roots of Urban Unrest*, Oxford: Pergamon Press.

Biddle, L. and Biddle, W. (1965) *The Community Development Process: The Rediscovery of Local Initiative*, New York: Holt, Rinehart & Winston.

Butler, D. and Sloman, A. (1976) *British Political Facts, 1900–1975*, London: Macmillan.

Calouste Gulbenkian Foundation (1968) *Community work and Social Change*, London: Longman.

Coates, K. and Silburn, R. (1970) *Poverty: The Forgotten Englishman*, Harmondsworth: Penguin.

Cohen, S. (1972) *Folk Devils and Moral Panics*, London: MacGibbon and Kee.

Community Development Project Information and Intelligent Unit (1974) *The National Community Development Project: Inter-Project Report*, London: Home Office.

Craig, G., Mayo, M., Popple, K., Shaw, M. and Taylor, M. (2011) *The Community Development Reader: History, Themes and Issues*, Bristol: Policy Press.

Crosland, A. (1956) *The Future of Socialism*, London: Jonathan Cape.

DES (1967) *Children and their Primary Schools. Report to the Central Advisory Council for Education, No. 1 (Plowden Report)*, London: HMSO.

DES (1969) *Youth and Community Work in the 1970s. Proposals by the Youth Service Development Council (Fairbairn-Milson Report)*, London: HMSO.

Demuth, C. (1977) *Government Initiatives on Urban Deprivation*, London: Runnymeade Trust.

Dennis, N., Henriques, F. and Slaughter, C. (1956) *Coal is Our Life*, London: Eyre and Spottiswood.

Donnelly, M. (2005) *Sixties Britain*, Harlow: Pearson Education.

Galbraith, J.K. (1999) *The Affluent Society* (updated with new introduction by the author) 5th revised edition, Harmondsworth: Penguin.

Greve, J. (1969) 'Community Development Project: research and evaluation' in *Experiments in Social Policy and their Evaluation* (Report of an Anglo-American Conference held at Ditchley Park, Oxfordshire, 29–31 October), London: HMSO.

HMSO (1969) *People and Planning (Skeffington Report)*, London: HMSO.

Hobsbawn, E.J. (1968) 'Poverty' in D. L. Sills (ed.) *The New International Encyclopaedia of the Social Sciences*, Vol. 12, London: Macmillan.

Home Office (1960) *Children and Young Persons (Ingleby Report)*, London: HMSO.

Jones, D. (1977) 'Community work in the United Kingdom' in H. Specht and A.Vickery (eds.) *Integrating Social Work Methods*, London: Allen and Unwin.

Kuenstler, P. (1960) *Community Organisation in Great Britain*, London: Faber.

Kynaston, D. (2007) *Austerity Britain 1945–51*, London: Bloomsbury.

Loney, M. (1983) *Community against Government: The British Community Development Project 1968–78*, London: Heinemann.

Marwick, A. (2000) *A History of the Modern British Isles 1914–1999*, Oxford: Blackwell.

Morgan, K.O. (1992) *The People's Peace: British History 1945–1990*, Oxford: Oxford University Press.

Nicholson, V. and Smith, S. (1977) *Spend, Spend, Spend*, London: Jonathan Cape.

Patterson, S. (1965) *Dark Strangers: A Study of West Indians in London*, Harmondsworth: Penguin.

Popple, K. (2006) 'The first forty years of the CDJ', *Community Development Journal*, 43 (1) pp. 1–18.

Popple, K. (2011) 'Rise and fall of the National Community Development Projects 1968–1978: lessons to learn' in R. Gilchrist, T. Hodgson, T. Jeffs, J. Spence, N. Stanton and J. Walker (eds.) *Reflecting on the Past: Essays in the History of Youth and Community Work*, Lyme Regis: Russell House Publishing.

Powell. E. (1968) 'Text of speech delivered in Birmingham, 20 April 1968', *Race*, X (1) pp. 80–104.

Radford, J. (1970) 'From King Hill to the Squatting Association' in A. Lapping (ed.) *Community Action (Fabian Tract 400)*, London: Fabian Society.

Rex, J. and Moore, R. (1967) *Race, Community and Conflict: A Study of Sparkbrook*, London: Oxford University Press.

Ross, M. (1955) *Community Organisation: Theory, Principles and Practice*, New York: Harper and Row.

Seebohm Report (1968) *Report of the Committee on Local Authority and Allied Personal Social Services Cmnd. 3703*, London: HMSO.

Sked, A. and Cook, C. (1993) *Post-war Britain: A Political History 1945–1992*, Harmondsworth: Penguin.

Smith, M. (1979) 'Concepts of community work: a British view', in D. A. Chekki (ed.) *Community Development: Theory and Method of Manned Change*, New Delhi: Vika Publishing House.

Taylor, M. and Presley, F. (1987) *Community Work in the UK 1982–86*, London: Library Association Publishing in association with Calouste Gulbenkian Foundation.

Thomas, D. (1983) *The Making of Community Work*, London: George Allen & Unwin.

Waddington, P. (1983) 'Looking ahead – community work in the 1980s' in D. N. Thomas (ed.) *Community Work in the Eighties*, London: National Institute for Social Work/HMSO.

Whittington, G., Burton, P., Means, R. and Stewart, M. (1986) *The Urban Programme and the Young Unemployed*, Inner Cities Research Programme. London: Department of Environment.

Young, M. and Wilmott, P. (1957) *Family and Kinship in East London*, London: Routledge.

Younghusband, E.L. (1959) *Report of the Working Party on Social Workers in the Local Authority Health and Welfare Services*, London: HMSO.

CHAPTER 9

Participatory Youth Work Within a 1950s Scottish Housing Scheme

Dod Forrest

This chapter focuses on the history of work with young people living on the Northfield estate in Aberdeen during the late 1950s and early 1960s. Research has been undertaken into two projects that existed on the estate in that time; one was a self-organised Church of Scotland Youth Group and the other a local authority youth club. The research explores how power was negotiated and delegated in these projects. The discussion considers how participatory youth work in these two settings offers some insights for contemporary practice. It is argued that the influential experiences encountered by members may have been short-lived but proved long-lasting in terms of interests, friendships and career trajectories.

The narratives of young people and youth workers describing how youth work was facilitated in the two locations form the basis of the research. Semi-structured interviews were undertaken with eight individuals involved during the period under review:[1] two Northfield Youth Group ex-members (one male and one female); an ex-Church of Scotland Youth Fellowship member (male); two Church of Scotland staff (male); and three staff from the local authority's Beehive Youth Club (a full-time male manager and two female part-time workers). Their accounts are supplemented by a range of primary sources. This adds credibility to the research as memories alone can play tricks with history. The collated stories convey an approach to youth work that sought to empower young people using methods that were found to echo, either consciously or unconsciously, a Freirean stance in relation to education (Forrest, 1999, 2005; Forrest and Wood, 1999; Lord and McKillop Farlow, 1990; Mullender and Ward, 1991; Rappaport et al., 1984).

Empowerment is a contested concept (Gallie, 1995–96), an idea that can underpin either liberatory or regulative social policy (Baistow, 1994). In this context it has been helpful to draw on Kieffer's (1984) analysis of community activism as a process of empowerment that begins with action often provoked by a sense of injustice. The core issues centre on who participates in this action and engages with the individual, and in what manner this experience is generalised and developed into group, associational and community action. Kieffer argues that empowerment is a process of learning and development. Kieffer describes this process as 'the construction of a multi-dimensional participatory competence . . . [which] encompasses both cognitive and behavioural change' (1984: 9). Accordingly, engagement of this sort with young people creates a more positive self-concept for the young person and sense of self-competence. It can also cultivate a critical understanding of the social and political environment leading to the utilisation of individual and collective resources for social, political and voluntary action.

First, to provide a context for the discussion of these issues, the chapter offers a brief summary of the development of youth work in Scotland post 1945.

Development of a Scottish youth service

Post-school education in Scotland in the immediate post-war years embraced a wide variety of forms that included adult education, technical education, continuation classes, youth services, community centres and voluntary educational agencies. Scotland's history of educational services for children and young people largely shares the same historical trajectory as the rest of the UK. Legislation to enable the funding of state provision was, according to the Advisory Council on Education's 1952 Report, influenced by:

> the pioneering work done by the voluntary organisations, in particular the YMCA, founded in 1844; the Boys' Brigade (1883); the Boy Scouts (1908); the Girl Guides (1910); the Scottish Association of Boys' Clubs (1927); the Scottish Association of Girls' Clubs (1930) and various pre-service training organisations.
>
> (Scottish Education Department, 1952: 12)

The first major governmental intervention appeared in 1936 when local education authorities (LEAs) were urged by the Scottish Education Department (SED), in their Circular 98, to extend their continuation class provision for physical recreation to cover youth groups. Thanks to SED funding, voluntary youth organisations received small grants to fund physical recreation classes, the construction of gymnasia and the purchase of equipment. With the outbreak of war in 1939, policy makers were concerned about a potential increase in 'juvenile delinquency' akin to that which had emerged during World War One. Politicians and civil servants alike believed that one of the best methods of preventing juvenile crime was to channel youthful energies into 'useful purposes' and LEAs were called upon to formulate comprehensive policies for their areas relating to services for youth (SED, 1952: para. 27).

In 1942 the SED recommended in Circular 244 that the authorities take responsibility for the development of what was now called the youth service. The LEAs were advised to appoint Youth Organisers and to establish Advisory Youth Councils and local panels. In 1944, the publication of *The Youth Service in Scotland* identified a widening range of aims and by the end of 1944 there were 29 Youth Councils and 200 youth panels functioning across the country (SED, 1952: para. 29). The following perspective outlines the reluctance to follow a narrow instrumentalist approach to working with young people:

> *A club existing solely for football or table tennis is not a youth club, because it is by itself incomplete as an agency for the development of social and recreational education . . . some youth clubs reveal this lack of sufficient purpose in as much as those who support them are concerned almost entirely with taking young people off the streets by the provision of little else than amusements such as darts, table tennis and billiards. The educational objectives which are the raison d'etre of the youth organisations call for more than diets of darts and sessions of snooker.*

(para. 363)

The Youth Service in Scotland (para. 02) asserted that, irrespective of setting, methods and activities should start with the young person's own world and his or her own problems and interests. Within the context of the youth club and community centre a 'self- governing' ethos was to be promoted. It set out its vision for such:

> *a Centre should be a community whose ways of life are not imposed on it from above but in a very real sense are the expression of the purposes of its members; for it is these purposes, occasionally a little sublimated, that there will be found the motivation for the educational activities carried on . . . and give the members practical social training in organising activities; opportunities of service to the community, and experience of shouldering responsibility.*

(para.663)

These perspectives on work with young people became the subject of development and debate within Scottish social policy and youth work practice throughout the 1950s. The emergence of such debate in Scotland preceded the similar discussions in England and Wales following the Albemarle Report in 1960. The following statement was made by Lord Craigton, Minister of State at the Scottish Office, to the debate in the House of Lords entitled 'The Youth Service and the Albemarle Report':

> *No Committee corresponding to the Albemarle Committee was appointed in Scotland, because the field of further education, including the Youth Service, had been comprehensively reported on by the Advisory Council on Education in Scotland in 1952, and in subsequent Reports. The most important of these were the conclusions of a conference of statutory and voluntary bodies convened by the Scottish Leadership Training Association in 1957, and a report on the Scottish Youth Service prepared by the Association of Directors of Education in 1958. It was as a result of these two reports that discussions were initiated which resulted in the setting up last year of the Scottish Standing Consultative Council on Youth Service. This body, under the chairmanship of Lord Kilbrandon, anticipated, more or less, the recommendation of the Albemarle Committee with regard to the setting up of a Development Council in England and Wales.*

(Hansard, 1960)

One dominant idea threaded through the influential Report of the Advisory Council on Education in Scotland was the notion of 'self-government' through participation in planning and programme development. This idea was to become the cornerstone of social policy for a whole era and one recommendation of the Albemarle Report described the development of a youth work approach that had participation as central to the aims of informal education within a youth club setting. The combination of debate and discussion generated by the work of the Advisory Council on Education in Scotland, and the recommendations of the Albemarle Committee, enabled the Kilbrandon Council to set the scene for an ethos of participation in Scottish youth work. The Council outlined its vision for the emerging new workforce in Scotland as youth workers acting in an advisory role whilst facilitating the empowerment of young people.

The following paragraph from the Albemarle Report captures the essence of the approach that influenced work with young people on the Northfield housing scheme:

Our recommendations for participation turn on responsibility and leadership. We should like to see more responsibility for activities and programmes turned over to the young people wherever this can be made possible, and real and actual charge of things within their compass (or just enough outside it to make them stretch their minds) given to them. The specialist group or self-programming group in which the adult enters as an adviser is an illustration of what we mean. We think for instance that after one or two trial runs young people are capable of initiating and running adventure schemes which are likely to be more probing because they themselves have drawn them up. We believe too that such groups will evolve their own discipline, which they will accept the more readily, because it grows out of the needs of real situations.

(Ministry of Education, 1960: para.174)

Moving to Northfield

In 1946, the corporation of Aberdeen acquired 386 acres from the Seaton Estates by feu charter[2] in order to re-house some of those living in poor and derelict properties in the city. The land was acquired for the construction of the Northfield housing estate which was to provide homes for 10,650 adults and children. Work began in January 1950 and was completed within five years (Aberdeen Evening Express, July 1965). Yvonne Allan, who eventually became the first President of the Northfield Church Youth Group, was only five years old when she moved with her family to her new home in Northfield. She told the author:

> *I can remember moving into the house and they were still putting the harling on the wall. So that's how quick they were filling them up.*

(Transcript 1)

At this time the housing scheme and surrounding countryside was effectively one giant adventure playground. Mike Middleton, who was born in Northfield around this time and was to become an enthusiastic member of the Church of Scotland and the Boy Scouts, described in some detail the excitement and the dangers of these childhood years:

> *there was the burn, the Bucksburn. Anyway it was a great haunt and my father and I used to fish further up towards Kingswells and picking cherries as well, quite regularly. Bucksburn Farm with a grain silo became a refuge for a while and then unfortunately like all buildings*

like that, kids set fire to it . . . Then the upper road to the Hillocks to Redmyres and what we called the 'Wimpy Hooses'. That was my haunt – up by my auntie and up to Brimmond Hill. That's where I broke two arms on my bike with two other boys, all on my bike, coming down that whole brae, the entire Newhills Brae right from the church at the top right to the almost bottom at the Wimpy Hooses and my mate stuck his foot in the spokes, spiked the wheel, catapulted us over. One of the guys was my uncle, just three years older than me, his face was completely torn – you'd think a tiger had attacked him.

We were not allowed to go to the Quarries, it was no longer a working quarry by then, but if you were down there you had to swear an oath that you would tell nobody. It was dangerous very, very dangerous. And there was a place of mystery far, far away towards the Bridge of Don called the Munganese [laughs] literally a very small quarry hole that had extracted manganese. But we called it the 'Munganese' and my mates would say 'We are awa' tae the Munganese', it was very mysterious and like an oasis in the desert. And I'd never been and I never got to go.

(Transcript 2)

Children and young people's participation in church activities

In 1951, at the same time as the first Northfield houses were being completed, the Church of Scotland arrived on the estate in the form of a wooden hut with seating capacity for 80 to 90. By December 1953 a new Church had been completed, with seating capacity for four times that number. In 1955 a small public library was opened and The Northfield Community Centre which catered only for adults. Therefore during the first decade of Northfield's existence, youth provision largely became the responsibility of the churches. The Church of Scotland and other churches between them ran Boy Scout troops, Boys' Brigade companies, Girl Guides, Girls' Guildry, Cub and Brownie packs, a youth fellowship and Sunday Schools. The Church of Scotland during this period alone had over 1,500 young people going to the various groups it provided. A popular item in the Church of Scotland's programme was the Saturday night Film Club which attracted hundreds of young people:

> *Children's Film Foundation . . . was important for the Church . . . there wasn't too much violence, there wasn't any other influences that they would have been unhappy with . . . which is fine . . . unlike the wee kirk roon the corner, they didn't even like to see you enjoying yourself (laughing).*

(Transcript 2)

The Northfield Youth Group (NYG) was formed from the Northfield Church Youth Fellowship around 1960/61. The Youth Fellowship consisted of young people who were already members of one of the uniformed organisations. The new Northfield ministry was in part born out of a growing movement within the Church of Scotland influenced by the Iona Community and the writings of Abbe Michonneau (1948) and Paul Tillich (2000).[3] During the late 1950s, Ross Flockhart, a member of the Iona Community, became the Church of Scotland minister in Northfield. Through Flockhart, many of the ideas and practices associated with the Iona Community came to have a profound influence on the development of youth work in the area. Also of significant importance in the development of the Youth Fellowship and NYG was Bill Howie. He first came to Northfield Parish Church as a ministry student on placement in 1962. After a period of time in New York he returned in 1964 to become the Assistant Minister responsible, alongside his wife Betty, for the Youth Fellowship programme he recalls:

> *the Church of Scotland in the early part of the century had just lost working class people, by and large. Part of the practical theology course we did in the last year of [ministry training] was looking at new forms of action. The Iona community in Scotland was a good example of people trying to relate to this . . . George McLeod, who was based in Govan and he was just aware of this tremendous gap between the Church and the working classes and he set out . . . and brought unemployed people to Iona . . . to rebuild the Abbey and they tried to develop styles of worship that were meaningful to people . . . but they also carried that back to Govan and House Churches, certainly in Scotland . . . perhaps that's where they originated.*

(Transcript 3)

This period coincided with the growth of the House Church movement in the UK which represented an alternative to the institutional churches for many charismatic and evangelical Christians. These outward-looking churches generally embodied a commitment to community action and new forms of voluntary effort that included non-traditional modes of engagement with young people. Bill Howie mentions that:

> *there were two (House Churches) there when I went back in '64 and we had nine or ten by the time I left three years later. So, I remember writing this essay, which was 'Revolution in a City Parish' which was about*

Abbe Michonneau.[4] And he was a Roman Catholic priest who was in this working class area where 5% came to the church and the other 95% wouldn't touch it with a barge pole and he assessed whether he should be active and busy with the 5% or whether he should put the 95% at the centre of his ministry, which is what he did. He felt that was really what the church was being called on to do. So he tried to break through the existing structures and to reach people in new ways, and to try to then build on new structures that would be relevant to them, that they could participate in, so I think the House Churches were an attempt to do that and by the end of the time we had as many people attending House Churches as were attending church on a Sunday – 50% were people who were coming to church but the other 50% were people who had no understanding of church worship and church life, who wouldn't go near it on a Sunday, but who were happy to come and discuss issues they felt were important to their lives.

(Transcript 3)

Bill Howie also notes the growth of local activism at the time:

The old folks houses [were] round about, and I used to spend most of my afternoons visiting them, when I was up in Northfield, but some of them (House Church families) just took them on board and became regular visitors, identifying people who needed extra support . . . one of the groups – they had a son who had learning disabilities and we knew of other people, where nothing was done at that time. They were all over school age, and they set up a small unit in the church hall once a week and within a couple of years they had 50 in it, coming from all over Aberdeen, that is what created the pressure on Aberdeen local authority to build Park House, to get a proper centre.

(Transcript 3)

A number of accounts from ex-members of NYG emphasise the influence of volunteering and community activism in the housing scheme. James Urquhart recalls this phase, and in doing so offered an insight into the impact his involvement had on his future.

Summerhill Club, I was involved in a disabled club there for a number of years . . . Of course the folk that came there came from all over the city – a regular Sunday afternoon and I went to teach some of those kids to swim . . . and I also played 5 a side football with them . . . I must have been 15, 16, 17 kind of age. And of course a lot of that fed into the sort of social work I did later at the Raeden Centre which was a multidisciplinary assessment Centre for disabled kids and their families.

(Transcript 8)

'Get oot! And let us dae it ourselves, and that's what we did . . . it was a good experience, it really wis'

Around 1962 the members of the Northfield Church Youth Fellowship decided to negotiate independence and become a self-organising association of young people. The first president of the new style NYG, in reflecting upon this new structure, vividly remembers the ideas and individuals that helped to foster change:

> *It was fascinating, I absolutely found it fascinating, my father was an elder and my mother went to the women's groups and a' that kind of stuff, so we were kind of brought up in the Church if you like. In the teenage years we were in this youth section with a woman called Jean Dick, who was our teacher. She was a Christian Communist and people couldn't understand this and her views were wide and varied and she certainly provoked us to think about stuff mair than just the Bible, Jesus and that kinda stuff.*
>
> *You see before the Youth Group they had what they called the Youth Fellowship and we didnae want to be a Youth Fellowship . . . because we saw that as far too much Bible and religion. We wanted to be mair oot 'er exploring and debating and discussing . . . that is the kinda group that we wis, so and that is when we had this kinda mini- revolution . . . if you like and we said 'No, we are going to be a Youth Group and we are going to structure ourselves wi' a chair and a secretary and a' that . . . so a' that kinda evolved at the same time as we were saying to the workers . . . And we are deing it wirsel, we will de it wirsel and you can go awa' and leave us alone.*

(Transcript 3)

The group developed their own structure, with co-operation a key value:

> *I was President of that group, yea, certainly was for a few years, but it was a kina group it was easy to be, because folk would take on . . . somebody would say, OK I will find oot when the buses are to Monymusk, or I will find oot how much food we need. They were really very*

Figure 9.1   Members of the Northfield Church Youth Group at Skerry Brae in Lossiemouth accompanied by the Beehive Manager Ian Kerr (at table left) and Betty Howie (at table right)

good and they distributed oot the jobs. And we would invite speakers in, and if onybody kent onybody, they would do it . . . We used to get some good stuff and folk were quite happy to take on board bits of responsibility and stuff like 'at. It was a good experience, it really wis.

(Transcript 3)

The Assistant Minister, Bill Howie worked closely with a graduate from the new Moray House Youth Work course, John Mack, who was possibly Aberdeen's first detached youth worker. Prior to becoming a full-time youth worker Mack had a background in Scouting. He described in an interview one particularly notable experience from his National Service days in the south of England.

If your background was in Scouts . . . you have a very narrow view. But my view had changed in the Army. It had to change or you would not have survived . . . you know (laughing). And even in the Scouts, we had lads that had never seen the sea . . . and the Brigadier gave me £400, which was a lot of money and said . . .' Take these boys to your home in Scotland, for a fortnight.' And we came up to Fife and they had never seen the sea . . . the fact they had lived in Woolwich. Never seen beaches, thought they were private – so that all changed my views.

Transcript 4)

Mack went on to have a considerable influence upon the thinking of many of the young people involved in the NYG. He offered:

. . . an opportunity for them to create their own agenda and to explore issues which were of importance to them. And that's how it worked, that's how the group grew and folk came in and went out . . . and we quite often met in my house.

(Transcript 4)

They found in John Mack, an individual whose views:

were totally, totally different at that time, frae mainstream views and he was quite happy to allow us to explore. I would not have said this then but . . . looking back, he was quite happy to let us explore were 'ain road' if ye like, ken, and were ain ideas.

(Transcript 1)

The same interviewee proceeded to define Mack's approach in these terms:

I think it is trusting youth, trusting them . . . they can de it, but if you dinna let them, then they winna . . . you have got to allow them to mak' their ane mistakes but be there . . . and they were there. They were kinda an age group in between, if you like . . . between the auld foggies (laughing) and us. We seen them as younger.

(Transcript 1)

New developments

Within the wider community the young people of Northfield, unlike many of their parents, had money to spend. Most left school at age 15 and went into work and the wages were sufficient for them to have money leftover to spend on music, films and going to dances. Some also gathered at night on the street corners of Northfield which, coupled with some acts of minor vandalism, helped fuel reputation for 'gangs' within the estate. A local journalist, Cuthbert Graham, discussing this 'reputation' some years later wrote that 'what gave Northfield a temporary notoriety was in fact growing pains. Sheer weight of numbers had a lot to do with it . . .' (*Aberdeen Press and Journal*, 7 March 1970).

Although the Northfield Youth Group continued to meet and expand well

Figure 9.2 The Beehive

into the 1960s, the opening of the Beehive Youth Club in 1962 meant that the focus for many of their activities shifted to this new location.

It was Thursday 15 November 1962 and Elvis Presley was starring in *Blue Hawaii* at Aberdeen's Odeon Cinema and the Beatles first single, *Love Me Do* had just been released. On that day a hundred plus teenagers queued outside Aberdeen's first purpose built youth club, the Beehive. Amongst those joining the queue were members of the NYG.

The funding of the Beehive had been politically contentious given the image of Northfield as a place of youth gangs and petty vandalism. Indeed, the decision to build it was deferred on more than one occasion by the council. Eventually the motion to proceed with the Beehive was passed by a one vote majority. In September 1960, the final design for a building, which eventually cost £35,378, was accepted by the Corporation.

Situated on the Northfield estate and managed by the LEA, the new club's ethos was described by the Deputy Organiser of Aberdeen's Youth Service in the following terms:

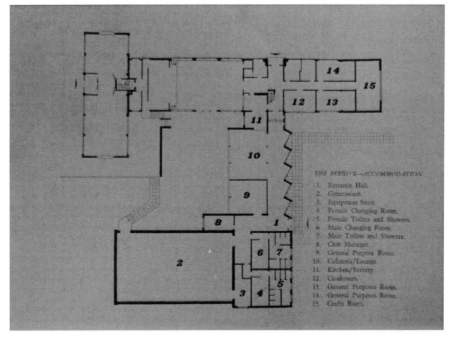

Figure 9.3   The Beehive Floorplan

When we opened these places we didn't set out to achieve anything other than to provide places for these young people to meet together and help them through their adolescent years. We had no aspirations to achieve anything beyond that.

(*Aberdeen Press and Journal*, 18 February 1964)

Initially those responsible for managing the Beehive Youth Club, Elma Brown and Cecil Murray, envisaged a self-programming organisation.[5] An active Aberdeen Youth Council, and far-sighted Youth Service staff, helped secure the substantial staffing and capital expenditure to enable this to happen during the first decade or so in which it operated.

Open seven nights a week, and Wednesday and Sunday afternoons, the Beehive Youth Club comprised a large coffee bar and lounge with alcoves within which upwards of a dozen young people could crowd around the tables, listening to the juke box, chatting and awaiting the arrival of friends (Transcript 1). The building also contained a substantial gymnasium, a room reserved for the use of girls and side rooms available for group activities and discussion.

Figure 9.4   Beehive leaflet

The self programming youth club

For the first few months, management of the Beehive was undertaken by the Deputy Youth Organiser for the city who oversaw the recruitment and training of part-time staff and the appointment of the first Manager.

One of the early part-time workers described her introduction to the setting as follows:

> . . . I wanted to be a gym teacher, just at my time it was too expensive, but I knew about the youth service in Glasgow, so I had a couple of courses there, Scottish Country Dancing . . . and then I got into Junior Clubs. Then when I went up to Aberdeen, I went to see them there . . . and they were just beginning the training, the people who were going to be in the Beehive and the 62 Club.[6]
>
> When it was the Beehive, I was going to be one of the team. We had to have a skill . . . I mean there was a super set of skills for that club . . . so a skill, but we were also trained . . . it was a Cecil Murray . . . Well I

cannot praise him enough . . . an older man . . . but he was picking up on the new ideas and he trained that staff before . . . [we] really got going. And he was very keen on the personal communication, and . . . we had a skill . . . and we did coffee bar work. Loved it, I loved it . . . I've often quoted, if Cecil Murray came into the main bit of the club, and there was two workers talking to each other . . . he would soon sort them out (laughing).

Transcript 6)

The part-time staff, many of whom had local links, became an invaluable resource. One of these, a social worker based in Northfield, described the benefits for young people of this arrangement.

I was also a social worker in that same area . . . so I was quite interested in networking and things and that was another link between me and the Church too as I got to know Nan Bryden who was the Deaconess and she ran a camp one year and took young people away to Strathconan. I was able to join in with that and take some kids that I knew through work who would not normally have got that kind of holiday.

(Transcript 7)

Many of the part-time staff had links to the church youth work. Indeed, Northfield Church's Minister, Ross Flockhart, encouraged his youth workers to apply for posts at the new centre, demonstrating a commitment to be in and of the community. The Church's Detached Youth Worker, John Mack recalls how:

when the Beehive was built, Ross stopped any formal youth work that they did. I mean they kept their Sunday schools and Bible Classes and he advised any of the folk that were working for the Church as youth workers to apply for posts at the Beehive. He didn't want it to be seen that the Church was in opposition to what was happening at the Beehive . . . It was never part of our job to make folk into Church members . . . it wouldn't have been Ross's view. I mean if they had wanted to become Church members he would have been delighted but it wasn't part of the agenda.

(Transcript 4)

'There was a massive question of where the hell to start'

In 1963, Ian Kerr became manager of the Beehive. This was the starting point for a new direction in his life and the lives of many Beehive members. Kerr had abandoned his engineering apprenticeship and acquired a love of poetry and literature, in particular the poems of Edwin Muir. He links this reorientation to the excitement, freedom and challenges of the Outward Bound Movement which he had become involved with through the Moray Sea School.[7] He described his feelings upon starting at the Beehive.

> So there was a massive question of where the hell to start and there was great difficulty there just in terms of trying to get to know the young folk. And again the double sidedness of things – recognising yes, some folk were interested in activities and that is why they came, and others were there because they wanted to meet their friends. And while that seemed to me to be perfectly legitimate in itself . . . and don't interfere with that, the other side was well there may be interests they have and was there any scope for them becoming more involved than that with whatever their interest was. And that is the kind of thing that I was pushing, that you must not see young folk as some kind of mass, that you must begin with all the different things going on. And sometimes that created problems with the staff as some felt they should be doing things. Behaviours that I would tolerate and not bat an eyelid at . . . that they become very upset with it and want to be kind of disciplinarian . . . and shut them out or discipline them or what have you. And I would say 'no'.
>
> (Transcript 5)

The stated aim of the Beehive Youth Club was to facilitate a self-programming, participatory membership. However, achieving this involved a slow process of listening and responding to the members. From the outset there were pressures on the staff to deliver activities that would justify all the money spent on this new facility and show it was keeping young people not only off the streets, but 'out of trouble'. Kerr remembers how

> there was always an expectation there that all sorts of things would develop that would be noteworthy and all the rest of it . . . So there was one occasion, it was a busy night and I can't remember even if a dance was on, but a few police arrived at the door, a sergeant in particular

and I can't remember his name, and he just barged in wanting to get hold of somebody and I said, 'Hey wait a minute, you may be after somebody but if you come in here you see me or another member of staff and explain what you are doing, you don't come barging in here.' And of course that got relayed back . . . Well it was, 'There are occasional fights go on there?' and I said, 'Aye', and it was, 'Well you canna have this sort of thing. You know it is bad for our image.' And of course that sets up the whole thing of what are you really interested in? Your image – the authority's image . . . or are you interested in young people and what is happening to them at specific times of their lives, and trying to do something about that. So there were often stresses and strains there . . . about the image of the thing.

(Transcript 5)

The coffee bar and the 'alcove space' offered an important element of security and group identity for the new membership of the Beehive as one ex-member explained:

Well I min' we always used to sit . . . there was the main coffee bar and the gym of course and there was the barrier door, which was the door between the Beehive and the Community Centre and depending on which worker wis on it was either open or closed. There was also these kind of alcove bits and we used to always congregate as a friend group, if you like, never went into the main, the big coffee bar bit . . . no we had our own group security within . . . a little cliquey bit, if you like, in the alcove bits . . . I never remember using ony o' the gym stuff very much. My active stuff was mair oot and aboot. Aye, and crack and a carry on . . . somebody once said . . . why . . . they were there . . . and she said 'a cup of tea and a carry on'. [laughing]. 'At wis it, because if you sat there you could see the door and you could see a'body coming in, as well.

(Transcript 3)

Another ex-member reflected on the experience of these 'Alcove Evenings' and their own involvement in them in rather more philosophical terms:

Yes, obviously the issue of mid adolescence and the tasks of mid adolescence, you know trying to establish some kind of identity, trying to work out exactly who you are, the way you think you know the exploration of ridiculous ideas, the kind of views that you have . . . [laughing], were very insular and they never explored the world, or explored any other place, ideas, I hadn't read widely, I hadn't studied . . . all before that . . . you are trying to explore some philosophical ideas and just trying to find out who you are.

(Transcript 8)

The emergence of self-organised groups and projects

The Beehive staff held a two hour monthly meeting, usually over the Sunday lunchtime, to review, evaluate and plan. It was at one of these meetings that concern was expressed over provision for young women:

> *Mrs Knight said she wondered if we were working hard enough with the girls in the club who are diffident to talk to leaders – are we trying to get them interested in something? It seems that we tend to give more attention to those who are taking part in groups and forget about those who are not attached to anything . . . It was pointed out that the severity and the position of the Ladies Room did not exactly encourage the girls to spend any time in it.*

(Staff meeting, 26/4/65)

Besides the generic youth work a number of autonomous projects existed in the club including a bi-monthly magazine called *Klub Krits*. The magazine reported on group and project developments. The *Girls Only* page of the magazine provides a stark insight into the 'Ladies Room' culture of the youth club where the headline appears 'Come on Girls, cheer yourselves up'. This feature article advocated change for girls but in these terms:

> *Change your make up colour . . . change the shape of your eyebrows; change your hairdo. Now here's a recipe for lemon coconut cookie. And after eating the cookies . . . try this Tummy Trimmer.*

(Klub Krits, Jan/Feb, 1965)

Other feature articles communicated useful information about such issues as safety when walking and climbing in the mountains of Scotland, and what to do if involved in a motoring accident. It also included reports from gym users, the Judo club and reviews of recent record releases. For example, here is one such review:

> *Billy Fury has a real swinging disc – 'I'm lost without you.' It starts quietly, but builds to a shattering climax, with strings and chanting voices. On the flip side is a real finger-clicking 'You Better Believe it Baby'. It's great for dancing.*

(Klub Krits Jan/Feb, 1965)

The finances of the club were scrutinised by both staff and members at the end of each financial year. No formal Beehive Youth Committee was formed but an Executive Committee was co-opted from local business people. Soon after being opened a plethora of small project committees came into being. The projects listed as operating in 1965 included the football team, the decorating and gardening group, the outdoor group, the Morningfield Hospital visiting group, the Keep Fit group, the dressmaking group, and the rather mysterious *'Group Z'* that organised such activities as tape recordings of stories, interviews and sound effects, photography developing and printing, film shows, magazine production and outings to the hills.

NYG members at the Beehive

For some members of the NYG the transition from Church to Youth Club offered new opportunities.

> *Yea, it was called The Fowk and it was Graeme, me, Maggie, Fred and Andy. We sung in pubs and folk groups and a' sorts and it really started wi' the three of us and the modern hymns, is what they called it, at the Church. Then moving into the Beehive and we got a practice room and 'athing . . . it got bigger and we created a folk group. The music was a big part . . . on the stage at the Community Centre bit we did stuff on there as well . . . a bit of drama and a bit of music and stuff, aye. It wisnae just a gym and a fitba' place . . . there was music and drama as well . . . I min' being involved in that . . .*

(Transcript 3)

In February 1964 a journalist from the Aberdeen Press and Journal conducted a series of interviews with staff and young people who were members of the Beehive and on the basis of these produced five feature articles. He encapsulated the public debate between those who saw the Beehive as 'A waste of public funds' and those who believed it was 'An imaginative experiment'. He commented that since opening the club, its stated objective was simply to help young people 'enjoy growing up' and that the reward of this endeavour would be 'the spiritual health and wealth of the people of Aberdeen'. One of the articles reported the current Beehive membership as 500, down from the 800 members of the first year. The Beehive, according to the journalist, '. . . was a full house; a rendezvous much used but not abused; of wear and tear from heavy usage, but not vandalism' (*Aberdeen Press and Journal* 17 February 1964).

A subsequent article focussed on the 'teenagers who confounded the sceptics' by taking so much responsibility for the wellbeing of the club. It quoted at length from a member of the staff group who described:

> The tendency among young people today is that if you indicate that you want them into this club to do them good – you are finished . . . We merely provided these places with leaders who were interested in and cared for young people.
>
> Aberdeen Press and Journal, 18 April 1964)

Yet another of the articles focussed on the 'young who help the old', and identified a significant amount of young people's voluntary effort and involvement across the city. The concluding article in the series featured an analysis that predicted 'specialist clubs' as a future trend for the youth service and the need for more trained leaders in the North of Scotland.

Conclusions: key elements of a participatory youth work approach

The youth workers in the two projects examined in this research sought to foster a sharing and exploring relationship with young people. Often volunteers themselves, they gave freely of their own time to help out with special projects and encouraged young people's leadership. Young people were invited into the homes of professional workers, something that mirrored the practice of those involved with the House Churches. Generally they extended the relationship with the young people into one of friendship. A friendship that often involved their own family, this process meant the private situation of family life, children and work was extended into the public domain. Consequently the lines between the personal and the professional were blurred. Regular residential weekends provided another setting for shared responsibilities and became a way of deepening these bonds of friendship.

As a result of their membership, many who belonged to the self-organised NYG were introduced to new responsibilities that enabled them to gain an early experience of public accountability and democratic processes. These young people learnt how to organise a meeting, find a speaker, chair an event, and find help and assistance where needed.

The youth workers were prepared to share not only time but their interests in such things as poetry, travel and literature. From this relatively small youth group a new generation of youth workers, community workers, educationalists, academics, skilled tradesmen and tradeswomen, city councillors and full-time trade union officials emerged. Self- organised young people in this setting created a 'multi-level participatory competence' from individual volunteering to collective association within a context that explored and developed new interests and skills. In this milieu, within both the NYG and the Beehive, the organisational goal was not upon the acquisition of members or their conversion or conformity. Nor was the prevailing ethos one that identified youth as a problem. Rather it was informed by a perspective that viewed young people as assets to their communities.

On reflection, the culture in both the NYG and the Beehive was one that encouraged autonomy and, in a non-patronising fashion, put the interests of young people first. Through involvement in democratic processes and the creation of mutuality between young people and staff, the former gained new skills that benefited their communities and that they took into later life. In the environment of the NYG, young people were encouraged to assert their right to shun the formal religion on offer and pursue their own enthusiasms. Religion was always one among many issues up for 'debate'. It was an approach to youth work supported by the church leaders. Workers adopted the roles of adviser, listener, informal mentor and facilitator. Roles allowed for young people's liberatory empowerment rather than their regulation or manipulation.

We now live in different times to the young people of the early 1960s. The parents of the 1960s generation endured a harsher post-war 'age of austerity' that their children refused to accept. In present times, with another 'age of austerity', the need for support and funding that prioritises the interests and concerns of the young person is paramount. Participatory youth work, in the form of the youth club and the independent youth group with the informal youth worker in their midst, is still a vital educational service.

Endnotes

1   All interviewees were made aware that material acquired would be used for this chapter on the history of youth work undertaken on the Northfield estate in the early 1960s.
2   This was the historical right to hold land for which the holder must pay in grain or money in perpetuity. The Abolition of Feudal Tenure etc (Scotland) Act 2000 abolished all the remaining aspects of the feudal system as at 28 November 2004.
3   The Iona Community was founded in Glasgow and Iona in 1938 by George MacLeod in the midst of the Depression. McLeod was a minister working in a Govan dockland parish and he took unemployed skilled craftsmen and young trainee clergy to Iona to rebuild both the monastic quarters of the mediaeval abbey and experience communal life.
4   Abbe Michonneau, Parish priest of Sacre Coeur de Colombes argues for 'mission communities' by means of 'parish activities' with the aim of 'creating a stir within the parish communities.

5   Unfortunately it was not possible to interview Brown and Murray as they are now sadly deceased.

6   The 62 Club opened in Summer Street in the city centre of Aberdeen on the same day as the Beehive. The first Manager was Callan Anderson, graduate in 1961 from the first year of the Moray House one year professional Youth Work Course. The idea of a self-programming club also underpinned his work within that youth club.

7   The Moray Sea School was established by Kurt Hahn, who fled Nazi Germany in 1933, and came to Moray and established the Gordonstoun School near Duffus.

References

Baistow, K. (1994) 'Liberation and Regulation? Some Paradoxes of Empowerment' *Critical Social Policy* 14: 3, 34–46.

Forrest, D.W. (1999) 'Education and Empowerment: towards untested feasibility' *Community Development Journal* 34(2) pp. 93–107.

Forrest, D. (2000) 'Theorising empowerment thought: illuminating the relationship between ideology and politics in the contemporary era' *Sociological Research Online*, 4(4). http://www.socresonline.org.uk/4/4/forrest.html.

Forrest, D. (2005) 'What does Paulo Freire have to say about youth work?' *Youth and Policy* (89) pp. 94–104.

Forrest, D. and Wood, S. (1999) 'An Empowering Approach to Working with Young People' *Concept* 9 (3) pp. 8–11.

Gallie, W.B. (1995–96) Essentially Contested Concepts, *Proceedings of the Aristotelian Society* (56) pp.167–198.

Hansard (1960) *The Youth Service and the Albermarle Report.* 18 May 1960, Volume 223, cc 935–1052 House of Lords, London: HMSO.

Kieffer, C.H. (1984) 'Citizen Empowerment: A Developmental Perspective' *Prevention in Human Services* 4(2) pp.9–36.

Lord, J. and McKillop Farlow, D. (1990) 'A Study of Personal Empowerment: Implications for Health Promotion' *Health Promotion, Health and Welfare*, Canada Vol. 29 (2) pp. 8–15.

Michonneau, A. (1948) *Revolution in a City Parish.* Blackfriars: Oxford.

Ministry of Education (1960) The Youth Service in England and Wales (Albermarle Report), London: HMSO.

Mullender, A. and Ward, D. (1991) *Self-Directed Groupwork: Users Take Action for Empowerment*, London: Whiting and Birch.

Rappaport, J., Swift, C., and Hess, R. (1984*) Studies in Empowerment: Steps Toward Understanding and Action*, New York: Haworth.

Tillich, P. (2000) *The Courage to Be*, Yale University Press: New Haven.

CHAPTER 10

In Defence of the Albemarle 'Settlement' for Youth Work

Bernard Davies and Tony Taylor

This chapter was first conceived early in 2011 as the UK Conservative/Liberal Democrat government's assault on state-funded public services was demolishing one local authority youth service after another and all but 'disappearing' youth work as a distinctive way of working with young people. For both authors, the Albemarle Report (Ministry of Education, 1960) had for over fifty years been a crucial, if often unrecognised, inspiration. The authors' personal and professional lives have been influenced by the framework of youth services which emerged after Albemarle. In particular, Davies qualified as a youth worker in the year that Albemarle was published and this also coincided with the growth of the Youth Workers' Union of which he was a member. For Taylor, whose career began ten years later, Albemarle was a source of contention, understood through a critical Marxist-Feminist perspective. However, over time, the person-centred aspects of Albemarle have come to seem more significant and relevant to the collective struggles of social movements.

In this context it seemed pertinent to look again at both Albemarle's recommendations and at the political and ideological conditions out of which these had emerged as well as for the insights these might offer into what is currently happening. For example – how far could the current ruthless unpicking of the past be explained by intrinsic weaknesses within the Committee's dominant perspectives and underpinning analysis? Over the half century since Albemarle the state moved from the relatively laid-back incursions of the social-democratic 1960s and early 1970s to the increasingly centralising and oppressive managerialist and market-driven controls imposed by the neo-liberal priorities first of Thatcherism, then of New Labour and as we write of the Coalition. Albemarle stimulated a substantial expansion of statutory youth services and we ask what the consequences of this have been in the subsequent period of retraction.

By taking Albemarle as our starting point we are not suggesting that it ushered in a golden age for youth work. For, as we make clear later, both its analysis and prescriptions and the application of some of its key principles were in some respects deeply flawed. However, it is clear that, when set against the bad times that had immediately preceded it and the many later 'down' periods, Albemarle laid the foundations for youth work to develop in more secure and in sometimes more innovative ways. Because the post Albemarle 'settlement', characterised by acceptance of the role of the state in youth work in partnership with the voluntary sector, was by no means inevitable, and because it didn't survive without repeated struggle, at this historical moment it seems important both to recall that history and to re-examine it critically.

Albemarle in its time

By the time the Albemarle Committee met in November 1958 the government's war time enthusiasm for the 'Service of Youth' (Board of Education, 1939) had long since cooled. As today, 'austerity' had hit it hard – and disproportionately. In the words of a resolution to National Association of Youth Leaders and Organisers' 1948 Annual Conference '. . . local authorities have made drastic cuts to their Youth Service estimates to such an extent that the maintenance of essential facilities has been impaired' (quoted in Davies, 1999: 27). Indeed, by 1957 a Ministry of Education spokesperson was admitting that: 'It has not been the policy to expand this service to any definition standard' (quoted Davies, 1999: 30). Moreover, beyond the financial constraints, influential commentators were asking some more principled, and threatening, questions – in particular whether a youth service would any longer be needed once the county colleges envisaged by the 1944 Education Act were providing part-time educational opportunities for all young people up to the age of 18 (Barnes, 1948: 3–4). By the end of the 1950s a tipping point had thus been reached: either leave the statutory youth service to die – or do something proactive to revive and develop it.

Far from being guaranteed, a decision in favour of revival and development required considerable pressure from a range of interests, some with very different starting points. Though small and with declining membership the trade unions within the field were pressing for renewed investment in facilities and programmes (Nicholls, 2009: 59); as were high profile national reports, in 1955 from the King George Jubilee Trust (1955) and in 1957 from a Commons Select Committee (House of Commons, 1957). All these helped change the dominant mood music of the time. In addition, a 1959 debate on youth in the House of Lords (Hansard, 1959) provided a platform for supporters of some of the national voluntary youth organisations and prompted strong criticism of the Ministry of Education's neglect of the youth service.

None of this was happening in a political or social vacuum. The ending in 1958 of the supposed 'disciplining' experience of National Service for young men was seen as an immediate and significant challenge. Wider concerns about youth as always played a part. Sometimes this was expressed in terms which have striking contemporary resonances: for example one peer in the House of Lords debate talked about 'the high rate of anti-social behaviour' (Hansard, 1959). Prefiguring David Cameron's obsession after the 2011 street riots with our 'broken' and 'sick' society and young people's supposedly misplaced sense of entitlement, anxieties repeatedly surfaced about Britain's slide into a 'permissive society' in which the young were less deferential to their parents – or indeed to anyone in authority.

Internal political pressures also played their part with the Ministry of Education worrying that the escalating youth crime figures could lead to a transfer of responsibility for the youth service to the Home Office (Smith, 1997: 29). It was thus seen as necessary to make the case for a service which, in the words of Lord Hailsham, a former Minister of Education, was 'a more attractive alternative to Borstal' (Hansard, 1959). However Ministry of Education officials had become sceptical about whether the 'youth leadership' offered by the historic charitable organisations was sufficiently responsive to or even aware of a newly assertive teenage culture (Smith, 1997: 30). As a sharp political operator, Albemarle herself could be trusted to be realistic and pragmatic (*The Observer*, 1960) but others were recruited onto the Committee on the basis of being properly 'tuned in' to the new spirit of the age. These included such notables as Richard Hoggart, author of *The Uses of Literacy* published in 1957, a study of working class life and culture which had attracted wide critical and popular attention; Pearl Jephcott, a long-time girls club worker and researcher; Leslie Paul, founder the Woodcraft Folk (see Paul, 1929), set up as a radical alternative to the Scouts; and Denis Howell, an MP with a long connection with youth work in Birmingham who was to become Labour's 'minister for youth' for most of the later 1960s.

The Albemarle bequest: money, buildings, structures

Retrospectively it appears that against the apparent direction of the youth service during the 1950s, the Albemarle Committee in confident and unapologetic

Recommendation	Implementation
Albemarle Report published	February 1960
To establish a Youth Service Development Council (YSDC) to monitor progress on the Committee's proposals and advise the government on future development (para. 157).	March 1960: Council set up with the Minister of Education in the chair.
To agree arrangements for emergency and long-term training of full-time professional leaders with the aim of increasing their number from 700 to 1300 within five years (paras. 247-58; 266).	February 1961: National College for the Training of Youth Leaders opened with first year intake of 90 students. 1962-1965: 140 students per year recruited. End of 1965: Albemarle 'emergency' target reached.
To set up a Joint Negotiating Committee on youth workers' salaries and conditions of service (paras. 279-85).	July 1961: Committee published its first report.
To fund 'a generous and imaginative building programme' providing 'better furniture, lighting, decoration and equipment' and more residential accommodation (paras. 224-5).	September 1961: Publication of Ministry of Education Building Bulletin No 20: *General Mixed Clubs.* August 1963: Publication of Ministry of Education Building Bulletin No 22: *Youth Club – Withywood Bristol.*
To provide more and better training for paid part-time workers (paras. 287, 289).	July 1961: Appointment of working party on the training of part-time youth leaders and assistants. July 1962: Working Party report published. December 1965: Second (YSDC) report published.

terms spelt out a highly ambitious programme of development in 44 detailed recommendations. Not only did the then (Conservative) government accept all of these on the day the report appeared. As the above table shows the government also acted with striking speed on those recommendation which the Committee highlighted as needing immediate or urgent action.

Other priorities – to be achieved through ten-year development plans – were to increase central government and local government funding for voluntary organisations (paras. 306–9, 320) and for the Ministry to put pressure on local education authorities (LEAs) to ensure 'their expenditure on maintained and aided services is sufficient to sustain the momentum of development' (para. 367).

Albemarle did little to strengthen the Service's legislative base. This has been a source of concern and agitation ever since which the 2012 Department for Education revision did little to relieve (DfE, 2012). It did however define a much more proactive role for the state. Within a much-vaunted if often strained 'partnership' with the voluntary organisations, this seemed to break the latter's taken-for-granted domination of the youth work field. The context here was a broad acceptance of the government's role in providing funding for public services generally. For example the Bow Group, an influential pressure group on the left of the Conservative party, took the view that:

> *If the community is concerned that there should be adequate facilities for meeting social and recreational needs of young people, the State must intervene by providing money and machinery to complement or replace existing services.*
>
> (Bow Group, 1961: 10)

It was thus not surprising that over the following decade governments came to assume that, as well as funding, they could – indeed should – offer the youth service oversight and policy steer. This, even though implemented initially with a sometimes very light touch, nonetheless represented a significant shift from past practice. Following Albemarle, it was assumed that LEAs would also be more active and indeed proactive. Such expectations, though eventually producing a postcode lottery of resourcing, prompted some LEAs to develop well funded and imaginative Services. As a result, despite many ups and downs, public money was increasingly injected into youth work, allowing the state, as we shall show later, to exercise much greater leverage over both the why and the how of the practice.

The Albemarle bequest: values and purposes

Many of these key structural and financial features of the 'Albemarle settlement' have remained the unquestioned bedrock of the youth service ever since. However Albemarle's impact went well beyond these. It was also crucial in shifting key ideological parameters, particularly through some veiled but carefully thought-out challenges to conventional wisdoms which had been inherited, often uncritically, from the voluntary sector – and which current Prime Minister David Cameron's 'big society' mantras are now explicitly designed to resurrect.

Driving this rethinking was the Albemarle Committee's recognition of radical shifts in the material circumstances and personal and social aspirations of many young people who were beginning to experience greater personal freedom and a wider range of leisure choices. Setting out a position which long pre-dates New Labour's and the Coalition Government's sudden discovery of young people's 'voice', the youth service's users, Albemarle declared, had to be treated as its 'fourth partner' alongside central government, LEAs and the voluntary organisations. Forms of practice were needed, it insisted, which were young people-led, even 'self-programming'. 'Open access' facilities were strongly affirmed – facilities which young people chose to attend and which embraced their group and social activities. Moreover these were to offer not just 'training' and 'challenge', but opportunities for 'association' and even 'social education' of the kinds routinely provided for university students through their student unions.

For any of this to take root Albemarle was clear that youth work would need to break with the often patronising and highly prescriptive mind-set handed down from its charitable and philanthropic past. Youth work was to become less dogmatic in its thinking and much less preachy in how it communicated with young people. The Albemarle Committee declared itself unimpressed with the prevailing language of many in the field. Terms such as 'dedication', 'leadership' and 'character building' were used, it said *as though they were a commonly accepted and valid currency'* (emphasis in the original). Such concepts, it suggested, 'connect little with the realities of life as most young people see them; they do not "speak to their condition"'. Rather, it said, they recall 'hierarchies of less interesting moments of school speech days and other occasions of moral exhortation' (Ministry of Education, 1960: 39–40).

Albemarle stressed that it 'wish(ed) not to be misunderstood', claiming that it 'in no way challenge(d) the value of the concepts behind these words' (para. 145). Nonetheless, at the time, these assertions caused consternation and deep offence within the traditional youth work sector and were strongly contested. In this context one crucial feature of the Albemarle philosophy needs to be highlighted: its acceptance that because many of its proposals *were* at variance with much that was orthodox in youth work practice challenges to them were appropriate and necessary. To its great credit, and in stark contrast to the prescriptive character of contemporary social policy, this ambiguity allowed, even encouraged debate and argument.

Those wedded to youth work's deep-rooted character-building tradition were for example distinctly underwhelmed by the post-Albemarle non-directive and non-judgemental approaches promoted by the National College (Ewen, 1972). This collision between tradition and trendiness seemed to be expressed many an evening in the youth club in disputes over whether swearing was acceptable and whether young people should be banned. Though today these questions might seem outdated, they symbolised an open and visible clash of cultures which was made sharper by Albemarle's unspoken, but unmistakable, assumption that the prevailing, largely taken-for-granted, link between youth work and religion needed to be supplemented by state-sponsored provision which was clearly secular.

These were important debates in their own right into which workers, managers, other professionals, ward councillors and local residents were drawn. Moreover, in due course, they eventually opened up new ideological spaces for youth work which came to be occupied by Black, feminist, gay and lesbian, and other political identity groups of workers whose legacy remains strong.

Finally, to develop the kind of practice it was recommending, Albemarle was clear that those providing it would need to bring to the table much more than good intentions and 'natural leadership'. To appeal to the new teenage generation, it concluded that youth work had to develop greater levels of sophistication and expertise, nurtured through more, better and more appropriate training. This opened up often difficult and still continuing debates on professionalism, qualification barriers and their relationship with volunteering. However against the background of what had gone before Albemarle also set an important benchmark for the skills required for a practice which, in a memorable phrase which policy-makers today would do well to consider, it described as '. . . peculiarly challenging because it requires a tense day-to-day walking on a razor-edge between sympathy and surrender' (para. 147).

Limits of the Albemarle analysis

Yet for all its sharp insights and vision, as we indicated earlier, Albemarle was not without its blind spots and defects. In particular youth work paid an increasingly high price for the limitations of both its social analysis and its policy prescriptions as social democratic policy-making collapsed in the face of the neo-liberal challenge from the 1980s onwards.

In many respects the Albemarle settlement has to be seen as a classic product of, and relatively late addition to, the wider post-1945 welfare settlement. The Albemarle Report was published at a time when the conventional political wisdom was that 'we've never had it so good' – that class conflict was being eliminated and Britain was becoming a classless society. With all fundamental policy issues thus settled, there was, it was claimed, no longer a need for a politics concerned with significant and indeed intrinsic imbalances of power and wealth. Rather what was now required were expert 'technicians' capable of social engineering solutions to some residual 'social problems'. As Anthony Crosland (1956: 155–6) a leading Labour Party 'revisionist' thinker and future Cabinet minister put it:

> We want advice, not of economists, but of psychiatrists, sociologists and social psychologists . . . The aid will take the form of . . . individual therapy, casework and preventative treatment.

To be included in Crosland's list apparently, post-Albemarle, was to be youth work. However this denial that any of these residual social problems might be entrenched in deeper structural inequalities was under challenge even before Albemarle reported. Though what it called 'racial outbursts', referring to the race riots of the late 1950s in Nottingham and Notting Hill, happened even while the Albemarle Committee was at work it completely missed their significance. Far from seeing them as expressions of deep-seated political or economic differences it called them a 'paradoxical' breakdown of inter-personal relationships between 'young people of all races and nationalities . . . (who) share common interests such as jazz and football and even a common culture' (para. 74).

These limited perspectives also constrained Albemarle's responses to those other enduring social divisions rooted in class and gender relations. Very soon after it reported, poverty was suddenly 'rediscovered' – including the understanding that away from the bright lights of London the lives of many young people were very far from 'swinging' (Davies, 1968). Here too – again with striking contemporary resonances – the off-the-shelf explanations were that, where they weren't simply the result of personal and family failure, such 'disadvantages' stemmed from 'technical' flaws in the education or the benefit system.

Moreover by the late 1960s questions were being raised about the wider political and economic assumptions underpinning the whole post-1945 welfare settlement. In 1967, for example, Peter Jay, *The Times* journalist and later the Labour appointee as ambassador to the United States, warned that:

> Social services expenditure in the next ten years is certain to rise relative to Gross National Product merely in order to finance current policies and standards . . . Any substantial improvement in the social services will require unprecedented draconian treatment of privately financed personal consumption . . . otherwise economic progress itself will suffer.
>
> (Jay, 1967)

As the 2008 banking crisis did for the 2000s, the massive rise in oil prices in the early 1970s brutally exposed just how weakly rooted was the much vaunted affluence of the 1960s, lending Jay's kind of analysis growing credibility in political and media circles. Well before Margaret Thatcher came to power therefore, a 'new right' radical critique of the welfare state – expressed most forcefully perhaps through a series of 'black papers' attacking the excesses of 'progressive, comprehensive' education (Cox and Boyson, 1977) – captured this new mood and gained increasing momentum.

One of its early 'captives' was Labour Prime Minister James Callaghan who in 1976, in a speech at Ruskin College, launched a so-called 'great education debate' particularly focused on making schools and other educational institutions the more responsive servants of industry and the economy. In due course the pressure even reached the youth service – for so long peripheral to most national education policy-making. In 1978, Barney Baker, a senior civil servant at the Department of Education and Science, reminded the Youth Service Forum (then the government's advisory body on youth work) that, because there were now 'so many claims on public expenditure', the youth service required 'a new look'. This, he suggested, needed to include: 'an increased emphasis on social objectives . . . Society's needs may have to be expressed in terms more or less unpalatable to young people' (Baker, 1978). What Stuart Hall (2011) has called the 'long march of the neo-liberal revolution' was now clearly well under way.

Politicisation of Albemarle

As this economic and political crisis deepened in the late 1970s a minority Labour government fell between pillar and post, between the capitalist demands of the International Monetary Fund and the common ownership of the means of production, distribution and exchange advocated in Clause IV of the Labour Party's constitution. The government was neither neo-liberal nor socialist in conviction. Into this vacuum spoiling for confrontation swept Thatcherism with its fetishism of the free market and avowed antagonism to the State. Unsurprisingly the youth service was not high on the list of prospective antagonists. There were much more important institutions to be tamed.

However whilst spurning youth work, the government began to piece together what became an increasingly coherent youth policy based on populist authoritarianism in schooling, employment, welfare and youth justice (Davies, 1986). Such was the Thatcherite distrust of what it saw as a refuge of liberal 1960s permissiveness, it sought to bypass or better, colonise youth work through the programmes of the Manpower Services Commission, notably the Youth Training Scheme. Illustrating its instrumental view of human activity, it advanced the narrower notion of social and life skills training in opposition to the broader concept of social education, inspired by Albemarle (Davies and Gibson, 1967). Both authors sharply criticised this offensive at the time (see Davies, 1981 and Taylor, 1981); Taylor in a Marxist vein, claiming 'the government is intent on nothing less than the behavioural modification of the young proletariat', an objective which remains alive and insistent three decades on. Though the Community and Youth Workers Union (CYWU) took the lead in fighting against this undermining of the Albemarle ethos the skirmish ended in a truce.

The core of this resistance was created through a politicisation from below of the Albemarle legacy. The attempt from above through the Fairbairn-Milson report (HMSO, 1969) with its half-hearted, radical insistence on a society perpetually transforming itself had 'proved to be distracting, diversionary, and even debilitating for the service's work with young people' (Davies, 1999: 133). In stark contrast, out of the social movements of the decade, activists entered youth work bent on radicalising its practice, particularly, as was indicated earlier, through autonomous work with young women, black youth, gay and lesbian, and disabled young people. At its most powerful and authentic this intervention infused the person-centred perspective with a sense of power relations largely absent from Albemarle itself and the ensuing full-time training curriculum. This swathe of workers were also deeply critical of the bureaucratic nature of the state at a local and national level, sometimes self-consciously claiming to be 'In and Against the State' (London-Edinburgh Weekend Return Group, 1981). Harking back to Fred Milson's desire to fuse youth and community work this sense of subversion was exemplified by Community Development Projects in the North-East of England, which spoke openly about organising for change in working class areas and forged close links with, for example, the Sunderland Polytechnic Youth and Community Work course (Taylor, 2009).

Inevitably this disturbing fusion threw youth work training and education into turmoil. Growing unease reflected a feeling that the training agencies were white, male and behind the times. By the mid-1980s the conscious recruitment of women and black lecturers had begun to alter affairs. Indeed by the end of the decade an 'anti-oppressive' and 'anti-discriminatory' (AOP/ADP) analysis of practice had become hegemonic within academia. Across the decade this shift was reflected in, for example the emergence in 1982 of the critical academic journal *Youth & Policy*, in the determination of Tony Jeffs and Mark Smith (1987) to puncture youth work's anti-theoreticism, in Val Carpenter and Kerry Young's avowal of independent girls' work (1986) with the concrete manifestation of feminist work in the creation of the Girls Work Unit at the National Association of Youth Clubs, and in the seminal exploration of the experience of black youth by Gus John (1981). Within this climate the proposals of the Thompson Report (HMSO, 1982) fell foul of all weathers; for the government it was too liberal in its continuity with Albemarle, for the radicals it was too much behind the times.

Practice could not remain aloof from this ideological convulsion. The tensions were highlighted in a major piece of research into the state of part-time youth work training which in practice mistakenly supposed that the content of this training mirrored the reality of what was happening on the ground. The authors argued that the traditional character-building model had been overtaken by the Social Education Repertoire (SER) – a mix of personal awareness, community development and institutional reform – very much an Albemarle cocktail (Butters and Newell, 1978). According to Butters and Newell SER itself had to be overthrown by a Radical Paradigm, within which young people themselves were transformed into a vanguard leading the struggle against the status quo.

The Butters-Newell analysis was incisive, yet skewed. However its use in the National Youth Bureau's Enfranchisement Project (Smart and Leigh, 1985) illuminated the contested nature of youth work practice. Utilising an exercise within which workers positioned themselves according to their ideological allegiance the Enfranchisement Project's workers exposed the plurality of conflicting perspectives that were out there – alive and kicking. Although a post-Albemarle radical interpretation of youth work was the dominant voice at a rhetorical level and had supported imaginative pockets of practice the emerging contradiction was that the conformist view of work with young people questioned by Albemarle was still hugely influential. In passing, we might ponder whether 30 years later the National Youth Agency (NYA) would now even consider supporting a national project which exposed the plurality of conflicting perspectives within practice, and thereby in the process daring to suggest that disagreement is a healthy state of affairs.

Radical retreat

The heady days of a radical practice shedding light on Albemarle were relatively short-lived for as the 1980s drew to a close the insidious effect of the neo-liberal agenda was seeping into the fabric of the work. First in the late 1970s and through the 1980s a significant number of activists had sought to unionise and politicise the workforce. This was expressed in the metamorphosis of the Community and Youth Service Association into the CYWU. This included the adoption of a 'horizontal' constitution with a Women's Caucus in the lead, overwhelmingly supported by the membership. By the end of the decade however the CYWU had reverted to a hierarchical structure deciding that this organisational form would better defend the interests of a discrete craft union of youth and community workers (Nicholls, 2009).

Second, whilst ambiguous, there was an implicit belief that a revitalised socialist Labour Party would be the friend of a progressive youth work. This conviction did not necessarily lead to membership of the Party, but it did see some workers gravitating towards municipal socialist councils such as the Greater London Council, Sheffield, Liverpool and Derbyshire. These islands resisting Thatcherism were viewed as havens of enlightenment. However, following the watershed experience of the defeat of the miners in 1985, in common with the left as a whole, the radical insurgents within youth work were on the back foot. The maverick socialist councils, losing confidence and finance, abandoned the project especially once the Labour Party itself under Neil Kinnock began the task, demanded by neo-liberalism, of reinventing itself as a party of the centre and of the market. Faced by similar pressures the social movements were also forfeiting their autonomy, taking the state's grants and seeing their leaders incorporated (Shukra, 1998).

It is possible to trace a compelling contradiction during this period of retreat. A prescriptive right wing agenda nationally was mirrored by an imposed left agenda locally. Radical praxis, which had sought to supersede the apolitical character of Albemarle's liberalism, forgot its roots in diversity, tolerance and the primacy of young people's starting points. Increasingly issue-based and fractured, it displayed an often authoritarian character. Having failed to win hearts and minds, some of its advocates opted to embrace neo-liberalism's partner 'new managerialism' as a way of insisting from above that their agendas be met. Ironically this period of 'one step forwards, two steps back' took place without any explicit conscious governmental intervention into youth work itself.

New Labour: Neo-Liberal

As we reached the 1990s, Conservative governments, via a series of ministerial conferences, dabbled with the notion of persuading the disparate elements within youth work to agree a national core curriculum against which performance could be measured. In one of its last moments of collective solidarity, an alliance of the statutory and voluntary sectors, perhaps remembering Albemarle and its pluralist inheritance, repelled this intrusion. From this moment successive governments opted to impose their desired ideological outcomes through the bureaucratic and managerial control of the funds they were making available. Thus following severe post-Poll Tax cuts in 1992/93 much new state funding for work with young people was channelled through such time-limited pro-grammes as the Single Regeneration Budget.

To win this money in the increasingly competitive market more and more youth services found themselves committed to achieving pre-determined tar-gets – usually as part of a corporate bid. In the early days monitoring was sloppy, but the writing was on the wall. Albemarle's holistic, educational vision was blurred in the shift towards a welfare and preventative view of work with young people. In their abdication to this instrumental view many managers and some workers took succour in the fact that the Labour Party under Blair was mouthing the same welfare mantra, retaining a belief that New Labour would be a progressive force. Thus it was that, in line with the political shift in the Labour Party itself, many in the youth work profession sidled towards the centre, cautioning against any criticism of instructions from above.

Once in power New Labour, in keeping with the neo-liberal aim of gener-ating 'individualised conformity', slowly, but surely, imposed an instrumental programme on youth work. In place of the old Labour dream of a state manag-ing capitalism in the interests of the workers, New Labour substituted a state managing the workers in the interests of capitalism. New Labour's mind was made up. Young people needed to shape up. As Jeffs and Smith noted (2008: 280), the last decade of governmental documents such as 'Every Child Matters' (DfES, 2003) and 'Transforming Youth work' (DfES, 2001) were 'simply prospec-tuses for the delivery of already agreed priorities and outcomes'. The strategy of 'integrated youth services' threatened youth work as a distinctive site of practice. Voluntary and open encounters with young people were perceived as inherently out of control and even dangerous. Increasingly New Labour all but deleted the term youth work from its authoritarian discourse, including it in the 2006 Education Act only very reluctantly and after considerable lobbying, insisting instead on the patronising and simplistic notion of 'positive activities'. The Albemarle legacy of social and informal education was dismissed as being soft, permissive and unaccountable. This new breed of neo-liberal apologists operating within our work were hard-headed and robust, and up to their ears in often irrelevant and dubious statistical information.

The New Labour years thus saw the evacuation of key principles emanating from Albemarle – starting on young people's terms; negotiating a critical dia-logue within which the educator is educated too; and, not least, the importance of the voluntary relationship (Davies, 2008: 79). Inevitably this fundamental alteration of emphasis put the youth work training agencies – bastions of a politicised Albemarlism – under great pressure. To this day they continue to fight the good fight, insisting on a definition of youth work as informal education

(Batsleer, 2009), on the centrality of process (Ord, 2007) and therefore on 'the need for a negotiation of usually complex and subtle human interactions if young people are to be motivated and supported to move on from their starting points' (Davies, 2008: 175). Nevertheless as Jeffs and Spence (2007) note, the impact of modularisation, the increasing fragmentation of knowledge, and the emphasis on competencies and NVQs combined to undermine a theoretically informed, argumentative youth work education – features essential to a continuing critical and creative reworking of the Albemarle legacy.

However, again under the radar, we have witnessed the increasing influence within in-service training of external trainers and consultants, disciples of neo-liberal ideology. With little scrutiny and less debate, a rehashed mix of adolescent and developmental psychology dressed up as Positive Youth Development (Schulmann and Davies, 2007), together with the eclectic pseudo-scientific amalgam of hypnosis, therapy and neuroscience known as Neuro-Linguistic Programming, have inserted themselves insidiously into the discourse of youth work.

Yet within youth work, criticism of New Labour's wilful Albemarle amnesia – revealed particularly in the priority given to pre-determined product over process – remained marginal. Notably many managers and workers throughout its period in office were fellow-travellers, apparently believing that, despite the Party's neo-liberal rebirth, a social democratic pulse was still to be felt. Refuge was taken in the fact that in some policy areas New Labour improved funding for work with young people, even though it invariably came with prescribed purposes. Their incorporation into the New Labour neo-liberal project made them reluctant to face a decisive question regarding: what was the purpose and character of New Labour's transformation of youth work? By the end of its tenure New Labour had all but completed the journey from youth work as social education, as a form of critical pedagogy; to youth work as a tool of social engineering, obsessed with the micro-management of problematic youth.

The drive to the market

In these ways New Labour paved the way for the post 2010 Coalition government to intensify the onslaught on the Albemarle legacy, both ideologically and materially. Continuity of intent was to remain the order of the day.

As we observed at the start of this chapter savage cuts to open access youth work meant that the youth service as understood by Albemarle was pushed to the edge of extinction. In parallel the very notion of youth work was denuded of its distinctive meaning as it was utilised to describe all manner of imposed interventions with young people across such fields as training for employment schemes, restorative justice and both curricular and extra-curricular activities in schools.

An overwhelming shift to targeted early intervention programmes also occurred, accompanied by the overnight metamorphosis of youth workers into youth social workers, complete with identified case loads of recalcitrant youth. At the other end of the scale, under the banner of youth participation, a surge of initiatives developed, focused on the creation of an elite 'new' breed of young entrepreneurs and young experts. These 'trained agents of social action' would evidently deliver public service reform via the 'youth-proofing' of policy and commissioning processes (National Youth Agency, 2012a) and be paid for their efforts – the commodification of both the concept of youth participation and of the young people themselves. Under the Coalition government all this has added up to a qualitative change in the youth work landscape since 2010, with the appearance in earnest of 'the Market' as the central organising notion. If Albemarle was a belated outcome of the post-1945 social democratic settlement, the *Positive for Youth* policy document (HM Government, 2011) marked the delayed arrival into youth work of the neo-liberal business model. If Albemarle had signalled an end to the dominance of the voluntary organisation and the rise of professional youth work, *Positive for Youth* announced the apparent return of a voluntary sector – greatly expanded by 'social enterprise' intruders – to centre stage in an unfolding drama of outsourcing, commissioning and ultimately the privatisation of work with young people. The script by 2011 was peppered with phrases like 'overcoming barriers to a more competitive market' and 'growing the market for social investment'. As we write, leading voluntary organisations such as the National Council for Voluntary Youth Services (NCVYS) and UK Youth had arrived in the front of the queue, as vibrant 'providers'.

Indeed by 2012 NCVYS was heading a consortium, Catalyst, which also involved the NYA, Social Enterprise UK and the Young Foundation. Its role being:

> . . . *(to work) with the Department for Education (DfE) as the strategic partner for young people, as part of the Department's wider transition programme for the sector . . . to deliver three key objectives over a two-year period. It aims to strengthen the youth sector market, equip the sector to work in partnership with Government and co-ordinate a skills development strategy for the youth sector's workforce.*
>
> (NYA, 2012b)

Rather than the resurgence of a critical independent voluntary sector, 'not afraid to make trouble' (Carnegie, 2010: 28) we were thus witnessing the co-option of key national organisations into propagandising in favour of, and seeking to deliver, 'privatised' services for young people.

Before concluding we must however acknowledge a glaring omission in our analysis: a failure to situate in this history of the struggle between social-democratic and neo-liberal ideologies, the renaissance of faith-based youth work. At the very least this significant development seemed to achieve a 'relative autonomy' from the neo-liberal imperative which largely coincided with its emergence from the 1990s onwards.

Resisting the hegemony

The 'In Defence of Youth Work' campaign (http://www.indefenceofyouthwork. org.uk/wordpress) in which both authors are involved, was launched in 2009. This campaign was inspired by the possibilities of challenge and change opened up by the banking crisis of late 2008. But, despite continuing deep-seated economic problems besetting capitalism, by and large, neo-liberal ideas continue as the common-sense of the age. This is reflected in the continuing uncritical embrace by many within youth work of the 'drive to the market' and the search for 'the entrepreneur within'. However as we write, there are signs that the tide may be turning. Increasingly we were hearing a revival of the notion of a common good that cannot be financially calculated – of moral arguments in support of public services based on need not profit (Williams, 2012; Sandel, 2009). Whatever the nuances of political differences, this shifting climate confirms the youth work priority of building collective resistance to the efforts to consign Albemarle to the dustbin of history. With all its weaknesses Albemarle catalysed a form of youth work: voluntary without imposition or sanction, which knew that its character was open to question, that its contradictions had to be embraced and examined critically, and that debate was necessary and legitimate. In contrast the neo-liberal agenda seeks to stifle this process of collective uncertainty in the name of inflicting programmed order on youth work and on young people. Such an authoritarian desire is a far cry from the humanistic aspirations at the heart of Albemarle, making the need to defend and extend its legacy even more necessary – and ever more urgent.

References

Baker, B. (1978) *Youth Service Forum for England and Wales – The Future Role of the Youth Service: Note by the Secretary*, London: Department of Education and Science.

Barnes, L.J. (1948) *The Outlook for Youth Work: report prepared for the King George Jubilee Trust*, London: King George Jubilee Trust.

Batsleer, J.R. (2009) *Informal Learning in Youth Work*, London: Sage.

Board of Education (1939) *The Service of Youth*, Circular 1486, London: Board of Education.

Bow Group (1961) *Responsibility for Youth*, London: Conservative Political Centre.

Butters, S. and Newell, S. (1978) *Realities of Training*, Leicester: National Youth Bureau.

Carpenter, V. and Young, K. (1986) *Coming in from the Margins: Youth work with girls and young women*, London: National Association of Youth Clubs.

Carnegie U.K. Trust [Commission of Inquiry into the Future of Civil Society in the UK and Ireland] (2010) *Making Good Society: Final Report*, London: Carnegie UK Trust.

Cox, C.B. and Boyson, R. (1977) *Black Paper 1977*, London: Temple Smith.

Crosland, C.A.R. (1956) *The Future of Socialism*, London: Jonathan Cape.

Davies, B. (1968) 'Non-swinging youth', *New Society*, 3 July pp. 8–10.

Davies, B. (1981) *The State We're In: Restructuring Youth Policies in Britain*, Leicester: National Youth Agency.

Davies, B. (1986) *Threatening Youth*, Buckingham: OUP.

Davies, B. (1999) *From Voluntaryism to Welfare State: A History of the Youth Service in England 1939–1979*, Leicester: Youth Work Press.

Davies, B. (2008) *The New Labour Years: A History of the Youth Service in England 1997 – 2007*, Leicester: National Youth Agency.

Davies, B. and Gibson, A. (1967) *The Social Education of the Adolescent*, London: University of London Press.

DfE (2012) *Statutory Guidance for Local Authorities on Services and Activities to Improve Young People's Well-being*, London: Department for Education.

DfES (2001) *Transforming Youth Work*, London: Department for Education and Skills.

DfES (2003) *Every Child Matters*, London: Department for Education and Skills.

Ewen, J. (1972) *Towards a Youth Policy*, Leicester: MBS Publications.

Hall, S. (2011) 'The neoliberal revolution' *Soundings* (48) pp. 9–27.

Hansard (1959) House of Lords Debate on the Youth Service, Vol 213, 4 February.

HM Government (2011) *Positive for Youth: a new approach to cross-government policy for young people aged 13 to 19*, available at http://media.education.gov.uk/assets/files/positive%20for%20youth.pdf (accessed May 2012).

HMSO (1969) *Youth and Community Work in the 70s*, London: HMSO.

HMSO (1982) *Experience and Participation: Report of the Review Group on the Youth Service in England*, London: HMSO.

Hoggart, R. (1957) *The Uses of Literacy*, London: Chatto and Windus.

House of Commons (1957) *Seventh Report of the Select Committee on Estimates*, London: HMSO.

Jay, D. (1967) 'Social services – a 70s crisis? *The Times* 31 May.

Jeffs, T. and Smith, M. (1987) *Youth Work*, London: Macmillan.

Jeffs, T. and Smith, M. (2008) 'Valuing Youth Work' *Youth and Policy* (100) pp. 277–302.

Jeffs, T. and Spence, J. (2007) 'Farewell to all that? The uncertain future of youth and community work education' *Youth and Policy* (97/98) pp. 135–166.

John, G. (1981) *In the Service of Black Youth. The political culture of youth and community work with Black people in English cities*, Leicester: National Association of Youth Clubs.

King George Jubilee Trust (1955) *Citizens of To-morrow*, London: Odhams Press.

London-Edinburgh Weekend Return Group (1979) *In and Against the State*, London: London-Edinburgh Weekend Return Group.

Ministry of Education (1960) *The Youth Service in England and Wales* (Albemarle Report), London: HMSO.

National Youth Agency (2012a) *A Practical Guide to Guide Commissioning Services for Young People – Part 10: Involving Young People in Commissioning*, Leicester: National Youth Agency.

National Youth Agency (2012b) *Department for Education – Catalyst Consortium*, at http://www. nya.org.uk/department-for-education-catalyst-consortium (accessed May 2012).

Nicholls. D. (2009) *Building Rapport: a brief history of the Community and Youth Workers' Union*, London: Unite the Union.

Observer (1960) 'Countess of many committees', 14 February.

Ord, J. (2007) *Youth Work Process, Product and Practice: Creating an authentic curriculum in work with young people*, Lyme Regis: Russell House Publishing.

Paul. L.A. (1929) *The Folk Trail*, London: Noel Douglas Publishers.

Sandel, M. (2009) *A New Politics of the Common Good*, Reith Lecture 4, BBC. Accessed at http://www.bbc.co.uk/programmes/b00kt7rg.

Schulmann, S. and Davies, T. (2007) *Evidence of the impact of the 'youth development' model on outcomes for young people – a literature review*, Leicester: NYA.

Shukra, K. (1998) *The Changing Pattern of Black Politics in Britain*, London: Pluto.

Smart, A. and Leigh, M. (1985) *Interpretation and Change: A History of the Enfranchisement Development Project*, Leicester: National Youth Bureau.

Smith, D. (1997) 'The eternal triangle – youth work, the youth problem and social policy', in I. Ledgerwood and N. Kendra (eds.) *The Challenge of the Future*, Lyme Regis: Russell House Publishing.

Taylor, T. (1981) 'Youth Opportunities: the argument for resistance' *Bulletin of Social Policy* (8).

Taylor, T. (2009) 'Youth Work and Class: The struggle that dare not speak its name' in R. Gilchrist, T. Jeffs, J. Spence and J. Walker (eds.) *Essays in the History of Youth and Community Work: Discovering The Past*. Lyme Regis: Russell House Publishing.

Williams, Z. (2012) 'The Guardian Interview: Stuart Hall' *The Guardian*, 11th February.

Essays in the history of youth and community work

Discovering the past

Edited by Ruth Gilchrist, Tony Jeffs, Jean Spence and Joyce Walker

Preface

Why history? *Mark K. Smith*

'The playground of today is the republic of tomorrow': social reform and organised recreation, 1890–1930s *Linnea M. Anderson*

From knowledge of the world to knowledge of self: perspectives on the professional training of youth leaders, 1942–1948 *Simon Bradford*

Chartism, education and community *Barry Burke*

The transition from girls clubs to girls clubs and mixed clubs: UK Youth, 1934–1944 *Michael Butterfield and Jean Spence*

'Why did they take that game away from us?' The rise and fall of girls' basketball in U.S. *Dan Conrad*

Cardijn versus Baden-Powell: The methodical turn in youth work history *Filip Coussé*

The rise and fall of community and youth work courses at Westhill College *John Holmes*

Starting out: origins of Newcastle YMCA *Tony Jeffs*

Familiar rooms in foreign fields: placing the 'BB Atmosphere' in The Boys' Brigade's Recreation Hut, Rouen, France, 1915–1919 *Richard G. Kyle*

T. R. Batten's life and work *George Lovell*

Long walk from the door: a history of work with girls and young women in Northern Ireland from 1969 *Susan Morgan and Eliz McArdle*

The counter-cultural revolution and the *Oz* school kids issue: the establishment versus the underground press *Keith Popple*

Withywood Youth Club *Sue Robertson*

Club, class and clothes: the origins of scouting in Sunderland *Jean Spence*

'Forgotten corners': a reflection on radical youth work in Britain, 1940–1990 *Tania de St Croix*

Youth work and class: the struggle that dare not speak its name *Tony Taylor*

The origins and development of the National Youth Agency *Tom Wylie*

2009   978-1-905541-45-4

Reflecting on the past
Essays in the history of youth and community work

Edited by Ruth Gilchrist, Tracey Hodgson, Tony Jeffs, Jean Spence, Naomi Stanton and Joyce Walker

2011   978-1-905541-73-7

Roots and wings

A history of outdoor education and outdoor learning in the UK

By Ken C. Ogilvie

Bringing alive the story of a movement that was driven by people and organisations who believe that a traditional academic approach to education is both too narrow and ignores important aspects of the whole person ...

Illuminating wider contemporary debates about:

- education theory, policy and management
- social trends and economic development ...

and raising questions about how we should help young people to learn at a time of global warming and climate weirding ...

This extensively researched book establishes clear foundations for a deeper understanding of the roots of experienced-based learning and personal development conducted out-of-doors.

Roots and Wings provides a fascinating and illuminating account of how ideas garnered from experience were championed and developed within the competing pulls of centralism and localism in both government and the voluntary sector ... how this led to differing approaches in the UK's various national jurisdictions ... and how safety, quality and accountability were developed without stifling innovation and constructive risk-taking.

Roots and Wings supports the case for early connection with nature in each child's life, and an on-going healthy and environmentally sustainable life style for all. It points to many activities that have sought to offset social trends that restrict areas of recreation for children and remove risk from personal development.

Published in association with the Institute for Outdoor Learning, this is the first single volume to address all aspects and sectors of the movement, and will be a foundation for future students and practitioners.

Kenneth C. Ogilvie ran Ghyll Head Outdoor Education Centre for over 22 years, and has held various offices with the Association of Heads of Outdoor Education Centres. He spent 16 years as editor of the National Association for Outdoor Education's newsletter, and was appointed a Fellow of the Institute for Outdoor Learning in 2010. He is the author of *Leading and Managing Groups in the Outdoors* (IOL: 1991).

2012   978-1-905541-84-3